USSR VLADIVOSTOK

GW00731362

S E A   O F

J A P A N

38° N

USSR VLADIVOSTOK

SEA OF JAPAN

H O N S H U

TOKYO

SAN

OSHIMA
JIMA

KURE

INLAND SEA

SHIKOKU

KIUSHIU

J A P A N

N

WAR ZONE

| 0 | 100 | 200 | 300 |

MILES

A

SEND PORT AND PYJAMAS!

Pheasant Shooting, December 1952. Colonel Hill, Captain McKay Forbes, the author (with gun), Sappers and pheasants.

SEND PORT AND PYJAMAS!

by

Dan Raschen

Buckland Publications Ltd.
125 High Holborn, London WC1V 6QA

ISBN 0 7212 0763 4

Printed and bound in Great Britain by
Buckland Press Ltd., Dover, Kent.

CONTENTS

PHOTOGRAPHS

MAPS AND DIAGRAMS

AUTHOR'S NOTE

I hope that what I have written here in my second book is close to the truth! I did not keep a personal diary at the time, but I have referred to the many letters I wrote home.

My greatest pleasure from the publication of my earlier book *Wrong Again Dan!* was to see my wife's face as story after story was corroborated long after she had first heard it. I have also enormously valued the many encouraging letters I have received, both from old friends and from complete strangers.

General Sir Hugh Beach wrote an exceedingly kind foreword to my first book. Any further comment at this stage would be unlikely to surpass it, but I would like particularly to thank my commanding officer in the Korean War, Brigadier Peter Moore, for the great trouble he has taken in checking my first draft of *Send Port and Pyjamas!* In addition my best man, Major Angus McKay Forbes, attempted to read it, even before the pictures were added! Many others have also helped me, and I thank them all.

CHAPTER ONE

PEACETIME

"The only shots fired today were by officers shooting pheasants." So the Korean War reports read in the British newspapers after Boxing Day 1950.

When North Korea had invaded South Korea six months previously, I had taken little interest. Now, with free pheasant shooting apparently on offer, I suddenly became keen to join in. That I had ever heard of Korea was sheer luck. At my prep school after Sunday lunch we received half an hour of religious education, usually based on the doings of the Society for the Propogation of the Gospel. The SPG seemed to have a fixation on Korea. Year after year, their missionary there (I think a kindly lady) had plugged along through very little thick and lots of thin. I grew to like Korea and, as it was further away than India where I had been born, I felt it was a long way away indeed.

Much had happened, though, since I had won prizes for having my hair properly parted when in the bottom form. As I had always hoped, I had joined the Royal Engineers and, in 1944, had been sent back to India to spend a happy, interesting, but not wholly successful three years with the Indian Army before the partition of the Indian Empire into India and Pakistan. My *Wrong Again Dan!** tells of some of the background but, to put us all on the same footing, I will explain why I went to the Korean War, which happened to be the first fought by the United Nations.

I returned to England in October 1947 and during my two months' leave at home in Devonshire it was confirmed to me that peacetime

*Published by Buckland Publications Ltd.

Britain was as austere as the papers abroad had reported. Although I had been commissioned when I was nineteen, I had only become a regular officer a year ago on my twenty-first birthday: now those who administered Royal Engineers officers seemed as keen to set their eyes on me as I was to discuss my future with them. The Adjutant General's posting branch, AG 7, was in Hobart House, SW1, so I quickly accepted the invitation to an interview, particularly as a first-class ticket to London was provided.

A year before, the same branch had entreated me, in Calcutta and later Assam, to prepare in my own time to sit the London University Inter BSc examination, so that I might read for an engineering degree at the Military College of Science. I had fondly imagined that many other Sapper officers would have jumped at this opportunity, so I had several textbooks posted to me in India. Now, the Captain who would fix my future congratulated me on my good intentions, saying, "All you need is to go to night school, and you'll have a real chance of passing the exam next summer."

"Where can you post me that is near a night school?" I asked. I expected him to answer immediately, as surely many others would have asked the same question, but he hesitated. He seemed already to have decided that No. 1 Training Regiment Royal Engineers at Malvern needed me, but added, "I'm sure there'll be a night school there, the place is full of schools."

"Please may I have a railway warrant to go and see them, then?" I asked. Normally such requests would not be granted, but he could make an exception. He gave me a telephone number, saying, "Make your own arrangements with their Adjutant."

Within a week I had presented myself at Malvern. The Adjutant saw me on arrival: I gained the impression that not many subalterns had taken time out of their leave to vet the Regiment before joining. He told me that I would be supervising newly joined recruits. I then asked about night schools. What, he wondered, had made me think that Malvern would sustain such a thriving night life, and had I not seen that the camp was some miles from the town?

As soon as I arrived home I wrote to AG 7 "respectfully suggesting" that, in view of the lack of facilities for preparation of my exam at Malvern, my posting should be reconsidered. Remarkably quickly a reply came changing my destination from Malvern to Aldershot. It just struck me that those in Malvern might have contacted AG 7 equally quickly.

No. 4 Training Regiment Royal Engineers was in the Victorian, Gibraltar Barracks, opposite the Garrison Church, and built in a vivid red brick. Aldershot was again proud to claim its role as "Home of the British Army", with signs such as "Court Martial Centre" and "Military Cemetery" predominating. However, I found my companions more encouraging: indeed, the Adjutant of the Regiment had been in Java when I had been in Sumatra. Yes, he understood that there was a Technical College in Farnborough, two miles away, and that it had a night school.

Early in 1948 there were still several Sapper Training Regiments and mine, No. 4, had two main roles, training firstly all drivers for the Corps of Royal Engineers and secondly those boy trumpeters who would later join the splendid RE Band at Chatham. The Adjutant advised me to keep clear of both activities. Instead, he thought it would be useful, and he hoped interesting, if I could please help a very senior major, the President of the Regimental Institute (PRI), with the Regiment's accounts.

Three months slipped congenially by, by which time even my friend the Adjutant realised that my talents were not being fully tested. Apart from new young conscripts, the Army was re-enlisting much older men, many of whom had been only too keen to leave the services at the end of the war, but had quickly become disillusioned with civilian life. "Dan, what makes most of them come back into the Army is wife trouble. We need a specialist Welfare Officer, and I am sure the PRI could spare you for a few hours a day to do it."

I was twenty-two, unmarried and with no close experience of broken marriages. "The padré says you can put an extra table in his office," the Adjutant concluded. The padré, a Church of England Irishman, certainly went out of his way to be helpful.

For several weeks I attended the Technical College in Farnborough but, despite the encouragement of an excellent tutor, knew that I would never pass the Engineering Drawing exam and, without it, I could not read engineering at London University. Pass all, or no place, was the rule, as the universities were overflowing with applicants held up by the war. Night school did not excuse me from the formal Mess Dinner Night each week, nor did I feel that my visits to London with friends, with a view to gaining the polish which I so obviously lacked after three years abroad, should be foregone. Meanwhile, my clients in the Welfare Office seemed to appreciate the chance of a chat and I, at least, became more worldly. I even achieved one mended marriage, then passed the happy soldier over to the padré without delay.

Summer approached, and so did the Inter BSc exam. London University extracted the entrance fee from me, which the Army promised to repay me if I passed. So exacting were the examinations that they stretched over ten days, which the new Adjutant, a much bemedalled officer called Martin, could hardly believe. I sat the two exams on the first day in an enormous room off London's Exhibition Road. The next morning, four hours were to be devoted to mechanical drawing and there was I standing in front of an enormous drawing board with around me at least a hundred similar, each with its victim unfolding the master drawing which we were expected to present on paper from different angles. I wrote my examination number on my sheet of paper, and, appreciating that the situation was hopeless, I printed "NO BID" clearly across my paper. I then walked from the room with an air of such confidence that the others imagined that I had finished the test in impossibly quick time. I stayed in London until the exams ended: the time did not count as leave, but was expensive. A month later I received the result "Failed (retired)" and managed to evade Martin's questions as to what exactly that meant.

As a junior officer I tended to miss out on some of the social life of Aldershot, so was glad to be involved in the Royal Engineers weekend, with a veterans' parade and a large party in the Mess garden. It was there that I was delighted to meet Colonel L. O. Clark, who had been Commandant of the Royal Bombay Sappers and Miners when I had first been commissioned. "Whatever are you doing here?" he asked, to which I replied, "I'm blessed if I know, Sir, and may I ask what you are doing?"

"I am the Colonel of AG 7, the postings branch." I was amazed, as I had never dreamt of asking the captain who posted me who his boss was. The Colonel and I exchanged a few reminiscences, and parted. A week later I was surprised to receive a personal note from him saying, "I find we have a spare place on a refresher course possibly leading to Cambridge. Would you be interested in taking it?" I was. That dull garden party had greatly changed the course of my life.

The summer wore gently on, but not as gently as I might have hoped: the Commanding Officer, having heard what Colonel Clark had fixed for me, thought that my experience should be further broadened. I was made Martin's Assistant Adjutant. My main task was to process the aftermaths of the Regiment's traffic accidents of which, as driver training was our job, there were many. Like most other commodities in 1948, fuel for the vehicles became so short that petrolless days were introduced once every week: with the possible exception of the ration truck, no vehicles were permitted to start their engines. This greatly reduced traffic accidents, but proved a rotten way to train drivers.

Even if Aldershot lacked action, plenty seemed to be happening in the rest of the world. In China Chiang Kai-shek's Kuomintang Nationalist Forces, whom we had been brought up to think of as allies and good men, were doing very badly indeed. In Indonesia the Dutch, who had taken over from us less than two years before, were on the offensive to regain their colonies but, in the attempt they had lost so much goodwill that the United Nations had withdrawn their support. The UN had also not supported Israel, newly independent and now attacked for the first time by her five Arab neighbours: it was the arms supplied from communist Czechoslovakia that kept Israel in existence. To us at home, though, it was of much greater interest that Berlin had been blockaded and that the air-lift, against all odds, seemed to be working.

I joined No. 11 Supplementary Class for Royal Engineers regular officers at Chatham in September 1948. There were thirty-two of us, of whom I, aged just twenty-three was about the youngest: some were touching thirty, and no less than eight of us had been at Wellington College together.

The Course had two purposes, first to bring us up to the standard required to read for an engineering degree at either Cambridge or Shrivenham, and second, to give us a more professional grounding in RE specialities than had been possible during our wartime training. We started with a few months of mathematics, taken with a dash of physics. Our instructor was himself a regular Sapper officer, Major Graham Sandeman, very clever and absolutely dedicated. He was determined that we should learn, and set us tests most days which he corrected well into the night.

Early in 1949 fifteen of us were entered for the Cambridge qualifying examination which, mercifully, did not include any mechanical drawing. We went to Cambridge for a couple of nights, sat the exam and all of us passed. I was fourteenth on the list, a remarkable achievement for Graham Sandeman.

It was a great relief to turn from our academic studies to the more practical arts that regular Sapper officers might need. We had several weeks in workshops, I made a bench vice, which broke the first time I used it, and an excellent watering can, and then spent a messy month on the Medway mud with bulldozers and cranes. The School of Military Survey was in Longleat Park, and we graced it with our presence before returning to Chatham for courses on water supply and electrical generators, as well as a cheerful week on sewage disposal. A construction tour of hydro-electric projects in some of Scotland's most beautiful scenery brought a happy summer to a climax.

If construction was our theme, destruction remained in vogue elsewhere. Shanghai fell to the Communists in May 1949 and any Nationalists who could leave the mainland for Formosa did so. The Indonesians had started to wear down the Dutch, and the French were finding Indo-China much more troublesome than they had expected. NATO was formed in the summer of 1949 just when, by coincidence, the first Russian atomic explosion was detected. There seemed to be very few parts of the world where soldiers were not needed but, needed or not, I was very glad to be going back to Cambridge.

Peterhouse, Cambridge's oldest College, where good chance had placed me during the war, took me back in October with much better grace than I deserved. Not a murmur was there of the list of misdemeanors from six years before which must have been on my file. Perhaps, aged twenty-four, I was now judged with the many mature men back from the war who were showing up so well. Two in particular, both Royal Engineers with distinguished war records, had gone down from Peterhouse just before I returned. Between them they had taken the top prizes in the Engineering Department, had run the College boat club and, just to confirm their true brilliance, had always time to spare for others. For my first few months I basked in reflected glory. Little could my tutor have imagined how late a developer he had on his hands.

Because the Army wished to have its officers back at work, and because considerable time had already been spent on our academic preparation, we were expected to study the "fast" course for the Mechanical Sciences Tripos. This involved doing the three-year course in two and, what sounded worse, the first two in one.

Our lectures filled almost every morning period of every weekday. In addition two afternoons a week were devoted to either practical work or to my old horror, mechanical drawing. We were not beholden to attend lectures but, as those who lectured also set the exams, attendance was advisable. Often the whole intake for our year, nearly 200 of us, were in the same lecture hall, so obviously we could not all sit at the front; not that I would have wished to do so, but there would have been more sense in it, as my eyesight had never been strong. That was due to measles I had when I was twelve, but my hearing can also be suspect and, although we were probably listening to some of the cleverest men in the world, it did not necessarily follow that they were good lecturers.

Although we were regular officers on full pay, the Army took the attitude that the less military we were at university, the broader men we would be. The University Officers' Training Corps continued to brighten up Grange Road but, other than watching rugger matches next door, I never crossed its doorstep and never asked the name of its commanding officer. Little did I think that fifteen years later I would be in his job. Reminders that we were combatant officers and should keep fit came not from the OTC but, and not very frequently, from Chatham. Rowing was my chosen answer.

A few oars were still needed for the Peterhouse bottom boat, and I was apparently the very man the Boat Club needed. How wrong they were! After a term every muscle I had discovered ached more rather than less, and my co-ordination of oar, body and stretcher seat became ever more ragged. Our great achievement was to row the Fairbairn Race at the end of term. Bogey time was around twenty minutes, but it took us twenty-eight: ever since, I have claimed with truth that I have rowed for longer, even if not further, than the University Boat Race. I resigned from the Club, and was not pressed to reverse my decision.

I was to have spent the Christmas vacation with my parents near South Molton, hoping to shoot a few of our very wild pheasants: there were still plenty of rabbits to entertain the dogs and if the weather was right, woodcock and snipe might come in. However, my Sapper friends at Cambridge thought otherwise, so I went to a series of excellent weddings, luckily buying my second-hand morning suit early in the circuit from Moss Bros for £15. It was when I was best man to Charles Holland in Carmarthenshire, an occasion which became literally riotous when gentlemen firing shotguns held us up until a ransom was charmingly extracted, that a bridesmaid called Judy was pointed out to me. I understood, though, that one of the bridesmaids had recently been sick in the car on the way to the wedding, so, thinking it must be Judy, pursued neither her nor the subject.

Back at Cambridge, without the almost daily trips to the boathouse, I thought I had time on my hands until yet another Sapper, Jamie Otten, introduced me to Jimmy Mackworth, also an army officer in his college, Christ's. Jimmy was the first officer ever to have been sent to Cambridge by the Royal Electrical and Mechanical Engineers. As he was on his own, and had a car, it seemed a pity not to accompany him on wide and comprehensive tours of the local hostelries. Jamie soon became a less frequent companion. He, too, was due to be married in the next vacation, and I was again honoured by being his best man. Bachelors on our course were becoming rare.

Interesting though much of it was proving, the engineering curriculum at Cambridge was not entirely to my liking. The subject which continued to baffle me utterly was mechanical drawing. Even if it was not included in the entrance exam, it was made clear that we would have to satisfy examiners at the end of our first year, that was unless we wished to do extra drawing for all our final year as well. The form of the exam was always the same, in that you were given a drawing of either the top, side or end view of some desperately intricate object like a car's cylinder block, a steam valve (steam was still great stuff) or a gear box, then you were told, without even the word "please", to draw it as it would be seen from some other direction. Because I had very little idea what such items were for, the whole thing remained an unhappy mystery. Not so for my friends, or some of them anyway: they would even talk mechanical drawing over their beer, and considered me narrow if I changed the subject to shooting, fishing, or even more beer.

The drawing exam was more horrific even than that in my London excursion. This time we, the victims, all knew each other well. You weren't meant to crib your neighbour's board, but in four hours you could hardly fail to notice the general shape of the masterpieces under composition on either side of you. However, the fellow on my right was left handed and kept leaning in front of his board as if he were terribly tired, and, and, blow me, if the one of the left wasn't right handed and did the same. I might be myopic, but fate had added to my problems and, bar some smudges from rubbing out, there was very little on my paper at the end of hour one.

By the end of hour three I had confidently concluded that my neighbours had been asked to draw something quite different to me. I had always thought that we would all be set the same questions, but perhaps the rules had been changed. At the end of hour four we were all told to put down our pencils. Now, in all the exams I had experienced, it had just not been done to check through another chap's sums before he handed his paper in. But, for this drawing exam, with enormous sheets of paper on enormous boards, there was no question of handing anything in. "Sir" would come and correct it on the spot in due course: in the meanwhile, anyone could look at anyone else's. I was surprised, and rather honoured, by so many of my friends quickly gathering in front of my board, but their silence was ominous. Compared to some of my earlier efforts, I thought that I had done quite well, with many splendid lines nicely joining at beautifully curved corners. Nor had I forgotten some neat notation of the outside dimensions which, although not essential, added a nice finishing touch I thought. At last Mark, a very old friend who was not prone to strong language, said, "My God!" The crowd then slowly and sadly dispersed, much as if from a graveside.

That evening several people took me out for a drink. It was Jimmy who explained that the item we had been requested to study, a "stuffing box", had been an assembly of many smaller components made of three different metals. Apparently I had drawn the whole thing as a solid chunk of iron.

Because ours was the "fast" course, we had been warned that we might be required to keep the long vacation term, which meant returning to Cambridge for six weeks during the summer. I was so required, principally with a view to spending the time on extra mechanical drawing. Of twenty-five army officers in my year, which included nine rather studious companions from the Royal Signals, only I had failed the drawing. "If I may suggest, Dan," one said, "it would pay you well to take extra tuition from Mr. Utting. He showed me what drawing was all about when I was up here during the war." "Were you as bad as me?" I asked, but my friend was already off on another topic.

The long vac term was, in fact, one of the most pleasant I spent at Cambridge. Mr. Utting proved to be as good as had been promised, as he induced some very dim light to glimmer around my mechanical drawing. I learnt that if you drew the bit nearest to you first, then you would be unlikely to need to cover it up with something in front.

Previously I had been obsessed with the back of the object which, when you come to think of it, you don't usually see.

The summer was lovely. I recruited and captained the Peterhouse Percolaters, a cricket team of such talent that it beat something similar from Trinity, a College five times our size. When I handed over the captaincy, we did even better. The term rushed by, but the Korean War, as we now knew it, had moved faster.

It may help if I now give a little of Korea's history. In the 1930s, whilst I was still at my prep school, the Japanese had strengthened their hold on the Korean Peninsula. Amongst other things, it had provided them with a very convenient entrance to China. When the World War was ending in 1945, the Americans and Russians had agreed that Korea must not remain Japanese. This would represent a considerable loss to Japan, Korea as a whole having about the same area as, and nearly the population of, Great Britain. The north of Korea had the minerals and the south the agriculture, the two together balancing nicely, but all that came to an end in August 1945.

The Russians had only declared war on Japan just as the other allies were bringing matters to a conclusion, but soon influenced the peace terms. It was agreed that Korea would initially be partitioned, arbitrarily, except in approximate area, on the line of the 38th Parallel north of the equator. London and the south of England lie about 51 degrees north, so the 38 line, which passes through Athens, Sicily and Southern Spain, sounded pleasantly torrid, but in Korea it had the knack of being very cold as well.

The Russians then occupied the north of Korea and disarmed the Japanese there, and the Americans did the same in the south. The Western Allies had not thought very thoroughly about the future of Korea, but had envisaged a single independent country. So, indeed, had the Russians, providing that it was communist. By 1948 the Americans had only a military mission left in South Korea, which was training a local force for internal security duties. Meanwhile the Russians had been much busier and had trained and equipped a quite large and efficient North Korean Army, all with a view to overwhelming the South quickly. Despite the different treatment, the people in the north and in the south were basically the same and, when the Korean War started less than five years after the Japanese occupation ended, might well have wondered to which part of the country they belonged.

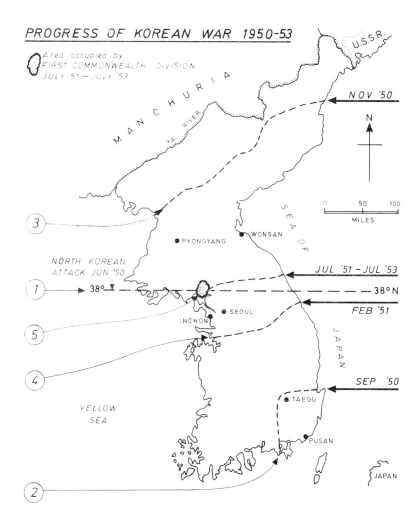

PROGRESS OF KOREAN WAR 1950-53

Area occupied by
FIRST COMMONWEALTH DIVISION
JULY 51 — JULY '53

The North Koreans attacked with eight divisions on 25th June, 1950 *(No. 1 on map)*, and the South Koreans had a few disorganised regiments with which to meet them. Hardly surprisingly they gave way, and Seoul, the capital, fell four days later. Almost immediately, and rather unexpectedly, President Truman of America promised support, and very quickly many other countries, including Britain, followed suit, all in the name of the United Nations.

The Berlin Blockade two years before had been a severe test, but this was the first armed aggression with which the United Nations had decided to get involved. Those concerned probably remembered all too well that the League of Nations had disintegrated when nothing was done about the Italian invasion of Abyssinia only fifteen years before.

To many people in Britain, Korea seemed more remote than Abyssinia, but to America it was very close to Japan, and Japan was so important to them that General MacArthur, who had "won the war" out there, was still in Tokyo. It was probably just as well that he was. He commanded the army of occupation of Japan, consisting of four extremely weak divisions, most of whose members were greatly enjoying the rights still accorded to them as a conquering force. War was a long way from the soldiers' minds, but it was to the Americans' great credit that they managed to move forces quickly into Korea and that those forces immediately prevented the imminent disintegration of the South Korean Army. Even so, when, two weeks later, the American Army influence became apparent, the North had nearly cleared the South, so that only an area about the size of Devonshire *(No. 2 on map)* around the port of Pusan remained. From the first day, though, the American Air Force had attacked communications to the North, and ships from the United States and Commonwealth Navies had bombarded the coast roads.

All this came as exciting news on the wireless and, with the war maps daily showing less and less left to the South, I and my military friends viewed matters perhaps differently to the others at Cambridge with us. Many of them had been in the services and were thankful to be out: we had chosen to stay in.

I may not have been a very conventional soldier, but I knew that wars were my business. I had already missed the fighting of 1939-45, and now I looked like doing the same again. The Cambridge Mechanical Sciences Tripos seemed to lose some of its priority, or so my conscience found it convenient to tell me. My conscience also found it convenient to forget that I was entirely out of touch with soldiering and that my uniform would be unlikely to fit me any more. "I always remember hearing," I said to Jimmy, "how rowing muscles turn to fat," and he nodded knowledgeably. He had not even undertaken my modicum of rowing, but was also broadening out perceptibly.

As a new war started in Korea, so did one in which I personally had been involved come to an official end. Indonesian Independence, which was first declared in 1945, was finally agreed in 1950 and the Dutch, who had tried so hard to regain their colonies, started to return to the Netherlands. Against great military strength, the spirit of local independence as fostered by the Japanese had prevailed, and it was now looking as if the same might happen in Indo-China, even though the French strength there was already greater than that ever reached by the Dutch in the Indies.

I had hardly picked up the threads again at Cambridge before another Michaelmas term had passed. A major disruption had been the Poppy Day appeal, when every college tried to collect more money per head for the Earl Haig Fund than any other. As a serviceman, I was appointed to lead the Peterhouse effort which, in the smallest college, was not too difficult to harness. The prize of eighteen gallons of beer offered by Dale's Brewery would represent useful drinking amongst our small number, and my personal knowledge of those public houses where donations might be generous around closing time would be an asset. I resolved that Peterhouse should win, and we did. That was the greatest achievement of my degree course.

Our pheasants at home that Christmas were even more scarce than usual, so to read of pheasants, possibly lots of them, being shot in Korea made me envious. That Boxing Day report, as mentioned in my first paragraph, was enticingly incomplete. Soon after it, in January 1951, a Royal Engineers posting officer came to interview us, to "discuss" where we would go at the end of the course in only five months' time. I asked, very politely, "Please may I go to Korea," to which the Captain answered, "Sorry, but we are only sending good officers there." Considering that he was new in the job, I wondered how he knew of me but, as if to encourage me, he continued, "You haven't been to Germany, have you? I'll try to fit you in there, and that'll widen your experience." I was disappointed, but not wholly, as in the last few weeks the news from Korea had sounded much less inviting.

Once the Americans had stopped the North Koreans close to Pusan at the end of summer 1950, such folk of the South who could be mustered had pulled themselves together and set about pushing the invaders back up the country. Contingents from other countries, including a British Brigade from Hong Kong, had started to arrive, so that the name United Nations had real meaning. Then, with the help of a difficult landing by the US Marines at Inchon on the West Coast, the UN advance had swept through the 38th Parallel, where the war had started, right through North Korea and up to the Yalu River on the Chinese border. The Korean War might have ended then, in November 1950 *(No. 3 on map)*, had not the Chinese Communist Volunteers joined in.

The Chinese had thought, possibly with justification, that the advance might not stop precisely at the border and, even if it did, they viewed the UN as potentially poor neighbours in comparison to their good comrades the North Koreans. However spontaneously they were said to have volunteered, the Chinese Communist Forces, CCF as they became known, were remarkably well organised and in much greater strength than General MacArthur had expected. When he realised that he could not hold the ground he had gained with land forces alone, he requested permission to send bombers across the Manchurian border. President Truman saw the dangers in this, and it was not long after he refused to agree that General MacArthur relinquished his command.

The President's decision was probably politically wise, but its effect on the already difficult battle was disastrous, and a mainly disorganised retreat back down North Korea in the depth of winter ensued. The bitter cold was made beastlier by an ever whipping wind, and very few of the UN troops had proper clothing for the climate. By February *(No. 4 on map)* the survivors were again below the 38th Parallel and Seoul again fell to the North, the third time it had changed hands in nine months.

All this, and much more, was reported in the papers. I remembered that in 1941-42 the war in Libya had gone from side to side with confusing rapidity, but Korea, particularly as it lay up and down the map, better fitted my idea of a Yo-Yo war. Korea was also different, as only five years before it had been fairly densely populated with people who all called themselves Koreans. Now they hardly knew whether to call themselves supporters of the North or of the South, but to be on the right side at the right time was a matter of life or death.

The United Nations forces gradually again advanced, and Seoul changed hands for the fourth time in March 1951 to remain in the hands of its "rightful" owners, the South, for the rest of the war, soon the line settled as shown on number 5 on the map. At Cambridge, our provisional postings were announced, with none of us going to Korea.

As the Lent Term of 1951 passed, it became increasingly apparent to me and most of my contemporaries that the engineering "fast" course was indeed fast. We had covered the normal content of two years in the first year and had hoped that the third year would result in a more pleasant tempo. What most of us had not realised was that the sheer quantity of knowledge imparted would be the problem. In our last vacation, Jamie, Jimmy and I devoted two weeks to a "reading party" at a farmhouse in Northern Cornwall. Very pleasant those weeks were but, in my case, the good intentions came too late. The excuse that I had not worked my hardest because I might be going to the Korean War now rang hollow.

I attended lectures in my last term more for their interest than for their relevance to the exams. The mature approach, I told myself later. It really was fascinating what was on offer for those who cared to listen. Never before did I know that the best timber for resisting worms under water was greenheart from the Amazon Basin, nor that the only ship-building timber that was "A1 at Lloyds" was teak. Evidently in a fire it flared, then charred to a non-inflammable ash.

It was during a lecture on fuels for internal combustion engines that my ears picked up the word alcohol. The lecturer was Paul Dykes of Kings', a popular don of character and substance who was for ever trying to drive his Bentley faster to see if he could blow the dust off it. "Sadly," he said, "as an engineer, I know I can't." What he then said about boundary layers has stuck firmly with me ever since. Alcohol brought us to the subject of proof spirit and the definition of "100% proof". I had always imagined that 100% meant absolute alcohol, the stuff one tried to entice girlfriends who were nurses to smuggle out of hospitals. Not so! Evidently 100% proof spirit was the perfect mixture with which to dampen the contents of kegs of gunpowder. In the right proportions, and that meant 49½% alcohol by volume, gunpowder remained relatively insensitive during handling, yet still burnt at vast speed when intentionally ignited. This was probably the most useful thing I learnt at Cambridge, and ever since I have surveyed the contents of bar shelves with a more knowing eye. Export gin, at 86% proof, had previously impressed me immensely but, at under 43% alcohol when rephrased, lost, at least in name, some of its lift.

One of the less likely things we were asked to believe was that an earth road, when subjected to the passage of sprung vehicles, would quickly gain a surface of perfectly formed waves. The lecturer, even when on a sensible topic, lacked confidence, but his efforts to explain why spring harmonics could cause perfect sine curves in a road's surface destroyed him completely. After muttering a few words at the blackboard and scribbling some integrals upon it, he gathered his gown around him and left us to our smiles.

After our trip to Cornwall and just before we returned to Cambridge for that last term, a message came, from just the same folk in the War Office who had previously spurned me, warning me to get ready for service in Korea. It was so worded that no one could imagine that I had made the suggestion in the first place, which was just as well, as my parents had welcomed my posting to Germany.

The prospect of Korea still pleased me, but I wondered why I was now wanted. Evidently it was now thought that the administration of the large number of Commonwealth units now in Korea, and also their influence, would be stronger if they were grouped together. The First Commonwealth Division was to be formed and, as it might well need reinforcements, my name had been considered. I was not much enthused by the other reason given, "As you will know, there have been some casualties." Nothing was definite, but I had to plan as if I were going to Korea. My immediate need was for a shotgun to deal with the pheasants, as I considered my own too good to take with me.

My uncle had just died and I went to stay with my aunt in Herefordshire. She asked me to undertake one or two jobs, and the first was to look in the cellar. She doubted if there would be anything there, as they had never had a bottle out since they moved house in 1927, and here we were twenty-four years later. I was given the key. I am not suggesting that this was a true parallel with Tutankhamun's tomb, but it became easier to understand how Howard Carter must have felt when he entered it.

Nearly three hundred bottles lay on the slate slabs or still in the large wooden boxes in which they had been moved. The gaping necks of many of the bottles and the stained bottoms of the boxes told the same story. I had always understood that whether a bottle was corked or not could be a matter of opinion, but no doubt was left with most of what I was to test.

I saved, for consideration later, under half the bottles I found, considering the duty so important that I made a list. The port that remained comprised of one Jereboam, a four bottle bottle, of 1868, the year of my uncle's birth, nine bottles of Cockburns 1896, twenty-nine Cockburns 1908 (there seemed to be no future to any of the 1904), six white port and a couple of various. In fact the rubies and tawnies had mostly gone so thin as to be nearly white themselves.

However gently I lifted them, the corks of many bottles crumbled out and the contents glugged onto the cellar floor, so much so that on the second day the soles of my shoes fell off, a terrifying demonstration of the power of corked port. My previous experience of vintage port had been limited to the Headquarters Mess of the Royal Engineers at Chatham. The port on offer was superb, but my education was sadly limited. I still lack practice!

The remaining bottles were nearly as interesting as the port, but I will only mention the three bottles of 1906 champagne. Who, you may ask, would drink 45-year-old champagne, when most is past its prime after a dozen years? As I handled one of the bottles, the rusty wire parted and out came the cork with a respectable thrust. I stuffed my thumb in the neck and hastened upstairs to my aunt, who was still in mourning. "I am very sorry," I said, "but one of those champagne bottles has come open. What shall we do?" "Drink it dear," she replied, and we did.

Another great discovery of that visit was the shotgun of a recently departed gardener. It was not difficult to understand why he had left it behind, but at least it was double barrelled and hammerless. In 1951 shotgun cartridges remained in short supply, so I was delighted to unearth a couple of hundred, all from well before the war. With my eyes shut and the gun held at the full length of my arms, I fired one of the cartridges and received a nasty jar in my wrists. As the gun did not blow up, I prescribed it "passed proof". I had explained to my aunt that my own gun was rather too good to chance losing in Korea, so she kindly presented me with both the gardener's gun and the cartridges. My impression was that she neither wished nor expected to see them back.

Charles picked me up by car from my aunt's, to return for our last term at Cambridge. Jane, his wife, had just produced me a godson, but planning for the May Ball in only seven weeks' time was already under way. Jane knew that my arrangements the previous year had become complicated, so asked if she could help. She soon discovered that I neither could decide who to ask, nor wished to book an expensive hotel room. "You'll probably be too late to book one now, so wouldn't you like to ask Judy, and then she could stay with us?"

Judy was the bridesmaid who had, I thought, been sick in the car on the way to Charles and Jane's wedding. She had stayed with them near Cambridge since, during which meetings I had established that it was, in fact, someone else who had succumbed. "Yes, please," was my answer to Jane.

Later in April the British units in Korea had fought a series of bitter actions, which culminated in what we later knew as "the Gloucester Battle". A gallant stand by the 29th Brigade, which included the Royal Northumberland Fusiliers, the Royal Ulster Rifles and the Gloucester Regiment, ably assisted by the 8th Hussars and, of course, Gunners and Sappers, had stopped the Chinese from once again driving through to Seoul. Most of the Gloucesters had been cut off, and those who were not killed were eventually taken prisoner. The long casualty lists in the newspapers brought what had been a very remote war home to many people. I did not receive my official posting order to Korea until 23rd May, which coincided with the final exams. The posting made, of course, no difference to my Third Class Honours, but provided a splendid excuse. That I had passed the Mechanical Drawing was entirely due to Mr. Utting.

I was warned to be ready to move on 7th July, and my three weeks of leave, which stretched into four, were mainly concerned with trying to become a soldier again. My battledress no longer fitted me, but the Royal Engineers Depot at Chatham gave me what was needed. I asked the fieldworks instructors for tips on the types of task with which I might be confronted, but as no one had yet returned from Korea, not much was on offer. The only definite advice was to learn about the mines.

For those who have been fortunate enough never to be involved in minewarfare on land, mines are explosive devices laid on, or just under, the surface of the ground with the intention of incapacitating men or vehicles. I don't know if you have ever planted a rude word in daffodil bulbs on a neighbour's lawn, and then left the district? The effect of mines can be equally delayed, and much more aggravating.

I discovered that both the Americans and Chinese were using mines that were new to me, and I slowly comprehended that I was going to a Korean war, or an American war, but not really to a British one.

CHAPTER TWO

REINFORCEMENTS

The troopship *Empire Fowey*, in which we sailed from Southampton on 13th July, 1951, was British, even though, like other "Empire" ships, she had German origins. Kure in Japan, and not Pusan in South Korea, as I had fondly imagined, was to be our final destination, but meanwhile we would be dropping off drafts on the way. Of over a hundred officers aboard, only fourteen were for Japan and Korea: of them, I was the only Sapper, so the chances of my getting there, whilst the war was still on, looked high. The chances of peace having been declared before my arrival, however, looked higher. After the failure of the Chinese Spring offensive, the two sides, North and South, had, rather surprisingly, agreed to have tentative discussions. There was I, trying to be a good regular soldier and see a war, and every time I nearly got to one, somebody tried to stop it. The Japanese had surrendered very soon after I was commissioned, and now it looked as if the Koreans were going to call a halt to things.

I was delighted to find that Charles from Cambridge, who was going to Hong Kong, was on the same ship, though sad that Jane and their baby would not be following until later. This was the first troopship on which I had travelled that abounded with families, and they certainly made for a livelier voyage. Most of the unaccompanied wives and their children ate at the first sitting for meals, and the unaccompanied officers, which included me, followed at the second. Waiting whilst the first sitting ate could be boring, so when a lady had left her knitting prominently on the table around which we had placed our drinks, the temptation was too great. My mother had taught me to knit as a child, so when I saw that the pattern was plain, with neither pearl nor other squiggles, I thought I'd just add a row for the lady. I did, and a highly bemused soul she was as she tried to continue from where she thought she had left off. Unfair and unkind, you may say, but very funny for those who knew the secret. I did tell her later, and was forgiven.

As on all long sea voyages with too many soldiers in too small a space, everything was dreamt up with a view to keeping them interested: this started with PT at 7.00 a.m., which ensured an unnecessarily long day. Charles and I and another Sapper were required to run a course of lessons on mines and grenades for the infantry. This was probably good for the instructors, but we sensed no great enthusiasm for the subjects from our pupils, especially from those who knew that they were going to pleasant peacetime stations. Lectures were arranged for the officers too and, although many were optional, I attended most. One in particular was for Gunner officers only, but I asked if I could be there and was graciously welcomed. Five years earlier, just before I left Sumatra, I had been taught the rudiments of gun drill, but had no notion of how gunfire was directed and controlled. Here, now, was a new system called "Target Grid", of which the highly authoritative Instructor of Gunnery said, "It is so simple that even the Sapper sitting at the back should understand it." This nettled me so much that I listened, and the chap was indeed right. It was simple! Either that, or he was a very good instructor. To share the secret, here is how I understood an observer (you) with a wireless (as we still called them) needed to proceed:—

1. Look at your map, decide where the target is and read off its grid reference. Grid references were taught to some lucky children in geography, or to soldiers whenever an idle moment needed filling.

2. With your compass, take the bearing from yourself to the target. As also with the target's location, pass this clearly over the wireless.

3. Call for fire, then listen for the pop of a gun behind you and observe the arrival of the shell.

4. Give corrections to bring the fall of shot onto the target, meaning that it would be jolly lucky if the first round landed precisely as intended, an impression which left me decidedly uneasy. If the normally proud and professionally proficient Gunners admitted that they, or the system, could be wrong, then just how big might my errors be? Little did I think that I would discover the answer not many weeks later.

5. Once you were satisfied that the rounds would fall on the target, you could call for as many guns as you liked to fire, and for as many rounds as you wished from each gun.

All this seemed to put great power in the hands of one junior officer. The instructor's intention was that we should be impressed, and I certainly was.

Charles and I both considered ourselves old hands on troopships. My trips to India and Sumatra at the end of the war had given me the experience of eight of them, so on the first day aboard the *Fowey* we set off to the Ship's Adjutant's office to enquire our correct address whilst afloat. He was out, but there was a notice telling us just what we wanted to know and how letters should be addressed: "D C I N F, British Army Post Office 3." We managed to get letters off to our families to tell them this before we left Southampton. At Port Said we expected mail, but none came. The situation was the same at Aden, and also at Colombo. It slowly dawned upon us that perhaps we had sent the wrong address home. When asked the Adjutant could hardly contain himself, as he confirmed that the address we had taken from the notice board was "for example only" and entirely fictitious. Too late we learnt the code letters by which we should have been known, and at about the same time the postal authorities must have become interested too, as large wodges of mail greeted both Charles and me when we arrived at Hong Kong.

Meanwhile at Singapore we had spent a very pleasant afternoon and evening. A Gurkha officer friend of Charles' had met us and given us a wonderful tour in his car across the causeway and a few miles further into Johore, so that he could point out, at a great distance, the nearest hills where bandits were thought to lurk. The Malayan Emergency had been much in the news, but this was the first time I had got a notion of what it involved.

I was very sorry to see Charles disembark at Hong Kong and, as those of us who were proceeding to Japan were not allowed to go ashore, I repaired to the bar in the earnest hope that it might soon open. One of the Gunners later found me and said, "There you are, Dan! I was right, I was sure you weren't stopping at Hong Kong, but why have they taken your box off here then?" I got him to go over things again slowly. He had definitely seen a large steel trunk with RASCHEN KOREA boldly painted on the top being wheeled along the quay. The ship's staff took a bit of convincing, but they reluctantly let me go and look in the transit shed, where miraculously I managed to find my box fairly quickly and got it reloaded. I only hoped the other one was still aboard.

You may well wonder why a young officer on his way to a war, where the necessities of life were likely to be provided, needed to take two large boxes, say three hundredweight, of personal kit. The answers were, first, that my main purpose in volunteering for Korea had been to have the chance of shooting the local pheasants. My shotgun and 200 cartridges weighed nearly thirty pounds. Then, there was no certainty that I would stay in Korea. The duration of overseas tours at the time was three years, the same as it had been when I left India five years before, but time spent in Korea counted double. Therefore, unless a chap did eighteen months in Korea, he was liable for a subsequent overseas posting, and who knew how peaceful and sociable that might be? As the Korean War had only been going for just over a year, no one had yet achieved a full overseas tour there and, with all the talk of peace, it looked highly improbable that I would be there long. With this clear reasoning behind me, I felt it would have been stupid not to take what might be needed elsewhere, including my dinner jacket, tennis racket and riding breeches. "Much better have what you might need with you," had said my father. Good advice I had thought, but when we received the rumour on the *Fowey* that reinforcements might be flown to Korea with only a 65 pound kit allowance, I thought again. There were some officers from the Royal Navy aboard on the way to join their ships, so I took the opportunity of explaining my predicament, hoping to cover the passage of at least my gun and cartridges, and various kind but provisional promises were given.

After a beautiful day steaming through the dead calm Inland Sea of Japan, we arrived at Kure on 14th August, 1951. Kure had been an important port during the war and we were told that the vast Japanese battleship *Kongo*, the largest warship of the war, had been built there. Certainly there were shipyards, large, bombed and rusty. When the British and Indian Division had joined General MacArthur's forces to occupy the country after the surrender in 1945, Kure had been allotted to the British, and when the Korean War started it had been the natural place to reopen as the British Commonwealth base.

We were motored in army lorries to the inevitable transit camp which lay a few miles outside the town: as usual, officers were separated from soldiers. There were certainly masses of depressed officers, so goodness knows how the soldiers felt. In all there must have been thousands of us, and I could only think that some prudent soul reckoned that he ought to insure against major casualties, as suffered at the time of the Gloucester Battle, and be in the position to send reinforcements immediately. He might well have been right, but luckily nothing like that was happening at the moment. In addition to the transit camp, there was a battle camp about twenty miles inland where all new arrivals were meant to spend at least two weeks.

I managed to see the Postings Colonel the next morning, who said that he knew the Division did not need any Sapper officers at present. The headquarters of the Engineer Regiment and a further British Field Squadron had only recently arrived and, of course, they were fully up to strength. The war, he said, was dead quiet, to the extent that there was difficulty in making any contact with the Chinese so, thankfully, there had been no recent casualties. However, as I was the one and only Royal Engineers officer in the pipeline, he saw no harm in sending me up for interview with the Commander Royal Engineers (CRE) at Divisional Headquarters near Seoul, "quite soon" after I had been to battle camp.

My previous operational experience had been under entirely different circumstances with Indian troops over four years before, since when I had filled my time mainly as an undergraduate at Cambridge. Now even though that battle camp was probably tailored just for me, I had set my heart on missing it, as my main fear was that the war would end before I ever reached Korea. I must have argued pretty plausibly, as the colonel eventually agreed that so long as I visited it and learnt about the types of mines which were being used, that would do for a start. I could return there after visiting the CRE. Even if I lacked experience in a Korean type war, I must have impressed him with my knowledge of transit camps, or possibly he sensed a trouble maker.

I felt that if I could ever get to the Division, I could probably talk my way into staying there. One of the main successes in my earlier doings had been to join a draft to Sumatra, when it was fairly evident that I was not the one asset 26 Indian Division lacked. Once I had arrived, it had been too much trouble to send me back, and I hoped that the same would apply in Korea.

Two of the four days more that I remained in the Kure transit camp were as interesting as the others were dull. Hiroshima, where the first atom bomb had been dropped on Japan just over six years before, lay only thirty miles to the north-west. I and some Gunners and a doctor off the *Fowey* found our way there. We were not so much impressed by the effect of the bomb, as by the manner the town had been rebuilt into an apparently cheerful place. Plenty of reminders of the bomb remained, mainly left on purpose, and the extent of the devastation was certainly as great as I had ever imagined. If that was what a "small" atom bomb could do, we wondered what bigger bombs would be used for. Almost the last lecture I went to at Cambridge was by an eminent scientist who proved to us that fusion weapons could never be made. Now I couldn't see the need for them anyway, but it was not long before the first H bomb was exploded.

Plenty of postcards recording the weird effects of the nuclear flash were on sale, but those selling them, who were mainly survivors of the bomb, were themselves more memorable. Of the population of 350,000, approaching that of Bristol at the time, only one person in four had escaped harm, and 100,000 had died. Many of the postcard sellers remained badly burned, but were keen to assure us that they were recovering. The doctor with us was not so sure. My overall impressions were of the amazing recovery of a town which might as well have been removed from the atlases after the bomb, and of the complete lack of any outward ill feeling to us, the conquering forces, just back for another war.

I visited the battle camp, twenty miles inland from Kure, to be updated on the mines which were being used or might be used and was glad to handle them rather than just to read about them. It was known that our side had laid many anti-personnel mines, but nobody quite knew what the North was doing, except that the front opposite the Commonwealth Division was being held by Chinese, and not by North Koreans.

The glimpses of Japan that these short trips gave me, confirmed the photographs and descriptions I had seen, but the roads were worse (there were very few cars), the houses flimsier (just wood and paper), and the cultivation even more intense than I had expected. To judge by the children, who were beautifully turned out and spotlessly clean, the Japanese people were in pretty good shape.

In the next room in the hutted transit camp was a Captain from the 8th Hussars, Dick, who had been wounded and awarded an MC around the time of the Gloucester Battle. At first, due to the strange green and yellow pillbox worn by his Regiment as headdress, I thought he might be a French officer. I still knew much more about the Indian Army than about the British, but that was of little use to me now. I was delighted to learn, however, that one of the Field Ambulances, actually field hospitals, in the Division was a unit from India. Dick proved most helpful in advising me on what kit to take, his main message being, "If you value it, or if you can't carry it, leave it behind here in Kure." Evidently one tended to be left with very few personal possessions after a few weeks in a mobile war, and for all those who had been in Korea up to a month or two back, the war had been very mobile indeed. Their most vivid memory was of the beastly winter retreat from the North: the last great "bug out". "If you see more vehicles than usual going south, it could pay to join them and ask the reason later" was generally given as good advice by the veterans.

I asked Dick about the pheasant shooting. Yes, there certainly were lots of pheasants, but last winter there had been other forms of shooting as well. The duck flighting near the mouth of the Imjin River was said to be magnificient, but "what a pity the Turks have laid mines everywhere there now". Despite their questionable judgement in ruining the duck shooting, everyone held the Turkish contingent in the highest regard. The number of nationalities represented in the United Nations Force was interesting and surprising, but it must have been an administrative nightmare for the Eighth United States Army, Korea (EUSAK), which had to take them under its wing.

I took considerable notice of Dick's advice about my belongings, and left my two steel trunks in store in Kure. Whatever else though, I was not going to dump my shotgun and cartridges, the main reason for my excursion to the Furthest East. I joined a draft which left Kure on 20th August, en route to the port of Sasebo on the south-west coast of Japan. I still appeared to have about three times as much kit as anyone else, so was glad to see others I knew from the ship, hoping that they might help. The mutual delight which I knew they would feel was not immediately apparent.

Sasebo was conveniently placed opposite Pusan, on the bottom of South Korea, across 150 miles of sea. Since the war started, fourteen months before, the Americans had built Sasebo up into their main supply port, and the train that took us there was also American run and provided an experience in itself. I had been in many troop trains in India, but apart from when I travelled "goods", had never met anything as uncomfortable. The Americans could not be blamed, as they had had to take what was available. Nor I suppose, could the Japanese as there are no two ways to it, the Japanese and the British just weren't built the same shape. The seats were so uncomfortable that none of us slept, but we had a magnificient view of the Inland Sea of Japan on our left as we progressed across the island of Honshu into the setting sun.

The train had presumably come from Tokyo, so had been nearly full before, we the few British, had joined it. Our companions were mainly Americans, who took the evening meal, or "Chow", which interrupted our scenic tour, without comment. When it was our turn we staggered to the equivalent of a buffet car, were issued with a steel plate, and were served in turn mince, spaghetti, onions and potatoes, all of which looked most promising, and then, without the option, a large helping of fruit salad on top. Our comments, albeit sotto voce, of, "Wot, no cream?" fell on truly deaf ears. Our hosts reckoned, with unquestionable logic, that if the food mixed in tummies, why waste clean plates unnecessarily? We crossed from Honshu to Kyushu, the most westerly of the large Japanese islands, during the night and carried on to its north-west tip to be deposited at Sasebo.

The transit camp at Sasebo turned out to be a place where the British did not normally stay, but as the typhoons that August were apparently exceptional, we had to stay. We arrived at 3.30 a.m., so were not looking for much social life that night. However, we were still there the next night; Sasebo only accepted dollars and we had none. My companion, an RAMC doctor, and I must have looked pretty pathetic, or perhaps we begged, as a most generous American gave us a chitty book for their Officers' Club, and what could have been a terrible second night in the camp became highly congenial. Before finding the club, we had located a Royal Naval frigate, the *Mount's Bay*, in the port and had been welcomed to her very pleasant little wardroom where John Collins was the drink in vogue at that time.

The transit camp was five miles out of the town of Sasebo, and how we returned to it I cannot remember, but we were duly jolted back to life in the morning. I had always imagined that American officers did themselves well, at least in comparison with us: I soon found that I had been sadly disillusioned. Amongst thirty-five junior officers in a barrack room, most of the others were Americans on their way home from Korea, so provided plenty of interest. Breakfast was from 6.30-8.00, lunch from 11.30-12.30 and supper from 5.00-6.00, and that was that for those who did not wish to visit the highly over-soldiered town.

The doctor and I tried to identify nationalities and apart from the preponderance of white and black Americans, who tended to be in separate units, we notched up French, Filipinos, Turks, Canadians, Indians, (both the latter for our Division), Puerto Ricans and some we thought to be Greek. There was much talk of the Abyssinians who were coming. I thought I knew just what they should look like, as Prince Mekonen, Emperor Haile Selasse's son, had gone to Wellington at the same time as me.

We sailed from Sasebo in a 7,000 ton Japanese ship, the *Koan Maru*, which was in use as a rather unsuitable troopship. The ceilings were so low that even I had to bend my head, proving how short were the average Japanese. We sailed in the evening, so were expected to have eaten for the night and, as the trip would only be twelve hours, we were told, "No, there will be no chow aboard, you'll be fed in Pusan tomorrow morning." As the majority of the other passengers were for the French batallion, they also did not think much of the arrangements. In giant letters along the top of the dockside warehouses we read "FROM THIS PORT SAIL THE BEST DAMNED FIGHTING MEN IN THE WORLD. PORT OF SASEBO. US ARMY." As we were their guests we agreed that everyone was entitled to his own opinion.

The tail end of a typhoon continued to blow and we could not dock in Pusan until the afternoon, twenty hours without food, and I had started to understand that the Americans, good company though they were, did not manage things in quite the same as the British. The "Snowdrops", an American Army negro band with gleaming black and white helmets, greeted us with *If I had known you were coming I'd have baked a cake*, which made us even hungrier. They put on a smart and entertaining show.

Once ashore, we rushed breakfast at 4.00 p.m. and, with some hiccuping, I managed, with difficulty, to get my kit to the train that was waiting. My bedding roll, bought at the Officer's Shop in Bangalore seven years before, remained in vogue, but not everyone had rolled so much into theirs. I favoured the old type of wooden framed camp bed with steel lattice sides, firm enough to sit on without toppling over, but others had the safari type which was certainly lighter. My camp bath also had the same lattice framed construction as the bed, and, when stood on end also doubled as a support for a canvas basin. A kitbag and a suitcase, the contents of which included my shotgun and cartridges, made it a certainty that I could not personally hump my kit in one go.

We left Pusan without delay, which was no bad thing, as the whole of the population of South Korea had attempted to retreat into the place early in the war, and many had thought it safer to stay there. We chugged very gently on our way towards Seoul and with me wearing serge battledress Korea, in August, proved to be exceedingly hot. After Taegu, fifty miles north of Pusan, we were crossing ground over which the war had been fought less than a year before, but, war apart, the general impression was of a brown country with paddy fields between the eroded hills, and of small, brown or apricot coloured, people.

Settling down for the night was again a problem, but when I had at last managed it, we stopped and were told to change trains quickly. The train to which we had to move lay two tracks away, and between the old and the new trains lay a long and firmly coupled goods train. Some of my friends tried going under the couplings, but found the antic none too easy and aroused the displeasure of the American movements staff. Not being of agile build, I had no alternative but to make a pile of my kit beside the first train, then set off with my first load around the back of the goods train. The light was good enough to see the contents label on the first wagon, and I was amazed to find it contained nothing but American anti-personnel mines. I knew these to be of the type which, when actuated by the pressure of a foot or the pull of a trip wire, threw a grenade about four feet into the air to a good chest height, where it then exploded. A railway wagon must have held thousands of these mines. The next wagon had the same label, so had all the others. A whole railway train full of jumping anti-personnel mines was quite a new thought to me, and I wondered who was going to lay them.

As the accent has been on a quick change, my friends, who managed their kit in a single load, were reluctant to come back to help me with my second phase, lest the train left. In my hurry I lifted my bedding roll wrongly, and ricked my back. I caught the train, but was stiff and bent when it delivered us to Yong Dong Po, just south of Seoul at 5.00 a.m.

We were taken by vehicle into Seoul, where we were thankful to be received back into British care. The UK element possessed a relatively undamaged building and some very ragged 3-ton trucks which proudly sported bullet holes. Later I wondered whether the holes had been administered by the Chinese or by the RASC drivers. The desired effect was certainly achieved upon me.

We were given breakfast, then offered another, which I accepted. Life was looking up, but my back was so painful that I doubted if I could dig a slit trench, which I fondly imagined might be required of me if I reached the Division that day. The Movements Captain was surprised to see me, but sympathetic about my back and never accused me of flinching in the face of the enemy, which I had rather feared. He assured me that as I would be likely to live in a tent above ground, at least in the immediate future, I would be glad to have such a good bed. Let alone being attacked by them, the problem was to make any contact with the Chinese. He thought that perhaps they had gone home for the harvest.

"Yes," said Movements, "I can see no harm in you going up to HQ RE (Headquarters, Royal Engineers) and seeing if they can use you. If not, come back here." I started to ask him if he had seen any pheasants during the summer and whether it had been a good breeding season, but there were others in the queue who were fidgeting, so I was waved on.

As I waited for the vehicle to take me up to the Division, I had a chance to think over my position. It was 24th August, 1951, and I would be twenty-six in a month's time. I was a slightly senior lieutenant in the Royal Engineers with three medal ribbons of no consequence on my chest. I had had precious little experience of commanding British soldiers, but hoped that "Carry on please, Sergeant" would work as well as had "Carry on please, Jemedar Sahib" in the Royal Bombay Sappers and Miners. My achievement was to have reached Korea, which had been my intention ever since I had read about the pheasant shooting last Boxing Day, and the Movements Staff had proved pleasant, a new experience for me. Things were going well and, if given the choice of sitting exams in Cambridge, as I had been under three months before, or of being in Korea, Korea would have won.

The First Commonwealth Division held about seven miles of the United Nations front some forty miles north of Seoul. Our line lay on or slightly north of the 38th Parallel, over which the North Koreans had attacked fourteen months before. Nothing much, other than a great deal of damage and a lot of casualties seemed to have been achieved so far and, as we left Seoul, previously the capital city of both North and South Korea, the damage was highly apparent. The Capitol, which must have been a fine building, was completely burnt out, and most other buildings showed direct signs of war. The overall appearance was uninviting, but it must have had its attractions, as many walls had been painted by the American authorities with slogans such as "NATIVE LIQOR KILLS" or, when in more moderate mood, "NATIVE LIQOR BLINDS". I had heard that the Japanese Asahi beer was of excellent quality and it did not, thankfully, fall into the "native" category.

There was a 20 mph speed limit on the roads, which reverted to earth soon after crossing the Han River and leaving the tarmac and cobbles of Seoul. I noted, as I sat in the back of a 3-tonner, that the road surface had formed in beautiful waves, just like the sine curves which our lecturer had proved would occur when he scribbled on the blackboard at Cambridge. We had laughed him from the room, but he certainly now deserved an apology.

As it was an American led war, we drove on the right and wondered what the myriad of "tac signs", or numbers on painted discs of various colours, and codenames, white painted on black backgrounds, meant. The number of our Divisional Headquarters was 40, and proved easy to follow, especially as the signs were newer than most. The Division had only been formed under a month before, on 28th July, and a lot of the old stagers rather resented its existence, having been very happy in their delightfully independent brigades.

The main way of telling where the road ended and the soft edges began was the signal cables which lay in their hundreds beside it. Some were on small poles, some tied together in clusters and some just lay on the ground. The wide valleys just north of Seoul appeared to be intensely farmed, but in the background were the browny red, scrub covered hills and an occasional minor, but craggy, mountain.

We passed Uijongbu, a town of which we had heard on the wireless during various stages of the war, now with no two bricks standing together. We were informed that the Headquarters of the Army Corps of which I COMWEL Div was part, "EYE" ("I") Corps, the American First Corps, was there, a place to which I was not attracted. As we continued, the scene became more desolate and the signs of war more frequent. A T34 tank and an anti-tank gun, both of Russian origin, lay to one side of the road and the line of the signal cables started to merge with the barbed wire fences complete with little red triangles which marked the edge of the minefields. "If you see a deer in a minefield, move away," advised our driver. "They can pull tripwires, and that can hurt you too." I hadn't even heard of deer in Korea, nor had an immediate wish to see one.

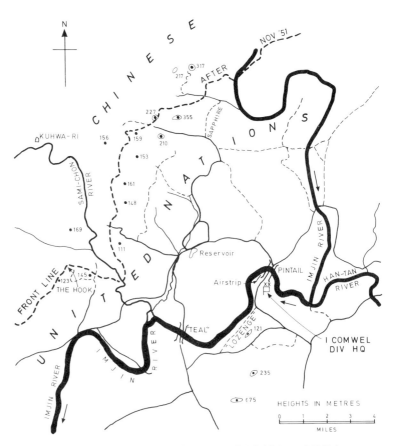

1st COMMONWEALTH DIVISION AREA

CHAPTER THREE

FIRST COMMONWEALTH DIVISION

I was delivered to the headquarters of the Royal Engineers, to find that the Commander, the CRE, was out. Perhaps this was no bad thing, as it gave his sergeant clerk a chance to check on what he knew of me. I had certainly arrived before I was expected, but a letter I had written to the CRE two months ago from Devonshire was proudly produced. Yes, they had heard of me. I had always understood that it was a matter of form for an officer to write to his new commanding officer soon after receiving a posting order, to say how delighted he was to be coming under his command. Apparently my letter was one of the first received from someone posted to Korea, and I gained the impression that others might not have been as delighted as I at the prospect.

My afternoon with the sergeant clerk proved to have been probably the best briefing that I could have been given. He made the somewhat unusual organisation of the Royal Engineers in that theatre of the war hang together so that I could understand it, and the rest of the Division then started to take shape. The CRE was, as his title implied, the Commander of all Royal Engineers in the Division and was also the General Officer Commanding's personal adviser on all engineer matters. He, the CRE, was Colonel E. C. W. Myers, CBE, DSO, an officer of whose war exploits, which included organising the early resistance in Greece, I had heard, and the General Officer Commanding the Division, the GOC, was Major General A. J. H. Cassels, CB, CBE, DSO. He had recently commanded 6 Airborne Division whereas, earlier, Colonel Myers had been CRE of 1 Airborne Division at Arnhem. The CRE had a tiny staff of his own, headed by a highly experienced Royal Canadian Engineer officer, Major Abbott. Permanently under his command he had 28 Engineer Regiment, with its own lieutenant colonel, as well as various American and Korean units attached on a more occasional basis.

The sergeant started to tell me about the personalities of the Regiment. Of the five officers in the headquarters, four held the Military Cross, and the other had been taken prisoner of war at Dunkirk. The Commanding Officer, Lieutenant Colonel P. N. M. Moore had two DSOs in addition to his MC. I could now understand what the Postings Captain in England had meant when he said, "We are only sending good officers to Korea."

I was feeling immensely impressed by the quality of the units I hoped to join, but also decidedly deflated, even before Colonel Myers arrived. He couldn't have been kinder, but there was no doubt that I was not wanted, not yet at any rate. The Regiment consisted of three Field Squadrons, of which one was Canadian, so I obviously would not be going to it. Another, 55 Field Squadron had been in Korea since the end of the previous year and had suffered casualties, but had been fully reinforced. The other British units, 12 Field Squadron and 64 Field Park Squadron, whose job it was to provide support for the Field Squadrons, had come with the Regimental Headquarters from Cyrenaica only a few weeks before. All were more than up to strength, particularly as the "Z Reserve", whatever that was, had been called up from civilian life to go to Korea.

Colonel Myers said that the best he could do for me immediately was to put me in charge of building a rest camp that was under consideration the other side of Seoul but, until plans were definite, I had better go as a supernumerary officer to the Field Park Squadron. I felt the same as I had when the Royal Bombay Sappers and Miners tried to keep me at the Depot at Kirkee just when I considered myself trained for war, and must have looked shattered. Colonel Myers said that he wouldn't forget me, and sent me on my way.

The Field Park Squadron greeted me most kindly. It turned out that the Officer Commanding, Major John Keer, was the brother of Martin, to whom I had been Assistant Adjutant at Aldershot, and who, coincidently, was now Adjutant to Lieutenant Colonel Moore, here in the Regiment. I knew that Martin was keen on shooting and that if pheasants were to be shot, he would be the man from whom to take advice.

Soon I was sitting on some pontoon bridging in the Field Park stores yard, bothering nobody and writing letters home.

The Korean War seemed to fall outside the rules of my previous training, particularly as regards security. Until 1945, and also in Sumatra, it had been drummed into us that nothing of any secrecy must be written down or discussed with unknown persons. Mail had been subject to censorship and the penalties for security breaches had been high. Here in Korea there was no censorship, and everyone seemed to do much as they pleased. I asked if I could tell my family where I was, and was told that there would be no objection whatever. The only problem would be to pinpoint our particular bit of the middle of nowhere in a way that meant something at home. "40 miles north of Seoul" was the best that I achieved.

At lunch the next day I was told that 12 Field Squadron had undertaken to use me as, nominally, their Intelligence Officer, and that I need not worry about building a rest camp. This most welcome news must have been due to, first the CRE offering me around, and secondly to the Officer Commanding (OC) of 12 Squadron, Major Howard Stephens, having overlapped me at Cambridge by a year. The variety of age groups at university after the war was proving to have its advantages.

12 Squadron were comfortably settled in tents or vehicles some six miles south of the Imjin River. On the north of the Imjin there were the Chinese, though exactly where was in doubt. That being the case, I dared to wonder at what some of our 25 pounder guns were firing. "Harassing fire" I was told.

Guns apart, the war was in a thoroughly phoney state. The peace talks had been on, then off, and were now on again and there had been no infantry contact near us for many weeks. Much the most dangerous things in Korea at present, I was told, were our own, or our friends', mines and booby traps. There were frightening stories of the Australians, the 3rd Battalion of the Royal Australian Regiment, an excellent and enterprising unit comprised mainly of ex-servicemen, who had been delighted to volunteer for service away from home. They occupied a feature on the south bank of the Imjin known as the Lozenge and, under the energetic direction of their Pioneer Officer had devised and laid an outstanding barrier of booby traps with a view to ensuring that no Chinaman should surprise them by stealth. Unfortunately the Pioneer Officer had then been killed by one of his own traps, taking most of the location plans with him in his head. The battalion had suffered severely from their own devices, and the subject of booby traps was no longer popular.

There was much talk in 12 Squadron of life as it had been in Cyrenaica, which meant nothing to me, but sounded as if it had been pretty good. They had been shattered when Lieutenant Colonel Peter Moore had called them together to say how proud and delighted he was that he and his units had been selected to represent the Corps of Royal Engineers in Korea. He had added that a training programme for war would start immediately. Everyone admitted that no CO could be better qualified to direct such a programme, and it had been undertaken with an intensity that would have made Field Marshal Montgomery envious. The only shore leave permitted whilst on the troopship had been for route marches, and these had been intentionally unpleasant. The Squadron had arrived in Korea expecting immediate involvement in a war, but found that only peace reigned.

Now, no longer under the direct supervision of their commanding officer, it was natural that a sense of relieved anti-climax had set in. Taking war seriously sometimes meant calling wolf too early, but those more experienced than me knew that that was the safest course. This was not my worry, as some trouble must have been taken to keep me busy. The Regiment had an excellent Intelligence Officer who kept the Squadron fully aware of any information that was available, so the Squadron IO turned out to be the odd job man, which suited me fine. I saw the country at the same time as having minimal responsibility and, now that I no longer had to carry my kit, my back was better. Added to which, unlike England where, six years after the war, severe rationing was still in operation, the food was good. Drink, including gin at 7 shillings a bottle (35p), was fairly plentiful, meaning that the NAAFI were starting to provide the necessities of life.

I was sent to make a reconnaissance of the road running along the south bank of the Imjin towards the infamous Lozenge feature. I would have thought that its state must have been well known, but supposed that it might have changed. I found it to be very rough and unfrequented, which was confirmed by two graves on the side marked with sticks bound together into a cross. Further along the road had been cratered by a large shell, but one of our Centurion tanks must have found cause to fire a large number of its 20 pounder rounds nearby, as some fifty of the large brass cartridge cases, representing nearly half a ton of brass, had been used to fill in the hole. I myself had, rather ashamedly, used coconuts as make weight for concrete in Sumatra but, if that was an original way to make concrete, so was this to fill potholes.

I went no further, as it struck me that perhaps others had heard of the Australians' booby traps.

The next day the OC said, "Pat de Clermont thinks there may be mines up the road behind his Squadron and, if there are, wants them cleared. He had asked whoever does the job to go to lunch with him first, and that better be you Dan." It was considered amazing that I did not know who Pat de Clermont was, but soon learnt that he was the Major commanding "R" Squadron of the 8th Hussars, and that I couldn't miss them, just go up the main supply route (MSR) on the left. Up the MSR I went and soon passed a yellow and red triangulated tac sign, meaning armour, with the letter "A" stencilled on it. I carried on another couple of miles, and saw plenty of other tac signs pointing up side tracks, but none led to armour, so I went back to the "A" Squadron sign and drove in. "Please could you tell me the way to 'R' Squadron," I asked and, for the second time that morning, was greeted by amazement. "This is 'R' Squadron." "But, then, why do your signs say 'A'?" I lamely muttered. "Sir, we are *Irish* Hussars, and we say 'A' as 'Ah'." "Ah!" indeed. Evidently this was a stock joke for which I had fallen, to the delight of all. We had its counterpart in Cambridge when, on their first Sunday morning, freshmen were directed to the morning service "at the first large church on the left down Trumpington Street". Some keen young man always said he knew it, only to discover that the impressive building was the Cambridge University Press.

Major de Clermont turned out to be just as I had been led to expect, a charming and self-assured cavalry officer who soldiered because he enjoyed the life. It appeared that 12 Squadron were doing him a great favour in sending me, and the lunch which he gave me, which well justified the designation luncheon, was very good. I had the strength of mind to refuse the port, as it was a warm day and I was not sure that port and searching for anti-personnel mines would go well together.

My host could not tell me much about the mines for which I was meant to be looking, just that there was a barbed wire fence across the track a couple of hundred yards beyond his tanks and he thought that it might mean mines. I asked if a minefield record form existed. None was held. I was taken to the fence, which turned out to be of the double-apron type, usually erected as a barrier against men, and it had no red triangles on it which denoted a minefield. It had obviously been erected by the United Nations forces, as our opponents did not seem to use wire, so the chances were that, as no one had actual evidence of mines, there were none. Thus reassured, I asked onlookers to depart and looking confident and, I hoped, brave, gently clambered through the fence, taking with me an electronic mine detector and a long metal prong suitable for prodding the ground.

The ground was dry and the track was flat, so I thought that I should be able to see any tripwires, but none were in view. So far as I knew, our side had only laid metallic mines, a type which would be picked up by my detector. I hadn't seen a mine detector for many years, but had tried tuning the headphones that morning, so managed to sweep a couple of hundred yards up the track quite quickly finding, as I rather expected nothing. That left the possibility of the Chinese having laid their wooden anti-tank mines. These were boxes containing about 14 pounds of high explosive, and they needed more than the weight of a walking man to set them off. They contained hardly any metal and would be unlikely to be found by the detector. I went through the motions of cautiously prodding the track, six inches at a time, sideways and forwards, very gently. This method always sounded splendid in our pamphlets and had, no doubt, been a wow in the sand of the Western Desert, but was of little use on a stone hard earth track which contained a lot of gravel. Had the prodding any hope of success, I would have tried it whilst advancing up the track with the detector. Now it had to be seen that I had made the attempt. It was all rather aimless, and I wondered what the shortest time on the task might be that would decently justify my host's hospitality. After just over an hour I climbed back through the fence, and reported that I could find nothing and was thanked for the great favour of my efforts. The double-apron fence was being removed as I left: I heard later that Major de Clermont had reported that he was delighted, so presumably no mines had been found.

Those first days in Korea were all that I could have wanted, with no responsibility other than for a jeep, a driver and myself. Some are never happy unless they can claim half the British Army under their personal command, but I was in no hurry to join that category. My journeys, all within the ten or so miles covered by our Division, gave me a welcome chance to take a look at the country. If the newspapers were to be believed, attractive scenery would seldom be seen, but I found the countryside much more pleasant than I expected. My initial reaction was probably influenced by the beautiful hot late summer days which greeted me.

True, there was a lack of large trees, but stunted and scrubby versions of many common species managed to cover the browny-orange hills. A form of eating chestnut, complete with masses of prickly chestnuts, were common, as were scrubby oaks and stunted pines. Amongst the oaks were some of the ornamental variety, with enormous leaves eighteen inches long. Previously I had been very proud of one in our garden at home, which turned to most beautiful pinks and reds in autumn, but I now realised that I had overrated its rarity. To show that men had once inhabited the land on which our army had established itself, there were the remants of villages with crops in the fields that had been sown the year before, or perhaps even the year before that, and had never been harvested. Some had been burnt off in the spring, but secondary growth had taken over, and the result was as good pheasant cover as any gamekeeper could desire. There were also a few small plantations of Japanese larches, and the odd row of poplars along the few older roads. Buildings, in the modern sense, didn't exist, and I soon confirmed in my travels that there wasn't a habitable permanent building anywhere back to Seoul, forty miles behind us. If the aim

United Nations. Major Howard Stephens, RE (British), Captain Freddie Mitchell, RCE (Canadian) and "Poppa-San" (Korean).

Korean village and bunded paddy fields.

Pheasant marsh beside the River Imjin.

had been to pick a battlefield where little harm could be done, high marks would have been awarded to those who positioned the 1st Commonwealth Division.

Despite what looked to me like a pheasant's heaven, I was getting worried: I had been in Korea nearly a week and I hadn't seen one. I found cause to visit Martin Keer, the Adjutant at Regimental Headquarters, to tell him how disturbed I was. "Dan," he said, "if the corn had not been cut in England, do you think you would see a lot of pheasants?" "No, Martin," I said. When I had been his Assistant Adjutant at Aldershot, I had always called him "Sir" on our first meeting in the morning. Although he was probably only three years older than me, that had meant the difference of availability for the war, of which he had seen his full share.

If Martin said one didn't expect to see pheasants at this time of year, I was reassured. Although that had, ostensibly, been the only question I had visited RHQ to ask, I was just a teeny bit interested in how long I was likely to be left in the non-essential job which had obviously been dreamt up particularly for me. Martin had grown a large moustache, which he managed to pull in such a non-committal manner that I was almost sure he knew something he was not going to tell me.

Sure enough, on arrival back at 12 Squadron the OC called for me. He started by saying, "David has had long standing trouble with his nose." Medical cases always worry me, being the queasy sort, so I tried: "There are worse places to have trouble, Sir." "He has got to go back to Kure for an operation, and I want you to take over 3 Troop from him." This was unexpected, but splendid.

David appeared to have mixed feelings on giving his Troop to me. Evidently, when he had taken it over in Africa not so long ago, it had mustered quite a proportion of individuals whom he would not personally have selected to represent him. Just as he was getting to discover the true talents of his manpower, along had come another five older soldiers recalled from the "Z" Reserve. Like me, he was unsure what that was, other than that it contained individuals who had at some stage in the 1939-45 War worn uniform and who had contracted, presumably at some slight advantage to themselves, to remain on recall to the colours, recall which they must have been assured was extremely unlikely. When the King had proclaimed that the "Z" Reserve should be recalled for the Korean War, consternation had reigned. The overall result had been the injection into units, that recently had consisted

Regimental Headquarters. Martin Keer and the author.

mainly of young conscript soldiers, of some fairly hardbitten men who acted as and claimed to be old soldiers. A Sapper Troop was established at just over sixty men. The working numbers consisted of three sections, each with a Corporal, one or two Lance Corporals and about ten Sappers, together with a further administrative section, including the drivers of about a dozen vehicles, a storeman, a signaller or two, the officers and sergeants. Officer, nor officers, was more the case, as Mike, a second lieutenant, was temporarily on detachment and was due to return to England in October, and we were in the last days of August. David assured me that the Troop Staff Sergeant was the best in the Regiment and "So long as he is about, you'll have no real worries. He looks after all the Sapper tasks, and lets the Sergeant, a storeman type, do the admin, NAAFI, clothing and all that." "Sounds splendid," I said, and so it was.

I had no sooner been delighted by my first few sunny days in the country, than it rained, and kept on raining. Although the Imjin River ran across our front, more or less from east to west, it originated from Chinese held ground well to the north of us, so we could always blame the Chinamen if the Imjin misbehaved. I had seen it as a lovely placid river, half filling a gap of over 200 yards between cliffs nearly fifty feet high. Where there was no flat water there as lovely silver sand, which made a perfect edge to a superb swimming pool. But now the Imjin rose, and rose. The sands were quickly covered and the water climbed steadily up the cliffs. Later, we became quite scientific in measuring the rate of rise and fall of the river but this, the first Imjin flood since the formation of the Division, was new to most of us and something of a revelation. It was just when we had generally agreed that the river had risen twenty feet in a day and was flowing at more than ten feet per second that I saw my commanding officer for the first time at full power. He had been wading up to his chin in the floods and rushed in to see our squadron commander. The cause of his concern was that the Canadian Brigade had mounted a substantial excursion by crossing in boats to the north bank, with a view to making contact with the Chinese. The latter had failed to oblige, but the Canadians, nearly a battalion of them were now cut off by the river, a point which the enemy might soon note. However, nothing happened, the river fell nearly as quickly as it had risen and the Canadians came safely home.

Another of these raids, as they become known, across the river was mounted a few days later and various members of the Regiment were encouraged to join the party. Some of these, including the regimental chief clerk, must have undertaken the walk more for the good of their health than for their contribution to the overall aim of taking prisoners. Very little indeed was known about the doings of the Chinese and their plans, but it was thought that a few prisoners might tell us all. I don't think we had any notion of how reluctant they would be to be taken, or how little they would be likely to tell us.

General Cassels, our Divisional Commander, who was already well known and popularly acclaimed as General Jim, announced he would personally present a bottle of whisky to the first man to bring home a prisoner. Whisky was sufficiently rare, certainly outside officers' messes, as to provide a real incentive, and there wasn't a man in the forward brigades who had not heard of the promise. I let it be known that I would very much like to go on a raid myself. Raids seemed to offer a touch of glamour and warlike excitement, without much real risk.

When I took over 3 Troop, its first task was to build, from Bailey bridging, a pontoon raft of sufficient capacity to ferry tanks across the river. That meant either the Mark 3 Centurions of the 8th Hussars, each weighing 50 tons, or the rather lighter Shermans of the Canadian

Squadron of Lord Strathcona's Horse. Luckily my Troop Staff Sergeant had undertaken the ferry building and completed it with great efficiency. He had then been kind enough to invite me to take command of the raft and navigate it across the river. At each of its four corners it had an eight horsepower Petter's engine which drove a propellor through a flexible coupling drive shaft, and at each propellor unit sat a Sapper studying the arm movements of the raft commander just as avidly as musicians study their conductor. Providing the raft commander knew the right signals, it was surprising what good and controlled progress could be made by such an ungainly craft. I had warned the Staff Sergeant that I was rather out of practice, an understatement, as the only time I had previously attempted the art had been on a still lake in India over six years before. The Imjin was not in flood, but it was certainly flowing, not just downstream but with a most unfriendly bias to the far bank. In my effort to counteract the drift I must have over-corrected, or perhaps my ever faster gesticulations were misinterpreted. Sufficient to say that we started to spin downstream in a most undignified manner.

My marvellous Staff Sergeant took over almost before I had made the request, brought the craft under control and suggested that we had

The tank raft at the "PINTAIL" crossing.

trained enough for the day. We took the precaution of making sure the raft was very securely anchored, which was just as well on that river. It was as we were leaving the river bank that the Staff Sergeant told me that he had heard that morning that he was to be medically evacuated to Japan due to recurrent leg trouble, and that the chances were that he would be sent home. He was kind enough to say he was sorry he would not be serving with me, but he was nothing like as sorry as I was to be in losing him.

I asked my OC for another Troop Staff Sergeant, and was told that, despite the reputedly massive number of reinforcements waiting in Japan, high quality senior NCOs were not included. "You'll have to manage with Sergeant Williams." I remembered what David had told me, and envied his sense of timing. Neither I nor Sergeant Williams were, in the course of a normal day, dynamic leaders, yet it was all too apparent to me that some of those under my command would need commanding. However, I felt so lucky to be with 3 Troop at all that my responsibilities worried me little. I assured myself that I had commanded larger sub-units in the Royal Bombay Sappers and Miners without causing a mutiny, so all would surely be well.

Then, though, I had been blessed with highly experienced and helpful subordinates. Then, also, we had been sleeping in good houses with electric light, and now I was in a tent with a candle. All officers were working hard and long, not least my Squadron Commander, who seldom arrived home until after dark, joined us for supper, took an orderly room to deal with those who had misbehaved, and then gave his orders for the next day. By the time I arrived back with my Troop, most of the NCOs were asleep, as they too had no lights and few candles. I hadn't the heart to wake them, but that meant a mad flap in the morning as I tried to gain details of the day's work whilst gobbling breakfast or shaving. Sergeant Williams saw it as his job to ensure that there was breakfast, and thank goodness he did. He was also quite happy for me to deal direct with the section corporals.

My greatest fear was of a rushed move. Soldiers did not have factory made camp beds, nor could they be acquired in the depths of Korea, but every man had made himself a bed, usually out of a timber frame lashed together with carefully knotted signal cable to support the bedding. A few had also made chairs and tables and most had acquired one or more large ammunition boxes in which to keep extra essentials. "What splendid initiative" you may say, but just you try loading that kind of kit on to vehicles already inadequate for all the kit with which a Field Troop of the Royal Engineers was issued. I remonstrated a little, but knew that I was on difficult ground, as the diversity of my own kit had aroused interest and mirth on my arrival. I should have insisted that officers were different. We held a practice move and, even in slow time, the results were horrific.

The early September days remained really hot, but the nights were starting to get cold. There was much talk of the lack of proper clothing last winter and of promises that everything was already available for the next. In the meanwhile I was glad of the sleeping bag I had bought in the Army and Navy Stores, though I had rather underestimated my size. I was still more than well covered and whatever the privations of the Korean Campaign, we could not claim to be starved. We probably had on offer the best food in the military world, as our dry rations, tea, sugar, butter and so on, were provided through British channels and the fresh food, meaning meat and veg, came from California or Hawaii, both of which we concluded must be lush by any standard.

With the peace talks continuing at Panmunjon, only about twenty miles as the crow flew to our north-west, I was finding it hard to inspire those under me with warlike thoughts and to explain the reason for our presence in what most soldiers considered to be a particularly unattractive part of the world. In the 1939-45 War we were told that we must make those under our command fully aware of the evils we were fighting, and many education sergeants justified their existence by doing just that. Like me, most of them never went to that war. In Sumatra, where we had been involved in a form of war, no one dreamt of discussing the reason for what we were doing. We just did it, and Korea seemed to be like Sumatra. Why we were there was not discussed. We were doubly thankful that this was the case, as we understood that the Chinese, even in the front line, spent hours and hours each day at political indoctrination classes.

CHAPTER FOUR

A RAID

It was when I was trying to interview the members of my Troop individually to find out a little more about those on our strength, that Howard told me that, as I had asked to go on a raid across the river, he had nominated me for the next one, tomorrow. The whole of the 3rd Battalion of the Royal Australian Regiment would be going, and so would a Troop of four Centurion tanks from the 8th Hussars. They would be taken across on the raft my Troop had built, but it would be operated by others. My job would be to look for mines, so I had better take three or four men with me. I was also allowed to take a vehicle, a 15 cwt truck, to carry the detectors and our kit, and we could expect to be back on the south bank of the Imjin within forty-eight hours.

From my point of view this was too good to be true. Despite their troubles with their own booby traps, 3 RAR were a unit of the highest repute, and their commanding officer, Lieutenant Colonel Frank Hassett had an outstanding reputation. Due to the speed with which I had been selected for the task, I had apparently missed the briefing and orders group but, as my OC said, "There's only one narrow road forward, so you can't get lost."

I had, by good chance, been introduced to Colonel Hassett earlier in the week and he crossed the river on the raft at the same time as my 15 cwt the next morning. Because of the cliffs, there were few natural crossing places on the Imjin, and each had been allocated a codename, mainly after types of duck. We were crossing at "PINTAIL", which had an easy approach over the silver sands on the south bank, and a dozer had cut a sufficient road into the cliffside opposite for the tanks to make a hair raising ascent. My 15 cwt took one look at it and decided that it did not like the idea. The poor young driver was highly embarrassed as he eventually managed to splutter the vehicle to the top, forcibly coaxed on by some very muscular Australians.

I had with me one of the "Z" reservists, a lance corporal who last soldiered in the Burma jungles, and three young Sappers who looked ten years younger than the average Australian. It was the 8th of September, 1951, so my twenty-sixth birthday in a couple of weeks was ages ahead.

One of the Australian companies had crossed earlier and had "secured" the bridgehead which, as no Chinamen had the slightest desire to be present, was merely a formality. From the top of the cliff at PINTAIL, the Australians pointed my mineclearing party up the narrow road to the left and waved us on our way saying, "There's a platoon in front, but stop when you get to the village."

Off we would have liked to have gone, but the 15 cwt had taken a real dislike to the enemy side of the river and made it obvious that it had breathed its last. We attempted to advance, with two Sappers going through the motions of mine detection, one with a mine detector, the other with a prodder, the lance corporal and Australian friends pushing the vehicle behind, and me giving fruitless advice to all and sundry. After a couple of hundred yards we concluded this embarrassing episode by ditching the vehicle, literally, so that it did not block the narrow road, and left the driver with it. Whatever else one did, it was not done to leave vehicles unattended, particularly near Australians, though they would have been more than welcome to that one.

The moment I had heard of the mineclearing, I had known that our task would be forlorn, and the texture of the road confirmed my worst misgivings because, despite the recent rains, the surface of well compacted gravel was much too hard to prod, and there were masses of potholes into which it would probably have been fairly easy to dig and hide a box mine. This was just like the mineclearing I had attempted for "A" Squadron of the 8th Hussars the week before, and likely to be equally hopeless.

So far as I know there are only two paces at which one can clear mines on foot. The textbook method was completely methodical, sweeping the detector over the whole track and then prodding at gaps of not more than six inches, a desperately slow undertaking. The other, which was not in the book, was to advance with care and caution doing little more than keeping a good look out for tripwires. We knew that we were expected to cover the couple of miles to the village in not more than two hours; there was no choice but to keep going. So we proceeded, gazing assiduously at the road surface, prodding it occasionally and dangling a prodder as if to sense tripwires, which on the nice sunny day, which it was, we could have seen anyway. Such Australians as we met looked duly impressed, but the Troop Leader of the Centurions, who were soon trundling along behind us, less so. It was a small world, as I had met him at friends' dances in the New Forest only last winter. He was as civil as could be, just saying that he thought he would be safer off the road, especially as the adjoining fields were firm.

Knowing that the tanks were off to the side of us made our efforts even more pointless, but we realised that they would have to come back onto the track fairly soon, or would get bogged down in the rice fields. Paddy fields are, by intent, soggy, and even after a year of neglect, the bunds had ponded up the rain well, so that great gooeyness remained. The village seemed rather further than I had expected. Like other items which I was already regretting, such as the wireless, I had left my map in the vehicle. Rather than be late, we quickened our pace. In front of us was quite a sizeable hill and the road skirted round it to the left at the bottom, but I was surprised to find that another very rough track ran off to the right. I certainly did not remember it on the map, and determined to report it as soon as I regained contact.

Despite the fact that the raid was in progress, the level of gunfire, all ours of course, remained much as on other days which, as we still hadn't found where the enemy were, was hardly surprising. It had been falling many thousands of yards in front of us and, though reassuring to hear the shells singing overhead miles up, we doubted if they were going to change the course of the war. Even though we hadn't found any mines, it was with the satisfaction of our diligent efforts that the four of us sat down to eat our sandwiches at the bottom of the hill. Our munching was interrupted by first a few shells, then the eight of a battery, falling around the crest line of the hill about half a mile in front of us. I had had a tingle that the village landmark might have been incorrectly explained to me, and my companions now confirmed my suspicions by suggesting that we were perhaps a little further forward than we should be.

We retired down the road, albeit with decorum, a great deal faster than we had come up it. We had gone nearly a mile when we were whistled in by some Australians, hidden in the long grass on the verges. I had learnt that a really serious Australian pronouncement was usually preceded by "My oath" and, sure enough, "My oath, why didn't you stop at the village?", together with other comments, greeted us. "We never saw the village," I said, "But you're in it" was the reply intended to achieve an effect, which it did. We looked around and noticed that, on average, the ground was more charred than elsewhere and the vegetation rather more varied. It had in no way struck me that a Korean village of timber and straw huts which had been burnt to the ground the previous year would look so little different from the rest of the countryside.

I know that many individuals have, by mistake, led their armies, but I was determined not to make a habit of the practice. I felt consoled, however, when I remembered that my aunt with her YMCA van during our advance up Italy in 1944 had been found serving tea to Germans. She always said that she thought they were prisoners.

With me and my small party safely behind them, the leading Australians advanced briskly up the road, confident that there were no tripwires across it. It turned out that the hill under which we had taken luncheon was our objective for the day, and that was where we were going to spend the night. There was no evidence of Chinese upon it and, although the leading company moved onto it prepared to fight, nothing happened. By early evening we were all up on top and, as we were three miles into country which the Chinese usually occupied, the chances were that we would receive some attention that night.

My small party was integrated into an Australian rifle platoon, and we needed little encouragement to dig slit trenches. In fact, the Chinese were proving very good hosts and had done most of the work for us. They appeared to have occupied the ground up to about a week before, and although you may not fancy sleeping in a hole recently vacated by a decidedly smelly enemy, to do so was preferable to digging a new one. Sanitation had not been their strong point and the flies reminded me of India in the hot weather.

My Australian companion in a two man slit trench was aged about thirty-five, an extremely self-composed soldier. It was the next morning that I learnt from others that he had had a very good war in the Royal Australian Air Force, had been a Wing Commander and held the DSO. Even without that knowledge he inspired me with great confidence, and I was delighted to be with him and do what he, a private soldier, suggested that I, Lieutenant Raschen, should do. There were plenty of interesting characters in 3 RAR.

The order for the night was that one man in each trench must remain awake, meaning guard duty of two hours on, two off. Unfortunately the flies and mosquitoes appeared to have made similar arrangements, except that the flies were on all day and the mosquitoes all night. I have always been one who needs a full eight hours' sleep and, after a long day with plenty of fresh air and exercise, I needed it then, but obviously was not going to get it. It was almost a relief when, in the depths of the night, there was a bang well down the hill behind us, which gave me an excuse to stand up. My companion told me that this was not necessary: "Just a grenade." After a couple of minutes there were three more bangs, not large as they go, but loud in the night which, apart from the mosquitoes and some of our own gunfire, had been remarkably quiet. A few shots were fired, as if by a sentry, then all had again been quiet for ten minutes or so when more grenades were thrown, and so the action, or lack of it, continued. Although it would have been tactically possible, it seemed strange and worrying that Chinese were behind us, but it was almost a compliment to know that the enemy appeared to be taking some interest in our no-passport excursion to the north bank of the Imjin.

Before dawn we all had to stand to and so a rotten night came to an end. Why the Chinese, who had a respectable reputation for night fighting, should be expected to wait for dawn was not clear, but once it was daylight we unfixed bayonets and set about breakfast and shaving. We were keen to hear details of the noise during the night and soon received the delighted report that the platoon concerned had been engaging their own Korean porters who had been bringing up supplies of ammunition and food. There had evidently been some misunderstanding over passwords, and everyone thought it a howling joke including, we were assured, the porters. They had, most commendably, carried on with their task, but had not delivered quite as many desirable items as might otherwise have been expected.

I had spoken to Lieutenant Colonel Hassett the previous evening and got the impression that he had nothing particular in mind for his Sapper party the next day, more that he expected the Chinese to make the running. They had not, and now it looked as if we might sit through the day doing nothing. I decided that the Colonel would like to see me, so went over the hill to where I knew he would be. Since the previous afternoon we had re-established contact with our vehicle and, in addition to the comforts of a blanket and rations, I had made a point of retrieving my map. This I had studied during the evening and saw that some tracks were marked on the far side of our hill. If anyone was going that way, I felt I ought to go and have a look at them.

Lieutenant Colonel Hassett was looking in just the right direction as I arrived, the reason being obvious, as two of his four rifle companies, each of about a hundred men, were wending their way down the hill. I had heard that some fighting patrols might be going out, and these must be they, in greater strength than I had expected. I was already slightly breathless, but burbled about going on a road recce, to which the Colonel replied, "I don't think there are any, but if you want to look, run and catch A Company, the one on the left."

According to my training, a lot of preparation and briefing went into deliberate sorties towards the enemy, but again I had managed to miss this completely. I am sure Lieutenant Colonel Hassett was being kind in granting my wish, but have just an inkling that he may have been glad to know that I was occupied for the day. When I had left my slit trench I had said that I would be back within half an hour, and had certainly not gone prepared for a day out. I had just my rifle, the bayonet hanging from my belt, and a few rounds of ammunition and a compass in the belt pouches, with my map case over my shoulder. Officers were issued with .38 inch revolvers, but most of us carried rifles or sub-machine guns in the forward areas, first because they were effective weapons, which the revolver was not, and secondly because, at a distance, an officer then looked like a soldier. As snipers were trained to pick off officers, there was no point in advertising one's rank. The British Army still had the .303 inch Lee-Enfield No. 4 rifle, which had been designed for easy production in the 1930s, but was no improvement on the old No. 1 rifle which had proved so effective in the First War. The No. 1 was the much better finished weapon and the Australian Army had stuck to it, much to our envy.

Rifle I might have, but I had no lunch and no water bottle and, delighted though I was to be chasing after A Company, it did strike me that perhaps I had been a little too enthusiastic this time. Its officer commanding was remarkably civil when I panted up beside him. He at least knew who I was, as we had met on other occasions during the previous week, but most of his men could have had no notion what I was doing. Apart from the Forward Observation Officer (FOO), a Captain from the Royal New Zealand Artillery, and his signaller, I was the only other "foreigner" present. Although he must have had other things on his mind, the Australian Major did his best to put me in the

25 pounder guns.

picture as we crossed the flat bottomed valley before the next ridge line. Both companies were going forward further than had been atempted in previous raids, right on to positions which were expected to be occupied, he hoped lightly, by the Chinese. The aim was to take prisoners, or just one would do, as the General's offer of a bottle of whisky was still considered a worthy prize.

At last our intelligence seemed to have been right and it was not long before the leading platoon started to be engaged with long range rifle fire. The Kiwi FOO took the opportunity to range his guns onto the slope of the hill in front of us, then call for his battery to fire, each gun firing several rounds. I had often seen guns fired before, but now that I had an inkling of how fire was adjusted, the sequence became more interesting: the Gunner lecture on the troopship had stuck in my mind much better than I ever expected. The gunfire appeared to achieve its aim, and a few Chinese were soon reported to be withdrawing: I wished that I could see them, but my eyes, even with specs, were not marvellous.

We carried on, with me near the OC in the middle of the company and the FOO moving across to the right-hand platoon to get a better view. Rather brisker rifle fire then started, showing that all the Chinamen had not crossed behind the ridge line. Our advance stopped and I expected the gunners to help us again, but nothing happened. After a few minutes a message arrived that the FOO was pinned down in the open, and couldn't see a target at which to fire the guns.

Just occasionally I know the answer but, being a modest and retiring chap, hate to admit it. If the conversation can be steered that way, though, it is nice to be asked. The OC of A Company was perturbed that he had, however temporarily, lost his artillery support, so perturbed that I did not think he would mind me offering to stand in as his Forward Observation Officer. "Even a Sapper (or much lesser mortal) can do it" had been my Gunner lecturer's taunt. The OC was delighted that I should wish to try my skill, but there was a slight snag. Whereas the FOO's wireless was tuned to the Gunner control net, ours was on the 3 RAR battalion wavelength. True, it was possible to switch to other wavelengths quickly on some sets, but not so easily on those that a man could carry.

I won't go through the whole rigmarole, but the sequence ran smoother than I ever expected. The most difficult thing, from my point of view, was seeing the target. My Australian companions assured me that I could see Chinamen, or at least the place from where they were firing. I had to admit that I couldn't. Soon I understood the defined area sufficiently to take the bearing with my compass and pass my idea of its grid reference. Once my message had been passed the pause before the first gun was fired in response was, for me, memorably anxious. I could hardly believe that a shell would arrive, but eventually, probably four minutes after I had passed the fire order, we heard the "pom" of the gun some miles behind us, closely followed by the whirr of the shell overhead and its detonation on the ground in front of us. That it had arrived in the right map square gave me immense satisfaction. That we were in the same map square rather concerned my companions.

I started to transmit my correction to bring the shell onto the target, "Add 400, go right 200", meaning yards in each case. The company commander listened intently and was particularily keen that I got the word "add" right, but before I had finished the routine, the New Zealander himself arrived. It never struck me at the time, but if you want to un-pin an FOO quickly, allow someone else to try firing his guns. The Kiwi suffered the full tongue of the Australians, who delighted in pointing out that not only a Pommie, but a Sapper to boot, had fired his guns.

With the guns back on a basis, the Chinese again withdrew and we advanced to just below the ridge line, over the top of which the Chinese continued to fire their rifles. The crack of the bullets, perhaps ten feet over our heads, was exactly as one used to hear them in the butts of a rifle range, and I longed for a pole with a flag on it to signal a washout.

We had been out for about three hours when a rumour went round that B Company, now about a mile on our right, had taken a prisoner. If it were true, that meant that the prize bottle of whisky had gone, but the report was unconfirmed and we still had to reach one more ridge. We crossed the next valley with much less trouble than the first and from the next hill had a splendid view of real live Chinamen walking about on yet another rise. That, at any rate, was what I was told. I peered through various pairs of binoculars, but never really saw our opponents.

It was time for lunch and, as I had not brought any, I was not beyond a little charity. The Australians were most generous. We were in nice deep Chinese trenches, had reached our objective and I, at any rate, had a feeling of well being. B Company seemed to be similarly disposed, to our right and rather behind us, when the Chinese began to shell them. This was most inconsiderate on many counts. First, I had understood that we were fighting an army of simple foot soldiers who, if they achieved anything, did so by sheer weight of numbers and, second, that the enemy even had artillery was an entirely new discovery for me. We had a splendid view of B Company, as also, presumably, had some Chinese FOO, as he quickly adjusted his guns to fire onto their position.

During our lunch break there has been much talk of the wirelesses. The Kiwi Gunner Captain had reported that his had packed up, after giving trouble all morning. Our Company set on the battalion net, a No. 62 set on the back of one soldier with another sweating friend carrying the lead/acid batteries and connected to him by a cable, produced even weaker signals, then succumbed entirely. Views on "Sigs", the 3 RAR Signal Officer were, considering his specialised subject, very general. Evidently sulphuric acid of a certain strength, liberally dosed with distilled water, was prescribed if complete satisfaction were to be achieved. "Sigs" had evidently had his own views on the ingredients, and we were now paying the price.

Luckily the hour for our withdrawal had been pre-planned and the time was reached shortly after the last tinkering with our hopeless radios. We were to retire by platoons, keeping as much as possible out of the valley bottoms by skirting the spurs of the hills. Just as soon as we started back, some Chinese guns were brought to bear onto us, very shortly to be joined by shorter range mortars, the latter inferring that the weapons were rather closer than I had imagined. As Lieutenant Colonel Hassett had predicted, I had not seen the suggestion of a road all morning, nor anything else of engineer interest. I genuinely had hoped to prove my presence necessary, but now, being decidedly spare, attached myself to the platoon who had kindly shared their lunch with me. It had no officer with it, but a Company Sergeant Major was in command, so it was clear that it would be sound for me to keep a low profile. What status, if any, a guest British officer had in the Australian Army I rather wondered, but was happy to assume that the answer was "none".

Just how low my profile could be, would, a few minutes earlier, have surprised me and my acquaintances, as I dived into the flattest pancake shape at the slightest suggestion of a shell's arrival. Although I had had long training for war, no one, so far as I could remember, had even given me a course of manners to be followed when under fire in the public view. I was immensely relieved to find that my extremely tough companions, many of whom had known real war, were equally nimble. I remembered that, soon after I started "primary training" at Colchester early in 1944, I had not shown up too well in the agility tests. How I wished that the selectors could have been with me this afternoon, as even fit men with excellent hearing appeared to be slower at lying down than I. For the first time I understood the true significance of the term "good old mother earth". Shells, coming in with a sharp screech, were easy to judge: mortar bombs, fluttering and only just audible at the last moment, were much more disconcerting.

Between the arrival of projectiles, our withdrawal continued with best speed, which did not actually mean at a run, as the dense cloak of vine-like ground creeper on the otherwise bare hillsides made a better pace impossible. On the way forward I had hardly noticed this creeper, now it caught me across the bootlaces at almost every step. I was decidedly hot, had nasty indigestion from the sandwiches I had scrounged, and wished I had stayed at home. It was almost inevitable that someone would soon be hurt and, within moments, three men did not stand up when the dust next settled, one of them in our platoon, and two in the platoon not far in front of us. I now saw the point of carrying two stretchers in each platoon, each consisting of a couple of poles with metal feet, joined together by strong green canvas, an inconvenient and bulky load at the best of times.

Our casualty had been hit by splinters in the head, was alive, very quiet and obviously very unwell. A shell dressing was wrapped on the wound and the poor chap moved onto a stretcher. In obstacle races I had always seen a dummy victim easily carried by two stretcher bearers, one at the front and one at the back. Now I discovered that carrying a stretcher over any distance was a four man job and even so, eight feet seemed hardly sufficient to maintain stability amongst the tangled creepers. The most useful thing I thought I could do was to carry the four rifles of the stretcher bearers, plus that of the casualty, not forgetting my own, six in all, together weighing over 50lbs. Each had a webbing sling, adjusted to the preference of its owner, too tight to fit over my head and across my body, or too loose to stay on my shoulder. They set me a hard test to balance and themselves proved remarkably knobbly as I practised my flapjack act with them. It wasn't long before it was my turn to take one of the corners of the stretcher, and I was very glad to shed the rifles, only to find the stretcher handles, too heavy for one hand, too awkward for two, were equally tiring.

However ignorant I was of the rules of self-protection under fire, I knew even less of stretcher lore. Obviously the task was to transport the casualty as gently as possible, but it was easy to argue that, if one were not there to carry him, little would have been gained by brave behaviour. So attentive did our listening for the next incoming projectiles become that we stopped swearing at each other every time we tripped on the vines. We had the personal attention of about six guns and four mortars, not a great number by barrage standards, but fully sufficient to add zest to an afternoon's walk of a full mile in the open. We could hear the "pom" of the guns firing, or the "pop" of the mortars, counted the number carefully and awaited "for what we are about to receive", gaining discernment of probable danger or comparative safety remarkably quickly. Our setting down of the stretcher together with diving to the ground was soon an established drill, but it cannot have improved our patient's health.

Our progress became depressingly slow, and I started to wonder how long it would be before the Chinamen followed us on foot. Luckily our predetermined fire plan had anticipated the same possibility, and our gunners were now soundly pounding the positions on which we had taken luncheon and from which our wireless had last condescended to pass a message. The guns were a mixed blessing, as their very noise made it more difficult to hear anything coming our way. Mercifully, though, we soon rounded a spur on the hillside and must have been lost to view of the Chinese observation officer as the shelling became increasingly wild, and then stopped.

All of us, I think, were very glad to stumble up the hill into our own positions which we had left that morning. Fresh men took the stretchers from us and I was just regaining my very puffed breath and thinking that the day must have been good for my waistline when a runner arrived with the Australian equivalent of his Colonel's compliments. I forget the exact words, but the gist was that one of our tanks had blown up a mine on the far side of the hill, and please would I go and make it possible to move it.

The word had already reached my lance corporal and two Sappers, and luckily we had brought some explosive stores up the hill with us. Much as I would have loved the cup of tea that was brewing, we set off over the far edge of the hill without waiting, and soon came to the road skirting the bottom. It ran about fifteen feet above the edge of a large lake, actually a reservoir constructed by the Japanese, which, with the steep slope of the hill above it, provided a splendid spot for an ambush that could not be bypassed. Sure enough, on rounding a couple of corners, we came up behind one of our turretless Centurion tanks, known as a tug, which was itself behind the mined Centurion, which had its 20 pounder gun pointing rather forlornly towards the next corner some fifty yards in front. This road was a prolongation of the same track along which I had cleared mines, or attempted to clear mines, the day before. My conscience was clear, in that I had explained how far I had gone, but now I expected to be accused of today's incidents, so was on the defensive. I need not have been, as the 8th Hussars admitted that they had taken a chance, adding that wasn't it a pity that a second tank had also hit a mine, but had already been retrieved. Another had slid down a steep bank and was stuck. Yes, it was all a great pity, but interested though I was, we curtailed the discussion.

There was no need to ask what was wrong with the gun tank. The mine which had exploded had been laid on the lake side of the road. It

Centurion tug and Centurion tank.

had removed the third from the front of the six large road wheels of the tank, at the same time as cutting the massive track. The trouble lay, though, in the fourth large wheel, which had not been removed, but its bottom had been blown flat. Try as the tug would, it could not pull the dead tank with a flattened wheel, and the more it tried, the more the tank slewed towards the edge of the lake.

"Dan," the tank Troop Leader said, "Please could you remove that damaged road wheel quickly?" "Can't the REME unbolt it?" I asked, but after two tense hours with spanners, that was considered an unnecessary question. No, the REME could not shift it, all the bolts had got locked by the explosion.

I had never really looked at a tank before. Even the wheels were a revelation, as nice, modest, tanks always kept their running gear, or most of it, covered with skirting plates. These plates, very heavy in their own right, had been conveniently removed by the mine and now lay, together with large quantities of newly turned earth, on the lake bank. There was nothing in the pamphlets on how to blow big wheels off friendly tanks, but I knew that if I could put enough explosive around the wheel bearing, something must give. I also knew that the tank was fully bombed up with high explosive shells, and that the detonation of my charge outside could well initiate an explosion inside, but with time short, this was no occasion for technical quibbling.

The 8lbs of plastic explosive which I managed to squidge into place behind the offending wheel proved pleasingly persuasive, and the wheel flipped over the lake surface like a flat stone before sinking with a satisfactory splash.

The Troop Leader and REME officer nipped round the corner to view the results of my efforts even before I could, all rather unethical but, with the light fading, time took precedence over protocol. "Splendid Dan, well done!" said the tank's proud owner, and I could have done with any amount of that. "Pity about the top roller," said the REME representative. I should explain that tanks have big wheels, known as road wheels, under which the track lays itself on the ground, and a series of little wheels, known as rollers, which support the track as it goes on round the top. My job had been to remove the offending, near-square, road wheel, and the effectiveness with which I had achieved that was beyond question. Yes, it was true that I had taken away one of the little wheels above it as well, oil still dripping from a severed bearing made it all too obvious, but it struck me that the REME were nitpicking. Some chaps can never be satisfied. He did condescend to say that there would now be no trouble towing the tank to safety, so I and my demolition crew took our leave and plodded our way up our hill, only thankful that we were meeting our friends before dark and before anyone became inclined to use grenades in lieu of the password.

My trench companion, the one with the DSO, had seen to it that some supper had been kept for us, and it really was a pleasure to be "home". I then realised how very tired I was, only to be disquietened by the abundant rumours of the action the Chinese were expected to take that night. After chasing us back from our daytime excursions, the general feeling was that they would try to dislodge us from our hill that night. My companion, however, most kindly undertook to remain on guard and my bedtime routine was restricted to leaving my bayonet fixed on my rifle on the parapet and to the careful stowing of my spectacles before I curled comfortably down. The mosquitoes were as bad as the night before, but I did not notice them.

It was hours later and pitch dark when I found myself being urgently shaken with my companion muttering, "Stand to." Actually the command was accompanied with other advice such as should not normally be given to an officer by a soldier, albeit a soldier with a DSO. "Stand to," he ordered and stand to I did. Too late I realised that I had stood directly upon my specs.

Some of you may remember* that soon after my 21st birthday party in Sumatra I, and others happened to be ambushed on the way to our airfield. This had been followed by me and a few of my Indian Sappers showing great initiative in trying to cut off the retreat of those who had ambushed us, and what was more, we had actually seen them, or at least some of them. I had even shot at them with our Bren gun, but had missed. Guess why? Because I had left my specs behind. It did seem something of a coincidence that, being confronted for the first time since then with the possibility of fighting, I was again specless. I explained my predicament to my Australian friend, who seemed almost relieved to be left to get on with anything that needed to be done by himself.

Actually, nothing needed to be done. The expected Chinese attack never came, and I never discovered who or what set off the trip flares which had been laid on some of the approaches during the day. They burnt with a lurid light and a powerful hiss, enough to make the stoutest heart a little jumpy. There must have been a few words said about trigger happiness the previous night, as no shots were fired and no grenades thrown.

Sitting in my trench, again aware of the mosquitoes, I had time to think things over, and decided that it would be very nice indeed if the peace talks succeeded immediately. I had had an eventful couple of days, quite sufficient to satisfy my curiosity about the Korean War and also to dine out on for some years to come. Talking of which, Judy, the bridesmaid I had misjudged, lived in Cheshire. Years later, after we got married, her father used to ask Colonel Sir Guy Lowther, the one time CO of the 8th Hussars who lived nearby, to drinks. Each time he set eyes upon me, Sir Guy, whose presence could usually be felt, would come across the crowded room announcing, "There's the man who lost my tanks!" It was no good trying to explain. Some of us are always misunderstood.

We obviously weren't going to have a long lie in the next morning, so we all were ready to move early. I would never have dreamt how much I wanted to get back to my own Troop and the rather comfier life

*Wrong Again Dan!—Buckland Publications.

to which I had become accustomed on the south bank of the Imjin. A messenger came over the hill from battalion headquarters and we all asked him when we would be moving back. "We're not," he said. "We're staying here and the whole Division is coming across." This was utterly new to me, and I was horrified at the thought of my Troop moving without me. "Really most unfair that no one warned me," I thought, but was prepared to believe that the General had made the decision on the spur of the moment. I now doubt if that was the case, but my mind was racing on what I should do next and not on what had obviously already happened.

I accompanied the runner back to Lieutenant Colonel Hassett which was just as well, as I and my detachment had been bidden to rejoin my Troop, which had crossed the river and was said to be at a most improbable map reference quite close to the PINTAIL crossing. I didn't dwell on my myopic problems, which were real, but did ask the Colonel about the soldier we had carried home the day before. The answer was not good. I thanked him for letting me join his country walk, and he was kind enough to say he hoped we would meet again.

CHAPTER FIVE

PREPARE TO ADVANCE

I stumbled back across the hill, feeling highly embarrassed by my near blindness. Sufficient to say that my party looked after me, and we went back down the road to PINTAIL very much quicker than we had come up it two days before. Apart from constantly having to stop to let the surprising quantity of oncoming vehicles pass us, the only item of note was a hen pheasant which planed off the hill on our left and passed just in front of us. Blind I might be, but not that blind, and it was encouraging to know that perhaps I had not come to Korea in vain.

My Troop was exactly where we had been told, on a tiny field on the cliff edge of the Imjin. The site would have been excessively confined at the best of times, but to keep everyone guessing, some unknown soldier had managed to set light to the spout of a jerry can of petrol right in the middle of our patch. Presumably he had hoped for a quick brew of tea, but in doing so had managed to knock the can over, thus making a minor flame thrower which glugged loudly and belched flame most ominously. The general opinion was that the can was likely to explode at any minute, and that it would be wise to wait at a safe distance.

So there I was, just when I should have been influencing "the battle", unable to see properly and trying to stop anyone approaching a burning can of petrol. It is all jolly well to say now, "Why didn't you put a sandbag on it?", but, if you are being truthful, do you usually carry full sandbags on hopelessly overloaded lorries?

Just to vex us, the can just spluttered out without exploding, making all those who had advised caution look stupider than ever. However, I had managed to locate my kit and to confirm my wish that I could have chosen a better batman. In reality, considering the unexpected task I had left him, he had done well, and it wasn't long before I unearthed my Army gas mask specs, ghastly discs of glass strung together with the thinnest of steel frames. My appearance became more toad-like than ever, but it was a great help to be able to see properly again.

My mother was keeping my letters sent home, and a couple of excerpts may give an indication of the varied aspects of our war.

17 Sept. '51

I've moved twice since I last wrote, and am now back on the home bank of the Imjin in rather lovely country, if seen under the right conditions. It's all very peaceful, bar some local Gunners who persist in making the night air hideous with "harassing fire". If the Chinks hate it as much as we do, the Gunners are winning!

Mike, my Troop Officer, and I have built ourselves quite a useful basha. The roof is a tarpaulin off a big trailer supported on pine logs, three of the walls are of pine brushwood, and the front wall-cum-doorway is of thatching reed and rolls away during the day. We only got the door on today, and it's a mixed blessing, as the last two nights have been too cold for the 'mossies', which now unfortunately thrive in here and are eating me fiercely. We do get repellant oil, but, as usual, it's got lost.

I heard a cock pheasant crowing his head off about 300 yards away this morning and was tempted to attack him, then found that the stock of the old gun had broken again in the moves. I'm getting a carpenter onto it tomorrow, but I'm afraid it isn't an easy job.

We just live from day to day, and don't believe a thing is going to happen until it is over. The early mornings are beastly cold and most demoralising: otherwise things are pretty good and I have a crate of beer and a bottle of John Dewar! I am most glad to have my flea bag to sleep in."

23 Sept. '51

This must be a quick letter as there's only about an inch and a half of candle left. My birthday tomorrow won't be a very different day, as we have quite a bit of work and my Troop Staff Sergeant is sick and Mike a witness at a Court Martial, so I'll have to be about. Anyway, Higher Command permitting, we hope to have a party on the 30th when a new officer will be twenty-one. As a matter of fact, there is one bottle of port in the Squadron Mess, which, if I can get there tomorrow evening, I hope to uncork.

With the season not yet open lots of pheasants are defying me and when I was on a road recce this morning a lovely bunch of about twenty mallard came flying along the stream right over our heads.

We've been at the same place on the south bank of the Imjin for nine days now and have built an oven and other comforts, but it can't go on for ever and I think you will hear of us one day.

We've had quite a pleasant week with lovely dry weather (still warm enough to bathe in the river) and not too much work, though we're never really idle. The nights are warmer again, as the full moon is over.

However, the Gunners still keep the nights hideous, though I now sleep through anything except rapid fire. Each gun in the local 4 gun Troop fired a round a minute for seventy minutes a few nights ago, and the other twenty guns in the same Canadian Regiment were doing the same. At £5 a 25 pounder shell, well done the taxpayers!, but it really does save Infantry lives.

Ammo supply is wonderful: all else (except food) is pathetic. We still have blokes with big feet with no boots and some men without socks (I suppose there will be lots for the winter), and endless minor things are missing for which there can be no adequate reason: all very difficult when you are trying to maintain your troops in good order. It all comes of being a minor concern in an American War, but it isn't the Yanks' fault.

P.S. A Chink deserter pottered into our 2 Troop's lines the other night. Thinking he was a local they told him to "shove off quickly", or words to that effect, and only realised their mistake just in time to get him back.

Living in the middle of the Canadian Gunners, and on the very verge of the only road to our PINTAIL crossing of the Imjin was no place for a country recluse, but it had its social compensations. First, anybody who was anybody passed my home and generally directed greetings to me and to 3 Troop, 12 Squadron in general, and secondly the Canadians offered generous hospitality to their obviously poor relations. So, the night after my birthday, I was asked to dinner in a Battery Mess. At dusk I was shown around the gun lines, eight 25 pounders of which only a couple were expected to need to fire the odd round that night. Trusted Koreans had been afforded the great honour of being allowed to assist in firing pre-loaded rounds of "harassing fire" at pre-arranged times during the night. This had the dual benefit of flattering the Koreans and allowing the Royal Canadian Horse Artillery, unmounted, but a unit of high tradition and reputation, to take sensible periods of rest.

It was just as I was being offered a second helping of fried chicken that a patrol of the Royal Canadian Regiment (Canada's First and Finest) bumped into trouble and called for supporting fire. This was unexpected, as contact during the past week had been minimal, but the effect was dramatic. The apparently relaxed Canadians came to life with frightening speed and the Battery Sergeant Major, even in the dark, made his presence felt most forcefully. To him I represented an extra pair of hands, and hands were for humping ammunition. The first time he added "Sir" to his orders, but not thereafter. The gun to which I became affiliated still seemed rather short of crew, just two Canadians and a Korean initially, so there was no doubt that I was expected to collect boxes of ammunition and open them.

25 pounder shells each weighed about that, so four in a steel ammunition box topped one hundredweight. I had often carried hundredweight sacks at home, but those ammo boxes with sharp corners protruding into my full tummy were awkward, more like a 9 gallon firkin of beer than a nice accommodating sack. Opening them, though, was the problem, as two metal clip hooks were firmly wired to staplelike loops on the box top. If correctly kicked with the heel of one's boot, these gave instantly, but I lacked practice. Once the lid was open, the top layer of two shells was exposed, their pointed ends, or ogives, protected by cones of heavily waxed paper. With these removed, the shell fuzes, with their screw-on caps wrapped with black sticky tape, became evident. For the duration of the gun flashes everything became visible, but in between I felt blinder than ever.

The shell boxes might have been heavy, but the steel cases of brass 25 pounder cartridges were much worse and would have won any competition for user unfriendliness. There were eight cartridges in each large steel box, and each of the cartridges had a form of cardboard cup filling its mouth. Although, during the last week before we left Sumatra, I had been taught some gun drill, I had never handled live cartridges before. I was surprised to find that the gun crew pulled out the cardboard cup to reveal, by the light of a torch, cloth bags of different colours, each containing the propellant to send the shell on its way. The NCO in charge of the gun then pulled out one of these little bags and placed it on one side before loading the cartridge and firing the next shell.

So rapid did the rate of fire become that I thought that, as part of my ammunition supply service, it might help if I removed the little charge bags myself. How that Sergeant Major saw me in the dark I do not know, but he made it very plain to me that he would prefer me not to delve inside the cartridges. That I received the message so clearly in all that noise was perhaps the most memorable part of my unusual supper party.

Almost as quickly as the little action had started, it was all over. As we groped our way back to the Mess tent I was interested to hear a message from the Forward Observation Officer who had called for the fire put out over the loud hailer, "Nice shooting. Very effective. Thank you!" An encouraging touch, I thought.

Back in the Mess, I asked why the Battery Sergeant Major had been quite so angry when I tried to help with the charge bags in the cartridges. "It was because," I was told, "if you had taken out a bag too many the shell would have fallen thousands of yards short, possibly on our own troops."

Three days later I and my Troop were back north of the Imjin. Everyone was talking of a further push forward to try to convince the Chinese that they had no hope of winning and, therefore, should make peace. Such serious discussion was swamped, however, by the news that 3 RAR, that splendid unit with which I had spent two days, had got their one hundredth Jeep. We knew that no vehicle that had not been positively immobilised was likely to remain in its rightful owner's hands for long, but had no idea that the Australians had been pursuing their proudly proclaimed national sport to quite such good effect. On "establishment" they had about fifty Jeeps. To have doubled the total was a fine achievement, or so I and the other irresponsible elements of the Division thought. Quite apart from enhancing the transport resources of the battalion, the extra fifty Jeeps cannot have proved all joy, as any man who captured a vehicle was allowed to remain its driver. To be a driver was more popular, and much safer, than being in a rifle platoon.

Just when we looked like being particularly active, I achieved a slightly swollen knee, caused by lying down rather too eagerly on some stones when some shells arrived on a road where I had business. I had always been taught that there were only two types of soldiers, the Quick and the Dead, but had never expected my unaccustomed agility to qualify for the first category. It was more comfortable to keep my knee moving than to sit still, so I was relieved to be asked to report if there were any minefields in front of the American unit on the right flank of our Division.

I took a couple of Sappers with me and duly found the unit, which turned out to be Puerto Rican, not fitting precisely into my definition of "American". The officer commanding the nearest company was surprised to see me, and assured me that there were no minefields in front of him. However, if I insisted, which I apparently did, he would be glad to provide a guide. The guide, a gentleman with no evident charm, spoke very little American. He did manage to ask why I was there, to which I could not manage a sensible answer, as the question had never struck me before.

The Puerto Rican led us to a large and straggly barbed wire fence on the forward perimeter, through which we started to pick our way. Swinging a stiff knee over successive strands, and trying to bend under others, proved tiresome enough before my injury. Just near the Sapper on my right, a pop was followed by the hissing of a burning fuse. To me this meant a grenade, a diagnosis with which that Sapper apparently agreed, as he swiftly managed to lie flat amongst the wire. I was less conveniently placed, so was thankful to hear our guide say, "No, no, smoke," from which I understood that we had triggered some form of smoke generator. The hissing continued and the Sapper nearest to it remained prone whilst the remainder of us stood and waited. Four seconds later I learnt that I should have had the courage of my convictions as it went off: it had been a grenade. The Sapper who had knocked it out of the tin in which, with its pin out, it had been hung on the wire, had seen that it was an American pineapple grenade: these devices were so called because of the segmented cast iron body which surrounded the high explosive contents. Just at that moment, though, he had been rather at a loss for words. He had been six feet from it on the ground, and the remaining three of us had been standing within twenty feet of it, yet none of us had been touched. Our guide's friends up the hill had heard the metal fly past, and thought it hilarious, as did we, that nobody had been hurt. We didn't pursue that recce. I reported that there were probably no mines, but that there were certainly booby traps. I also reported that I would have very little faith in American pineapple grenades and was sure that ours, the descendant of the Mills bomb, must be better.

The old Japanese road which touched the north bank of the Imjin at PINTAIL was turning into a busy highway. The American Engineers from "I" Corps had put in a floating bridge of rubber pontoons, which looked flimsy compared to the floating Bailey bridging to which I was accustomed, but was buoyant enough to carry tanks. After crossing the river to the Chinese side, most of the traffic turned left, mainly because the majority of the units in our Division were located that way, but also because there was a very weak old timber bridge on the road to the right. I mentioned this bridge to Howard, my squadron commander, who fully agreed that it would be a good idea to replace it with a short Bailey bridge, strong enough to take any tank.

As the road took very little traffic after dark, I decided to undertake the task that night. I then allotted the job to my troop officer, so knew that I ought to keep clear: on the other hand there was nowhere particular I should have been that night. I promised Mike that I would keep out of the way, but be on hand, and attempt to act accordingly.

Pulling the old log bridge out of the way with a crane had proved relatively easy, as we had anticipated, but digging down the bank seats on which the Bailey bridge would sit proved a more difficult task than we expected. It was obvious that the completion time was going to be later than we had estimated, and I became increasingly perturbed. It was not long, however, before my attention was diverted, as I was informed that Sapper Pocklington could not be found. I had seen him earlier in the day and thought I had seen him on the bridging site as dusk fell, but now was increasingly aware that we might be nearer to the enemy than we liked to believe. True, we had a couple of sentries out with a Bren gun, but it was now very dark and there was no doubt that Pocklington was not in easy view. I made it my personal job to find him and became increasingly annoyed and worried when I did not. He was not the type to curl up for a cosy snooze and the longer I stumbled around gently calling him, the more convinced I became that perhaps he had been snatched by a Chinese patrol. There was some considerable gunfire two or three miles to our north-west, much more concentrated than our normal harassing fire, so the activity gave rise to every form of imagination.

It was as I was fearing the worst for poor Pocklington that a vehicle with dimmed lights approached the bridge from the direction of the earlier gunfire. I went to send it away, only to find that it was an ambulance from the "Van Douze", the Royal 22nd Regiment of Canada, one of the three battalions in the Canadian Brigade and a unit of great repute. It carried five wounded men, one on a stretcher and four sitting up, and the driver, who like the remainder of the Regiment was by birth French speaking, explained to us in halting English that he had been told to take the casualties to the MASH (Mobile Army Surgical Hospital) in the neighbouring Division down the road on our right. He also pointed out that our removal of the bridge which he was accustomed to use made this difficult. His five wounded friends, none of whom appeared to have been weakened by what had befallen them, then consolidated their views on those who blocked roads, and on the Royal Engineers in particular.

Mike reported that it should be possible for the ambulance to cross our bridge in twenty minutes, and kept his promise. The driver, who previously had led me to understand that he had done this particular trip many times, then asked for help in finding his destination. Apart from Sapper Pocklington, I still seemed to be the most superfluous person present, so I undertook to help them find the MASH. We drove east for a couple of miles and were greeted by the first American unit we found. They had their own dressing station and promised to put the casualties on their proper way if we left them there. The driver and I were only too glad to do this and, after a wealth of "Au Revoirs", we returned to our bridge before dawn. Mike had a wearing surface of boards, two inches thick, spiked onto the Bailey decking and, after a hard night, everyone was pleased with a useful job done.

The next morning, as I toured around after a late breakfast, there was Sapper Pocklington, well and apparently happy. Yes, he had been at the bridge all the time, but as he knew I had seen him earlier, he thought his pals were pulling his leg (he used his own terms) when they told him I was looking for him. I didn't pursue the matter, but just a tiny tingle suggested that his absence might have been a put up job to keep me off Mike's back.

When seen by daylight Mike had very evident pink-eye, a nasty contagious disease so I understood, and not one with which I wished to share a tent. I persuaded him to report sick, and wherever he reached in the medical chain detained him, which was worrying, as the management of 3 Troop, with the Staff Sergeant already evacuated to Japan, was becoming increasingly weak.

It was upon the management, meaning myself and Sergeant Williams, that kindly man who would have been much happier in a quartermaster's store, that most of the activity of the next few days was thrust. It was known that we were going to advance, which, in almost roadless country, meant masses and masses of Sapper work.

Why ever we should wish to advance was quite beyond me. There we had been, sitting strongly and comfortably behind the River Imjin with commanding high ground behind us. Then, only recently, we had decided to occupy the relatively flat and dull country immediately north of the river, country which the enemy appeared not to want. Another theory was that the Chinese particularly wanted us to occupy it, so that they could wait for an Imjin flood, then mop up anyone so stupid to be on their bank. Perhaps we, as Sappers, realised the true potential of those floods better than any of the others.

Whatever the reason, I was delighted to be asked to mount a road recce for 3 RAR, my recent hosts when we crossed the Imjin. I joined Lieutenant Colonel Hassett and three of his company commanders on a forward slope overlooking what I understood to be Chinese territory. Major Butler, a Squadron Leader in the 8th Hussars, was also with the Australians. The Colonel said he would like to know as much as possible about the land which lay between us and a small rounded hill which we could see two valleys away. To reach it we would have to cross a road, and that was where the Sappers were needed. Anywhere else it would have been lucky to be called a track, but in Korea in 1951 it was a "road".

Lieutenant Colonel Hassett wanted information quickly and, as all his soldiers were intensely occupied with preparations for the impending attack, asked if I could provide protection, perhaps the equivalent of an infantry section, for the recce party of one of his company commanders, plus Major Butler and me. This sounded a welcome diversion for some of my rather bored men, so I readily agreed and we fixed the start time for four hours later.

When we had been south of the river, some of the least soldierly amongst us had been selected to accompany raids across it. Hardly anyone had been hurt, initially at any rate, and it had all been good fun. The situation was now different, with the Chinese very likely to react if probed. Had I had sense, and time, I would have taken my best men with me, but I had to take those who were in camp when I reached it, some of whom would not have been amongst my first choices.

We needed to take a machine gun and to carry it (a Bren gun itself weighing twenty-two very awkward pounds). I selected a large but notably idle Sapper. In addition he had to carry several loaded magazines, each of twenty-seven .303 rounds, making a full load for a fit man. My other companions were a lance corporal and four Sappers, all carrying rifles. I had a Sten sub-machine gun, and just hoped that we were all correctly equipped.

The two majors thanked us very graciously for coming, and off we set at a much more cracking pace than I would have suspected. We were moving in full daylight, an unusual time of day for a small patrol to walk straight towards the enemy, however far away they might be. I, with next to nothing to carry, was soon puffing. Even earlier it was evident that my Bren gunner, who had not been a volunteer for the excursion, was even more unfit than I had earlier believed. I was highly embarrassed, as it suddenly struck me that the Royal Engineers might not be showing up too well in the eyes of the two very experienced officers we were supporting. My lance corporal did a splendid job as a sheep dog, keeping us all up to pace, but it wasn't long before he himself was carrying the machine gun.

In the first valley we reached the road. It turned out to be an unditched track of fairly flat earth about twelve feet wide and completely unmarked by vehicle tracks, so unmarked that it wasn't even potholed.

As our purpose was to only cross the road, we did not walk far down it. I suppose I should have been paying attention to the little of it I was going to see, but was more intent on keeping our escort along with me. My preoccupation was disturbed by Major Butler asking, "What do you make of this, Sapper?" He was pointing to the ground in front of him and, now he had mentioned it, I could immediately see that the ground on either side of the middle of the track had recently been disturbed, and appeared to be marked with a distinct pattern. "Those are Chinese rope-soled shoe marks," said Major Butler. I was greatly enlightened, and had no reason to doubt the profound statement. "Do you think there might be mines underneath?" he then continued. "Good Lord, Sir, indeed there might be," I replied. I felt decidedly excited as I then said, "If everyone would please take cover, I will investigate." This sounded desperately pompous, especially in front of

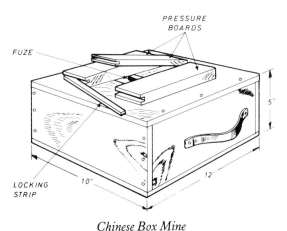

Chinese Box Mine

an Australian, but two officers had recently been killed when both inspecting the same mine.

I borrowed a bayonet and probed the nearest rope-soled shoe mark. About three inches under the surface I sensed resistance. When prodded very gently, the resistance sounded wooden and hollow. It didn't take long to determine the extent of the silhouette of a box, and I knew enough of the Chinese anti-tank mines to know that I had met my first. I moved across to the second shoe mark and established exactly the same set of circumstances. I went back to the two Majors and reported, "Yes, there is a box mine under each of the shoe marks." "Thank you," they said in unison, "that's exactly what we thought." From that moment on my escort party seemed more cohesive and less reluctant to move so swiftly.

We crossed a rise and then the next small valley, before climbing the gently rounded hill which was to be the limit of our reconnaisance. It was nearly bare and, apart from a few recent shell holes and a few gullies caused by torrential rain, represented a fine example of soil-eroded latterite, or so the little geology I had learnt suggested. The smoothness of the surface made the one dead Chinaman, lying apparently comfortably on his tummy with his face on one side, look all the more incongruous. He was a fine, good-looking man, much bigger than my idea of the average Chinese, and there didn't appear to be a mark on him. He looked so well and peaceful that he did not even make me jump when I first saw him. We talked about searching him, but it was so unusual for dead Chinese to be left when they could have been recovered that we thought he might be booby trapped, so made our way home without touching him. The more I thought of it later, the more I wondered if he had not been alive and well all the time. If so, he would have been a very brave man.

We crossed the track at a different place, but saw no shoe marks, but then no one would have expected every few yards of a road to be mined.

On arriving back with Lieutenant Colonel Hassett, the two majors kindly allowed me the kudos of reporting the mines, even though I would probably have overlooked them without their guidance. Nobody seemed very interested in the dead Chinaman.

That evening, when I went back to the Squadron HQ for supper and the OC's "prayers", I confirmed that the road which we knew as SAPPHIRE was mined. "Mined or not," said Howard, "we were going to have to check it, and now we know there are some there, it'll be more interesting. It'll be just the job for your Troop." At his briefing he then told us that the whole of the American I Corps, which included our Division and was the most westerly of the four Army Corps stretching across Korea, was to make a limited objectives advance, starting in two days' time. SAPPHIRE was one of the only two possible vehicle routes available for our Brigade, so it was important that it should be opened early.

Although it was still before 9.00 p.m. when my driver and Jeep deposited me back in my Troop lines, a couple of miles up the road from the Squadron, most of the men were settling down for the night. Apart from a few small tents, everyone was sleeping in bivvies so, with no light other than some ineffective hurricane lamps and candles, there was little to stay up for.

I summoned the NCOs to the cookhouse tent and told them of the impending attack, which resulted in a general feeling of relief. The state of doubtful war and doubtful peace had been most disquieting and it was reassuring at last to know what we were expected to do, even if we were not sure why we were doing it.

CHAPTER SIX

OPERATION "COMMANDO"

It was whilst we were preparing to move the next day that I was told to help some Gunners get into position to support the attack. I knew the capabilities of the 25 pounders, whose maximum range of over seven miles allowed them to be positioned well back from the front line, but we were now talking of a troop with four 4.2 inch mortars. These were short, muzzle loading weapons with the barrel bearing on a heavy baseplate which sat directly upon the ground. A metal bipod supported the barrel at the correct angle when the bomb was fired. The maximum range of 4.2 mortars was limited to just over 4,000 yards, and the Gunners would never have deigned to man them had it not been for the very considerable power of the bombs. It could be proved, so we were assured, that, due to its favourable design, the 20 pound mortar bomb was a very much more lethal projectile than the shell from a 25 pounder. Having been on the receiving end of the Chinese (or probably captured American) equivalents, I thought both were beastly, so doubted the need for justification.

At dusk I met the Gunner Troop Officer, who turned out to be a friend from the troopship answering to "Stew". We were about 300 yards from where he wanted to put his mortars, and a steeply banked stream lay in between. I had a small bulldozer, so there should have been no problem. However, the bulldozer broke down, and it then rained.

"Surely, Stew it's not worth going to all this bother just to get you three hundred yards forward?" said I. He looked disappointed by my ignorance, as he explained that his bombs had to reach the top of Hill 355, which on level ground was nearly 4,000 yards from where he needed to be. "That 355 means metres, Dan, hundreds of feet above us here, so the poor old bombs won't get up there unless we are well within maximum range." It took no more to convince me, but I was also soon convinced that the gentleman who had decided that the lorries, towing the 4.2 mortars and carrying their ammunition, only needed to have a two wheel drive had missed the point also.

Needless to say, each vehicle in turn got stuck in the stream, and every man nearby who tried to push them out slithered on the muddy banks just as ineffectively. With the rain clouds overhead, it was a completely dark night, and every time torches were shone we were beseeched to remember that there were plenty of Chinamen well on our side of 355 and there was no need to tell them that they would be attacked in the morning.

At midnight we had three of the four mortar towing vehicles stuck in the stream. The mortars they were towing had been uncoupled and had been manhandled on their trailer wheels, one up the enemy bank and two back the way they had come. Everyone continued digging, to try and ease the slope on the enemy bank, but by 2.00 a.m. no real improvement had resulted. The mortars were due to start firing at 4.00 a.m. and Stew, normally the most balanced of fellows, started to become perturbed. He even mentioned that, until now, the promised Sapper assistance had not achieved much.

At 3.00 a.m. the spare part that the bulldozer driver had requested arrived, and at 3.15 there was the chuckle of his donkey engine starting, soon followed by the more powerful surge of the main engine picking up. I had long before established with Stew what the absolute minimum requirement would be, and that was one mortar in position with a good stack of ammunition nearby before 4.00 a.m.

The dozer, with its tracks, was easily able to climb up the enemy bank of the stream, whence it towed the mortar that was already across into position. Rather than mess about in the dark trying to build a roadway up the bank, the answer was to winch one of the stuck towing vehicles, complete with its load of ammunition, up and out. The strain placed upon the vehicle's chassis can have done it no good at all, but nobody cared at the time.

At 4.00 a.m. on 2nd October, 1951, the supporting fire for Operation COMMANDO, as we had discovered our advance was to be known, opened up. The Forward Observation Officer (FOO) who was directing the mortars had no doubt that he needed their fire, and I soon realised the true implications of only having one out of four guns in action.

I am not sure if the FOO had even been told of this sad fact and, even if he had, it would have made no odds to him. Every time he called for "one round gunfire" (the Gunners called their mortars guns), he expected four rounds, one from each of four mortars, to fall on the target. The crew of the single mortar in action had to work like beavers to pop the bombs down the barrel fast enough, and even faster when five rounds of gunfire, meaning twenty rounds from the single tube, were demanded. The mortar barel was getting very hot, the FOO said that rounds were falling very satisfactorily on the target, and as dawn was breaking I left.

SAPPHIRE was a mainly earth track, rather softer in texture than the old gravel road I had tried to check for mines when we crossed the Imjin, but still a rotten surface through which to search for wooden mines. Our detectors, which were designed to indicate the presence of metallic mines would be of no use, so the only possible method would be by prodding with outgrown steel knitting needles, our issue prodders. I had made it clear to one and all that I personally had found mines further up the road, so there was no doubt that it was mined and it was in all our interests to find them.

The prodding teams had been working for nearly two hours when I arrived from my sleepless night with the Gunners. Only a few hundred yards had been covered, nothing had been found and the track stretched ahead for more than a mile more. I was sure that mines must have been missed, and spent some time re-prodding the places I thought most likely, but was thankful to confirm that nothing was evident.

I already knew the speed for effective prodding, and that was painfully slow. I tried to hurry the search, knowing that I was wrong to do so. Had my escort party not been discussing the rope soled shoe marks further up the same road on our recce the previous week, my report of mines would have been considered either imagination, or a doubtful means of whipping up enthusiasm for a very dull and possibly dangerous task.

By noon no mine had been found, though the odd large stone had been gingerly dug from the road. We were at last approaching the corner where I had prodded the two box mines and I was most anxious that they should prove to be there. I had marked the side of the road with a distinctive line of stones, so there was no doubt when we reached the place. I went forward and repeated my prodding act of a few days before and was thankful to say that nothing had changed. The shapes beneath the surface still felt just like wooden boxes.

To disarm a Chinese box mine was very simple. Just uncover the lid, gently remove the locking bar, or lath of wood, which kept the fragile top shut, raise the hinged lid of the box, lift out the pressure switch which acted as the mine's fuze, then pick up the mine. So obvious had the laying of those two mines been, though, that we all thought they might be booby trapped, perhaps with a pull switch attached to another explosive charge, to be activated during the lifting of the mine. The drill under such circumstances was to "pull" the mine with a cord from a safe distance. I had never tried doing so, but it always sounded so easy that I couldn't believe there was anything to it. All that was needed was a good length of cord with a hook on the end, which would be attached to a suitable projection near the bottom of the mine. To turn the horizontal pull into a vertical lifting force, the cord would have to be passed over a suitable stone or similar object which should be positioned near the side of the mine.

Guess what? A flat sided box has no suitable projections on it, nor were there any good stones handy nearby. Anyway, I earmarked a position behind a small hump in the ground about ten yards from the mine from which I could pull and where I thought I would be safe if its 14lbs of lyddite, a nice yellow block of solid picric acid, went off. I then gently scraped the earth off the top of the first box and dug down until I could get my fingers underneath on the far side. I positioned my improvised hook, shouted for everyone to take cover, withdrew behind the hump and gently pulled. Just as gently, the hook came loose.

Back to the mine I went, repositioned the hook at the same time speaking pretty firmly to it, and retired once more. This time I managed to exert a really strong pull, rather like dislodging a spinning minnow from a sunken branch in a salmon river. Unlike most minnows, which never oblige me by coming loose, the hook freed itself most effectively and flicked back quite dangerously towards me.

My companions were geting bored in their take cover positions and wondered quite audibly, above the considerable background noise, what I was doing. Ever since dawn, with our attack being pressed all along the front, the day had been particularly noisy but, as the Chinese reserved their own bombardment for our attacking infantry, nothing came as far back down the track as us. On my next attempt with the hook I said some very kind words to it, and when I pulled in on my line

I knew it had worked. The box mine had toppled on its side in the hole and I could see that it had not been booby trapped.

The second mine came out much more quickly, so we disposed of them and carried on with our forlorn prodding. It had taken us a total of seven hours to clear the required length of track and the only two mines we had found were the two I had by chance located the previous week. The coincidence was remarkable, and there were even suggestions that I had laid the mines myself, just to keep my Troop on its toes.

Operation COMMANDO continued, we were assured, according to plan. The Division on our left, 1 ROK, or Republic of (South) Korea, achieved its objectives quite quickly; ours which included some very steep hills, took four days and the American 1st Cavalry Division on our right had even harder going and took much greater losses than us as well as two more days. Apart from our own Division, which was wholly formed from the Commonwealth, all the Divisions had an amazing selection of nationalities included. Even in I Corps we had units from the Netherlands, Colombia, Thailand, the Phillipines, Greece, Turkey and Ethopia. To them, though, we must have appeared equally motley, with units drawn from the United Kingdom, Canada, Australia and New Zealand and the Indians with their Field Ambulance, or Hospital. In addition several officers from South Africa had recently joined us.

As expected, the Chinese had had no wish to leave the good deep defences they had dug themselves for winter, so fought hard and we received many reports of the individual bravery of our troops, some of which resulted in immediate gallantry awards. The Kings Own Scottish Borderers had taken Hill 355, known as little Gibraltar, a beastly rock climb at any time and a great achievement against a determined enemy, and the Australians had cleared the feature to the north of it using their bayonets. The hills were covered in stunted firs, which, unless they had been burnt by napalm from our air raids, restricted the field of view to ten or twenty yards. Evidently the citation on one Australian read "Private X, having had his rifle knocked from his hand by a bullet, closed with a Chinaman and kicked him to death". In the official version the last four words were changed to "killed him with his bare hands". Malcolm Velvin, a Royal New Zealand Engineers officer, whom we were delighted to have attached to 12 Squadron, personally accounted for two small parties of Chinamen who were proving very troublesome. My own Troop's involvement in opening up jeep tracks was much duller, and also much safer.

The official statistics for our Division during this operation were that we had advanced about 6,000 yards and were now twelve miles north of the 38th Parallel, had taken over 100 prisoners and had ourselves suffered fifty-eight killed and 262 wounded. Written like that the casualties may not sound great, but when a good proportion of them were going past us on stretchers in jeeps, we quickly realised why the road we were opening was important.

That our Sappers achieved wonders could not be credited to my influence, as I was away from the wireless in my jeep and in which I tended not to stay any longer than proved essential. I had learnt that I could hear incoming shells, and particularly mortar bombs, much better away from the background noise of an engine, so did most of my recces on foot, usually with one man as escort, enjoying the walks in the autumn countryside.

Although the Chinese had lost their positions, there was continual evidence of some of them remaining inside what were now our front lines. Anyone who cared to stay in the woods might not have been found for weeks, and a party of four Chinese led by a woman in black was reported so frequently that its existence can have been in little doubt. It was when I was alone, climbing one of the lesser hills we had taken earlier in the advance, that I had my greatest fright in Korea. It was caused by a tremendous rustle in the undergrowth behind me and I spun round expecting to be mown down by some hidden Chinaman with a burp gun, as their Russian-pattern sub-machine guns were called. Instead I saw a small deer bounding away, the first I had met, though they were said to be common.

I had a chance of inspecting the Chinese way of life on that particular hill, as no one had waited to tidy it up since the enemy had departed in front of the Australians. Most of the digging consisted of tunnelling into the reverse slope of the hill, leading to dank and dark chambers where three or four men apparently dwelt. Apart from a few spare bits of clothing, there was neither bedding nor furnishing of any kind, not even boxes: just a part bag of rice to each hole, and quantities of small arms ammunition and grenades. For sanitation the occupants appeared to frequent a further recess near the entrance to their tunnel, so the whole place was extremely smelly. Quite apart from the dirt and the few dead Chinese lying around, the main element of smell came from the recent habitation. I hurried back to my Troop position still quivering from the fright that the little deer had given me.

Now that it was thought that there were no more mines for us to find, our main job was again roadwork. To align and open up a new track could be really interesting, almost exciting. To improve an already existing road so that it could carry many more times the quantity of traffic for which it was ever designed was, we were assured, highly important, but was also deathly dull.

Whilst our attack was still in progress my Troop had had to open up a road behind the Royal Northumberland Fusiliers as they attacked their final objectives. This fine battalion of the Fifth of Foot had been amongst the early British troops to reach Korea and had fought throughout the winter and then through the intense actions associated with the Gloucester Battle. They had been in reserve for operation COMMANDO and, as they were due for relief in a few days, everyone had hoped that there would be no need to commit them, but, when the unit in front of them had run out of ammunition just as they had reached the Chinese positions, the RNF were required. I could imagine how I would have felt if I was just about to go home, but they seemed to take the commitment as routine. A few Chinese shells and mortar bombs were arriving in their forming up area when I and some Sappers and a bulldozer also happened to be present. To ward off the projectiles the RNF Company Commander put up his black umbrella of Whitehall pattern, and even the least experienced amongst us felt considerably reassured.

A particularly pestilential official cameraman was trying to make war films, and asked the RNF to "smile please" as they approached the ridge line with the Chinese over the brow. Their reactions were varied, as they knew much better than the cameraman what they were about to face. A little later the stretcher jeeps gave him plenty of scope.

We had been allocated a largish bulldozer with a particularly good operator to build that track. He was Sapper Bell, a Z reservist who, on recall to the colours, had found himself as a helper in a cookhouse. It was only by chance that an officer heard him say that he knew something about bulldozers, about which there was nothing on his military papers. Once he had been allocated a machine, Bell proved to be as good as anyone in the Regiment.

A soldier's most important possession, or so he was told, was his Part 1 paybook. For the sake of confusion, his pay was not registered in it but on a separate little book, the Part 2, which he was seldom allowed to keep. In his Part 1 were recorded, amongst many other snippets, his next of kin, the dates of his innoculations and the results of his range courses. Whatever else a soldier knew, he knew he must not lose his Part 1 paybook.

Although it was October, it was warm by day and Sapper Bell was working under pressure, so he took his shirt off and laid it on the side of the road: unfortunately on the downhill side of the hill he was cutting. About half an hour later he realised that he ought to have put it on the other side, but his shirt was gone and Horrors! it had his paybook in it.

I was immediately informed of this calamity and all present spent a full ten minutes scrutinising the vast banks of earth which Bell had turned so well. I thought I had my priorities right in telling him to carry on dozing, but it took quite a lot more of my personal time later to stop Bell being charged for the offence of losing his paybook. About ten years later, others noted that much of the information recorded in paybooks was duplicated elsewhere. They were discontinued, nobody missed them, and most of us sighed with relief.

Bell had sloped the road at a gentle gradient on the friendly side of the hill, but the quickest way to the bottom and out of sight on the Chinese side was straight down. The slope was 1 in 3½, which, if the surface was dry, caused no problem to a jeep, but was not such fun with a trailer. Visitors started to arrive, amongst them a splendid little man, Brigadier Pike, the Commander Royal Artillery and the officer who took over command of the Division whenever General Cassels was away.

Brigadier Pike was in a "Dingo", a Daimler scout car armoured to keep out small arms bullets, thus very heavy for its squat size. He went down the hill when it was dry, but it was raining when he came back. The Brigadier pushed as well as any of us to get back up the hill, and the flying mud from the wheels much enhanced our spirit of military comradeship.

It was beside that same stretch of road that I first met the Sherman tank dozer. The Canadian regular Army in 1951 was based on three Infantry Regiments, each of three battalions, and one Armoured Regiment, Lord Strathcona's Horse. These were supported by three Regiments of Gunners, of whom I already knew the Royal Canadian Horse Artillery quite well, in the same way as I knew 57 Field Squadron of the Royal Canadian Engineers. Each of the Infantry Regiments had sent its 2nd battalion to Korea, and Lord Strathcona's had sent one of its three squadrons, with about twenty Sherman tanks.

Road building. "Ramona" on "Green Five".

"Brown Two" road in the thaw.

These, with their 17 pounder guns, had less firepower and a worse silhouette than the more modern 20 pounder Centurions of the 8th Hussars, but the Strathcona's remained a potent unit which everyone was delighted to have around. One of their tanks was fitted with a bulldozer blade, which made an already menacing vehicle look a warwinner. Those of us who had been taught a little about earthmoving knew, however, that the design of the Sherman track was totally unsuitable for pushing large clods of earth along a side slope, knowledge which the driver of the tank dozer had quickly confirmed. No sooner was the vehicle slightly off level, or the push slightly on a skew, than everything wiggled to one side and off fell a track weighing a ton or more resulting, on muddy ground, in no easy job for the crew of four to replace it. The remedy was to split the track, straighten it up in manageable lengths, then link them up again; but splitting the track was nigh on impossible if the weight of the tank was pulling it tight in the wrong direction.

I found the driver and a crewman aiming frenzied blows with sledge hammers at the track links, achieving nothing other than very bad tempers.

"Would it help," I asked, "if I were to cut the track with explosive for you?" The driver didn't appear to listen, but kept calling his vehicles two words which I had never heard in that connection before. At last his natural charm returned, and I got the impression that he would be delighted to see not only his track, but his whole vehicle, split in twain. I so happened to have some explosives with me, Sappers usually did, and the three pounds of plastic high explosive I administered proved to be slightly more than was essential, but no major damage was done, and the track was left in a state from which the crew could easily mend it. They were most grateful.

Only two days later I met the same Sherman dozer in the same state again. The crew's actions were also exactly the same, except that the driver had dreamt up two different, but similarly descriptive, words with which to address his vehicle. This time I only used one and a half pounds of explosive, and the whole job looked neater and more professional. Soon after that, the Strathcona's Squadron Leader must have realised that his dozer was no great asset, and allowed it only to be used for the easier earth moving tasks. Long after I had moved away from the Canadians, however, I knew that I had friends whenever I saw that tank.

I tried to write home at least once a week. By writing OAS (on active service) on the outside, the dirty grey airgraph forms could be sent free, but we usually wrote letters, which cost only 2½ old pence providing airmail paper and envelopes were used. It seemed rather dull and unimaginative, 11,000 miles from Britain, to have to use the English King George VI stamps, though perhaps the postmark "Field Post Office" followed by a surprising variety of numbers were of some philatelic interest. The system lacked glamour. So did our conditions of service, which were UK related and, at that time, the Army was very poorly paid. The Treasury attitude was understood to be "if there is nothing in Korea to spend money on, why give extra pay?" All very sensible, but with so many different countries serving together it was too easy to compare with other rates which were usually many more times our own. However, the difference was more a matter of interest than of great envy.

One great advantage we British did have was our dry rations, which included butter and tea. These were highly attractive to Americans, as was the occasional bottle of spirits which could sometimes be spared. My Troop proudly boasted, in addition to the issued Bren guns, a .30 inch Browning machine gun: it had been swapped for a bottle of gin from the NAAFI.

With winter coming, clothing was much on our minds when I wrote:—

10 Oct. '51. British Army Post Office 3.

Please could you post me a heavily nailed pair of Lotus Veldtschoen boots. I think they'll be about £6. My seven-year-old pair have just passed right out. I do have a good pair of marching boots, but the supply position is pretty chronic still. Please could I also have a pair or two of strongest socks. I reckon I've walked fifteen-eighteen miles on road recces today, and feel very fit on it. You have to go over the ground at least twice trying to align the tracks, and the curves and gradients need to be smoother than those of any pin-up. Advances of even a few miles through trackless country mean an awful lot of road work. There are very few mines, but those there are are almost impossible to find and several vehicles have been lost, including a precious bulldozer, like gold out here: so, to look at, is the ground we are dozing. It certainly glitters, and must contain minerals.

The days are absolutely perfect at present, and the nights fairly cool. We still wear cotton, with a battle dress top at night. All the Noggies (Chinks) have got their quilted winter clothes already and a lot of our Infantry are nicely decked out at their expense, though it is much too hot for it by day.

The country also looks really lovely, lots of hills up to 1,000 feet with pine forests. The rice is ready for harvest, but all the locals have been removed as refugees so, with the millet as well, the pheasants should thrive. Sending the civilians away is the only way to stop them from being shelled (and, anyway, we can't be sure which side they are on), but it is rather pathetic making them leave all they have.

Those box mines were proving maddening. Apparently the exceptional thing about the two with which I had been involved was that we had actually found them without harm being done. I never heard of any others being found at the time, except by claiming a target. It was further along the road that I had "cleared" that was proving particularly nasty. Dozens of vehicles would have safely crossed a given spot, then suddenly a mine would detonate and wreck whatever was on top. The theory grew that the wooden box mines must have been buried very deep with some kind of pusher bar balanced on top, with the top of the rolling pin, as it was popularly thought to be, well below the surface of the earth road. Only after the road had worn down would the top of the stick be exposed and then pushed down onto the mine lid by the next vehicle which came along.

As even my own experience showed, we had no satisfactory way of finding buried wooden mines, unless the Chinamen obligingly left footprints. To find mines deeply buried was proving even more impossible. I wondered how many I had left behind in the length of road I had reported as cleared and had a deep personal interest, as I took my jeep up and down that particular stretch at least twice a day. From every point of view it was lucky that nothing materialised. However, with the loss of our small bulldozer "David" ("Goliath" was much larger), which made the fourth mined vehicle in a few hundred yards, some thoughtful fellow ordained that the whole road must be dug out to at least a foot deep, with all the earth being shifted at least a foot to the side as well. At Wellington College at the start of the war in 1939, Rupert Horsley, the dedicated and demanding master in charge of Land Work, had us all double trenching fields which had never been turned since builders through the generations had rolled in their rubble. That had been a terrible job for pick and spade, and this road digging was equally beastly. The job was given to our Koreans, who were politely designated "Katcoms" (Koreans attached to the Commonwealth Division), but known as "Gooks". A Sapper lance corporal was in charge, and I told him that I would fully understand if he stood well back from the diggers. None of us were quite sure what would happen if a box mine were hit with a pick axe, but it was generally agreed that the result could prove dangerous. Amazingly the Gooks didn't seem to appreciate that aspect, and worked much better than I had expected.

The double trenching of the earth road was duly completed, and not one mine was found. It almost seemed a pity that the Chinese could not be told how successful their few mines had been: if any of those concerned read this, perhaps they will be interested.

Whatever else, those mines had caused real concern, as no Sapper likes to admit that he is beaten. It was known that the CRE had sent for a platoon of mine dogs, dogs which had been specially trained to detect inconsistencies in the soil, which was one way of describing a mine. It struck us that the same definition might cover a large stone, so it was with mixed feelings that we all undertook to "wait and see".

If the Chinese minewarfare methods were resulting in some original thinking on our part, so did building jeep tracks widen my education. The one I now had to build was to supply Hill 317, a steep and prominent spike of one thousand feet on the front, and near the right, of our positions. After Hill 355, 317 was easily the most commanding feature in our part of Korea, thus a good place to hold. A company of the King's Own Scottish Borderers were on it, with two other companies on lower hills on their left and another behind them covering the valleys through which I was to build my thoroughfare.

The minimum specification for a jeep track was "anything along which an ambulance jeep can pass", which explained why mine was needed quickly. Every day brought casualties from bombs and light mortars, casualties which needed evacuating, and supplies and defence stores were required in great quantities to be taken up if the hills were to be held. All this being so, my answer was to tell the dozer driver I had been allotted to go as straight as possible, cutting the shortest path. On the higher ground the result was excellent. All that was necessary was to ease away any nasty obstacles, such as banks and rocks, and, Presto!, there was a road.

Soon, though, we came to the first valley with its flat bottom covered with paddy fields, bunded up with little walls to aid the irrigation. We had had a few dry days, the locals were absent, so had not recently moistened their crops, and the paddy was hard. We were across the first little valley, perhaps a hundred yards wide, before Howard, my OC, came to see what had been achieved. He was old enough to have seen the war in Burma, and was evidently disquietened by my efforts. Did I not know that to route a track across paddy without undertaking major drainage schemes was well proven to be a waste of time? No, I suppose I should have known, but I did not.

Back came the dozer with its driver, who was understandably disappointed. Round one side of the hill, up the right-hand side of the valley had to be cut, then back down the other side of the paddy, which took about five times as long as straight across, and quite a major operation that took the whole of the next day. Overnight, though, it had rained, and there was not the slightest doubt that Howard had been right, as my original way across the paddy had become a quagmire. I had thought that to emulate the Romans with their nice straight roads must be right, but now wondered how they would have tackled my paddy fields. Anyway, I got a glimmering of how the 'rolling English drunkard' must have felt when he built his road.

The area occupied by the KOSB was of considerable tactical importance, meaning that the Chinese might well wish to reoccupy it whilst we were still very thin on the ground. "Surely Sappers have often been used as Infantry?" someone must have mused, and in no time me and my No. 3 Troop of 12 Field Squadron, Royal Engineers found ourselves referred to as No. 14 Platoon of the KOSB. When their Commanding Officer, Colonel Macdonald, took me under his wing he asked only one question, "How many machine guns have you?" I remember he was greatly impressed when I answered "Five", meaning the four Bren guns we had on normal issue and the .30 inch Browning that had been traded with the Americans for gin.

As its defensive task, my Troop was to hold a spur of hill on the home side of the valley up which my track ran. The four companies of the KOSB were up the road in front of us, which edged round the corner of my spur and ensured that we held a socially commanding position. It was pointed out to us that, if everyone had to go past us to get to the front, then, if the Chinamen managed to get through that front, the chances were that they also would wish to come past us. The message sank in, and we all dug ourselves standard slit trenches up on the hill, which, as usual, took much more than the standard time: the hill was covered with some rather measly pine trees which had plenty of roots that hampered the digging, as did the liberal presence of large pebbles in the soil.

Prior to receiving our added infantry task, my Troop had been living behind the spur we now occupied and beside a pleasant stream, good for paddling and washing, if not for bathing. Even so, with a full list of engineer tasks, mainly on roads and ditches, which were dull stuff but hard work, everyone was tired by the time it became dark. Now each evening we had to climb up our hill and spend the night in our slit trenches. Sentries had to be awake in each of the four sections and they needed to be visited by someone senior which, so far as I could determine, meant me.

I had always needed lots of regular sleep, and was soon missing it. Stumbling round those trenches, which had been dug wherever a gap between the pine roots permitted, was hard enough in daylight. On a dark night without a torch it was a feat which ensured that many more than the prescribed minimum of sentries were kept awake, as stones and clods of earth, sometimes followed by the Troop Commander, fell into the excavations.

Howard, my Squadron Commander, was all too aware that, with its Staff Sergeant ill, my Troop was short of supervision, and now Mike, my Troop Officer, was himself evacuated to Japan. To add to the problems he was closely followed by Howard himself, who was wounded by a mortar bomb.

Peter Leslie, one of the very experienced officers in Regimental Headquarters, came and took over 12 Squadron. He looked round my defensive positions the same evening and, quite rightly, said he did not like the look of the place and wanted the barbed wire and digging improved. So, indeed had I, but my attempts to balance our limited effort between the Sapper work, which looked of low priority to the uninitiated, and the Infantry work, which was very much in the public eye, could not please everybody. Certainly the Brigade Commander and Colonel Macdonald came to inspect our defensive positions daily.

My main concern about the vulnerability of our spur was not the left tip, around which the track ran, but the right-hand end which just merged into the rest of the large belt of trees on the hill. In daylight we couldn't see more than twenty yards from our forward slit trenches, and we obviously needed warning earlier than that if the Chinese decided to come along the ridge line. There was no doubt that small patrols of them had been seen nearby, often with the women in black thrown into the sighting report, so I was rather proud of my brain wave, trip flares to put in the trees on our right, and managed to obtain a dozen from the Regimental Sergeant Major of the KOSB. His job of supervising ammunition supplies in war was more popularly rated than that of supervising the parade ground in peace.

There was a special knack in laying those trip flares of British design, and I knew that I personally had not got it. It was only too easy to make the tripwire, thin, black and strong, rather like the trace one used on a salmon minnow, too loose or too tight. I was assured, though, that two of my Sappers were experts with trip flares, and was delighted to allow them a day to cover all approaches off the wooded hill and down to our spur.

Except when I was visiting the sentries, I slept much more reassured the next night and, apart from the harassing fire from our own guns going overhead, to which we had all become oblivious, perfect peace reigned. The next night was more windy, everything rustled and not just the sentries stayed awake. Suddenly out beyond our positions there was a pop, a hiss and the lurid flame from one of our trip flares. I scrambled from my trench, rolling in the usual twenty or so large pebbles which made such uncomfortable bedfellows, and crept to the trench nearest the flare. Apart from trees, nobody had seen anything and, commendably, no one had fired.

The breeze became a wind and off went two more flares, closely followed by another. We now knew what had happened. A trip flare came complete with a two footed spike of steel rod on which it was suported, but the pegs to which the other end of the tripwire should have been tied were missing. My two experts who had laid the flares had thought it a godsend that they were laying in the midst of small trees, each a ready made and splendidly well rooted peg. Unfortunately neither they nor I had thought that the wind might shake the trees sufficiently to pull the wires tight enough to set off the flares.

I wondered what the KOSB battalion HQ must be thinking of my firework display, and stumbled down the, again completely dark, hill to ring up their Adjutant from the phone which a kind linesman had provided that day. The Adjutant was distinctly relieved, as an assault down onto us by large numbers of Chinese had been rumoured. The next day we relaid the remaining flares, using proper posts and not trees to which to secure the wires. Apart from one of our own men setting one off in daylight, we had no more trouble.

Peter, our new OC, came to see us daily; otherwise I was seeing very little of our other two Troops in the Squadron, but one evening Roy

Gout of 2 Troop said I really must spare a moment to call on him. We had known each other at Aldershot and I was delighted to visit him, though green with envy at what I found. Compared with my own circumstance, everything looked so very organised. His living arrangements, with a tent well dug in and electric lamps from not one, but two, vehicle batteries were, to my eyes, palatial. We chatted over what we were doing, and he brought out a notepad with a long list of tasks which he kept, all marked with the priorities he gave them. I was amazed. I knew Roy as a splendid fellow to spend an evening with in a pub, but had never credited him with literary ability. He certainly hadn't, so far as I knew, been back to a university, yet here he was, infinitely more organised than me. He must have read my thoughts as he said, "Dan, any fool can be uncomfortable." I only wish that he had said it to me long before.

CHAPTER SEVEN

MY MINEFIELD

I had heard that Barry Pollard and his Troop were laying anti-personnel mines somewhere on the right boundary of the Divisional front, and that all the Infantry, who knew how exposed they were in their new positions, were clamouring for us Sappers to lay minefields to guard them. Sure enough, I was told that my Troop was to lay a minefield to stretch eastwards from the bottom slopes of Hill 317 to join up with the minefield which Barry was laying about 600 yards to the right.

I went with Peter in his jeep to the head of my track behind 317, then started to climb up the 800 feet or so on the home side of the hill. Luckily a winding track, sometimes with rough steps, had been constructed or trodden down by the Korean porters on whom our logistics depended. I soon asked, "Why don't we have mules out here?" as I was not sure whether Peter, whose war had been nearer home, had had the advantage of a one week's mule course, as had I in Bangalore soon after I was commissioned. Why we didn't have mules was because, presumably, we thought we could always build a jeep track, which was not true, not initially anyway. We understood that the Chinese were increasingly using mules, or some equivalent animal, and that their communication trenches had to be deep and wide enough for laden horses.

Climbing a hill like 317 on a hot day, and the days still were very hot, was a feat in itself. You may remember that I had arrived in Korea in a rather well nourished state. Two months of fairly active service had rendered my waistline slightly, but no amount of exercise was ever going to make me an athlete. I was thoroughly puffed when Peter and I met the company commander, Major Roddy McLeod, on the top of the hill. As we had stumbled our way up we had, with hurt pride, been overtaken by strings of Koreans each carrying a heavy load, such as a coil of barbed wire, a bundle of steel fencing pickets or a couple of long thin wooden boxes with rope handles on each end, each containing a dozen No. 36 grenades: these were near enough the same as the Mills bombs which had been in service nearly forty years before. In all our eyes, though, the most interesting loads were cases of a dozen large bottles of Asahi beer. On top of Hill 317 we were generously offered a bottle, and I seldom can have needed a beer more, but, for once, decency prevailed and we resisted the very kind offer in favour of those who had to live up that steep and lonely hill all the time. I wished that Sir Philip Sydney had not set so good an example.

As if to show appreciation of our visit, the Chinese started to shell 317, quite gently but with persistence. The very top of the hill was about the size of a tennis court, and we were on it. We all agreed that it would be uncommonly difficult for a Chinese shell to land on the top, though we chose to overlook the fact that several of our own had done so: the craters were still evident from when the Australians had taken 317 during Operation COMMANDO two weeks before. Whatever the Chinese gunners' intentions, it was decidedly exciting to hear a shell coming in, go past the top of the hill and then burst hundreds of feet below on the bottom of the slope we had just ascended, or further down in the valley behind us. Some landed so near to the Korean porters, whom one could not but admire, that we wondered if the Chinese had a forward observation officer on our side of the hill, a worrying thought.

So far as the minefield went, Roddy said he would be very happy to accept anything we could offer him. There was a great chunk of land on the eastern face of the hill which flattened out into a ridge line of a lower hill that he would be delighted if we were to make it unpleasant, particularly as he saw no chance of patrolling it properly himself. "What kinds of mine have you got?" he asked. I didn't even hazard a guess, but I knew what the answer would be whatever we could lay our hands on. Peter was more specific: "Anti-personnel," he said, "with tripwires." "Sounds splendid," said Roddy, as we waved him and his cheery Scotsmen farewell, promising to let him know how the minefield progressed.

Roddy had a reputation for being a considerate host, and we gave him the credit for the Chinese shells no longer falling as we slithered down the hill. Near the bottom Peter and I turned left and back towards where my minefield was to start. The hillside was steep and, with no form of track, the going would have been difficult enough had all the small pine trees been standing. As it was, the lower slopes of 317 had been subjected to an air raid with napalm, so the trees had all been scorched, and we were constantly stepping over, or ducking under, filthy black branches.

After about half a mile we reached the spot where my minefield would be the nearest to the top of 317, hundreds of feet above us, and Peter pointed out the general line the field was to take, basically along the ridge line of the spur and on the home, or reverse, slope, which had also been liberally napalmed.

I must have looked highly concerned, if not rather horrified. I had never laid a live minefield, but had been trained in some depth in the war to lay anti-tank mines of a design I knew well, always in grass fields which were flat and reasonably soft. Such exercises started by a lorry driving up to the end of the field and the mines, never in any great quantity, being unloaded. Great play was made, very sensibly, of recording exactly where the minefield was laid, so that, not just in training, we could lift it again if needs be. First a reference point had to be chosen nearby, perhaps the corner of a building or any other prominent object sufficiently permanent as to be unlikely to disappear completely in war. It was from this reference point that the survey of the minefield, made with a compass, started. I was pretty sure that, on that napalmed slope which had gone out of its way to be featureless, I was never going to know to the nearest couple of hundred yards where I was, let alone pinpoint the end of my minefield exactly on the map.

Map reading wasn't my greatest worry, as a minefield half a mile long would be needed and that meant hundreds of mines which, of whatever type they were, were sure to be heavy. So would be the steel pickets and barbed wire to put a single strand marking fence around it. How they would ever be got to the spot, I had no immediate notion. Oh for a nice road for lorries, just as we had always had in training! Helicopters for a task like that were unthinkable: the Americans were using some, probably for the first time in war, but they only carried very senior commanders, or evacuated casualties.

Before we scrambled back the way we had come, Peter told me not to forget to complete the fence before I armed the mines at the end of each day, meaning the removal of their safety pins. This was quite a point, as the field was obviously going to take us several days, so we would have to put up a temporary fence on the open end each night.

We reached Peter's jeep behind 317 at the top of the road, as I liked to think of my track, which was certainly much appreciated by the KOSB. I had plenty to think about, but the best piece of news Peter had given me was that a new lance sergeant of excellent repute had arrived with the Squadron and would come to 3 Troop that evening. Lance sergeants were only found, so far as I knew, in the Royal Engineers and the Brigade of Guards and, in our Corps, the rank was rare. This young man was evidently considered to be an outstandingly good corporal, so had been given his third stripe. If he was good, I didn't mind what rank he was in.

Nearing the far end of the road, just before it turned round the spur of the hill that was 3 Troop's very own little bit of Korea, we were surprised to find our route diverted by a stationary Oxford Carrier, an open topped armoured vehicle of the type which succeeded the Bren Carrier. From the signs on it, we could see that it belonged to the KOSB, so we were surprised, on their home ground, to find it festooned with the red tin triangles with which a minefield fence was marked. These had been high in my mind, wondering just how many I would need. We edged round the Oxford with some difficulty and asked a Sapper at the end of our spur whatever was up. "Oh, it broke down and the KOSB thought 3 RAR would pinch it, so we've marked it up as a minefield. The spares are coming and it will be away tomorrow." To lose a vehicle to the Chinese would be a matter of shame, but to the Australians, worse. In fact 3 RAR had no Oxford Carriers, so, had they taken to the roads with one, others might have noticed.

Soon after Peter Leslie had returned to Squadron HQ, we were told the types of mines we would be getting for the minefield. The first hundred or so would be American M3 anti-personnel mines, then the rest of the 200 that we would need for laying with tripwires would be another type of American mine, the M2, and also some of our own old British Mark 2s. This must all sound very confusing, but I knew that the first, the M3, was just a block of cast iron filled with TNT, whereas the others were what we called bouncing mines and much more complicated. Our Mark 2s had been obsolescent for years, so we were surprised to find some had landed up in Korea. All this started to set an interesting scene, as did the news that the usual igniters for the M3 mines were not available and that we would be given items known as M1 pull fuzes.

In no time I had managed to find M1 pull fuzes in the excellent little American mines book, to be told that "this fuze has some employment in Korea by friendly forces. It is especially useful in booby-trap set ups." The last words gave the clue, because further down the page the keen reader could discover that after withdrawing not one, but two, safety pins, a pull of two to three pounds on the little ring at the end of this igniter would release the striker and fire whatever explosive charge it had chosen as its raison d'être. Normal pull switches of the type one used with tripwire mines needed a pull of fifteen to twenty pounds to set them off, so the care needed in setting the booby trap switches would be comparable to that of playing a salmon on a trout rod.

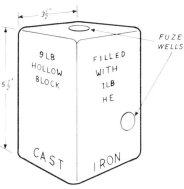

American M3 Mine

That afternoon Lance Sergeant Marshall arrived, and I immediately liked the look of him. I left him and Sergeant Williams, the storekeeper type, with such working numbers as we could muster to practise setting out the V patterns to which we would eventualy lay the tripwires and the mines. My driver then took me and a lance corporal back up the valley to start planning the layout of the minefield.

I knew that it would be difficult to get the stores to the start of the minefield through those napalmed trees on the awkward hillside without a footpath, so the corporal and I spent even more time aligning it with little lengths of white tracing tape, than I, only a few days before, had spent aligning an equal length of jeep track. We chose as the reference point for the end of the minefield a large rock, which was nothing like as unique as ideals would dictate, and also fixed the location of the "datum point", from which the end of the first row of mines could be pinpointed. The datum point would be marked by a clump of steel pickets which, like the reference point, would hopefully not be removed by the odd shell.

As I set out the line along which the first row of mines would be laid, I found that I was walking over what must have been a Chinese defended position, which may have accounted for the attention the area had been given by the napalm. Amongst various items of rather dull equipment still lying around were a dozen or so small wooden boxes, which I knew must be the Chinese version of the old German "schu" mine. These devices contained a small charge of TNT and a rudimentary fuze from which the safety pin was pushed out as the lid was pushed down by a walking man. The usual effect was not only the removal of a schu, but of a foot and part of a leg as well. I was surprised that the Chinese had left their mines behind, but perhaps they didn't rate them very highly. I was sure they must be commonplace and wouldn't have mentioned them now, had I not read in an intelligence report over a year later from another part of the country: "This is the first time that the presence of enemy schu mines in Korea has been confirmed." I then knew it wasn't, but saw no point in advertising my failure to report schu mines earlier.

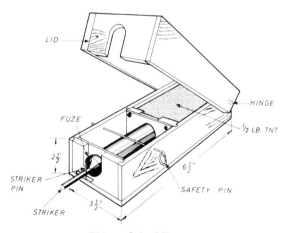

Chinese Schu Mine

My preoccupation was not so much the presence of a few unarmed enemy mines, but whether my Troop would have any mines to lay. I gave top priority to building the footpath and by the next afternoon our Koreans had hacked, picked and shovelled an excellent access route along the hillside. That day we started the barbed wire perimeter fences and laid a mere nine mines, covering a front of under fifty yards. As we had laid none of these mines before, let alone with booby trap switches, the concensus of opinion was that it should be the Troop Commander's honour to arm them. This involved pulling out the safety pins from the booby trap switches, which had been screwed in one to each mine, and, once done, meant that the mine would explode at a tiny touch of its tripwires. I was thankful that the wind was not blowing, and quickly appreciated that a hand as steady as one that spills no froth from a brimming mug would be required.

Some may remember my earlier efforts with explosive charges and tripwires in Sumatra over five years before. There it had been my task to lay what we called silent sentries, or one ounce guncotton charges, complete with igniters and tripwires, the aim having been to dissuade nasty Indonesians from entering our lines by night. Most unfairly the same folk had arrived by day, just after I had armed my first charges and, in my hurry not to be caught on the job, I had hastily retreated through my own tripwires. It was only after the second loud bang that I had realised that it was I who was setting them off. In the meanwhile the bangs had started a riot in the adjoining jail and, one way and another, my reputation had not been enhanced. The fact that no Indonesians ever seemed to come that way again gained me no discernible credit. Now, on a dirty hill in Korea, I had to remind myself that these mines were not just silent sentries, but specifically designed to kill anyone who pulled a tripwire.

We laid the mines in threes, much as A, B and C are shown in the sketch. Each had its switch screwed into the socket on the side nearest to the enemy, and the switch had a little split ring in the end. To this a couple of five yard lengths of tripwire were loosely attached, and then splayed out to form an approximate right angle. At the far end of each wire a small peg was driven in, so that the tripwires formed a broad V, with its bottom at the position of the mine.

All this had been done by the Sappers laying the mines. My job in arming each one was gently to make fast the wires to the ring, making sure that they were just tight enough to be off the ground, but on no

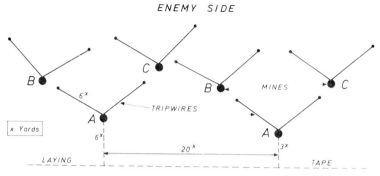

Typical Tripwire Minefield Pattern

account exerting a pull of more than two pounds, then to ease out the safety pins. After that, it was a case of edging away extremely carefully without touching the tripwires, or rolling anything onto them. To start with, this was all rather hair raising, but after the first few the main problem was to keep concentrating. The tripwires were specifically deisigned to blend with their background and, even just after handling them a moment before, were extraordinarily difficult to locate. I was thankful that we were doing the laying and arming by day, and wondered how folk ever coped at night. After having learnt British minefield drills for eight years, here I was laying my first live minefield with unknown mines to almost unknown drills. All very strange!

I was not proud that evening when I had to tell Peter that we had laid only nine mines, and I could sympathise with him having to tell the KOSB how little we had strengthened their defences. I wondered if we had been over cautious, and would have loved to compare times with others under the same circumstances but, apart from Barry, knew of nobody who had recently tried.

As it was, Barry had been attacked by a cow, or that was how the message had reached us. Evidently he had only just armed his mines at the end of a laying session, when a cow had appeared from the direction of his Chinese enemies and walked through one of his cunningly laid tripwires. The mine had wounded Barry, and we never heard precisely what became of the cow. Many years afterwards I asked Barry, who had become a General, his version of the story. He said that he had often wondered about the exact circumstances himself, but could only assume that the Chinamen had cut the front edge of his minefield fence and then driven in one or more poor cows. This tallied with what we had always believed and, as he had not been severely wounded, gave cause for further mirth.

The next day a Sapper and I laid out several hundred yards of the proposed minefield. The main belt of mines would lie just on the home side of the ridge line, which was still relatively bare due to the napalm, but the fence on the Chinese side had to run through thick trees, so some care was needed in aligning it to make sure that it kept properly clear of the forward mines.

The fence on the home side looked a much easier task and we were making much better progress in setting it out when, close on the ground beside us, there was the characteristic pop, followed by the hiss, of a hand grenade being ignited. The last time I had heard that sound, I had recognised it all too well, but had not had the courage of my convictions, lest my Puerto Rican guide thought me scared. I had vowed that in future, discretion would be the better part of valour, and here, suddenly and surely, was the time.

I needn't have worried about warning my assistant, as he had got the message remarkably swiftly, but I still shouted loudly. Otherwise, I again muttered "Good old mother earth" and attempted to simulate an ever flatter pancake. Have you ever thought, when lying on your face, whether you bottom sticks up more with the muscles tensed, or when all floppy and relaxed? Until then I hadn't, and am still not sure which I would advise. However, the hissing continued for an interminable time, and I was convinced that the bang at the end of it all was likely to be enormously large. It never came, so eventually I looked up very cautiously, to find that a trip flare had started the makings of a forest fire.

Almost at the same moment an exceedingly irate Australian private soldier arrived, who told the British officer and his companion what a couple of Pommy cissies they were. We helped him put his fire out and told him that it was better that it had happened before we laid the minefield in front of him, than after. I was also pleased to discover for the first time exactly where the Australian positions were, information well worth knowing.

That day a really useful number of mines were delivered up my new footpath, and thirty-six of them were laid, adding a couple of hundred yards to the length of the minefield. Sergeant Marshall and I had only just finished arming them at the end of the afternoon when not only our Commanding Officer, Lieutenant Colonel Peter Moore, but also his superior, Colonel Eddie Myers, our CRE, came striding up towards me from the direction of the Australians. Those two combined immensely varied operational experience and, even if they did not look overjoyed at seeing me, I felt most honoured by their joint visit.

I soon discovered that they had come to see me for a purpose, and that all was not too well. I was apparently to be given a piece of their minds, the impact of which was likely to be considerable, so they told me to sit down before they started. It was just as well that they decided to sit down also as, no sooner had they done so, than there was a powerful bang from very close to us. One of the scorched branches of the napalmed pine trees had at that moment decided that it could hang on no longer and had fallen across the tripwire of a mine I had just armed. Judging by the twigs which fell off other trees all around, including over our heads, the fragments of the cast iron mine must have flown well.

Such little happenings appeared to be all in the day's work, and I only hoped that I would not be asked to go into the minefield to replace the exploded mine. Instead the Colonels had come to tell me that an officer who had more right to command a Troop than me had just arrived in Korea and that, with mixed feelings, they were going to give him my 3 Troop, where admittedly I had always been the temporary incumbent. Once the new officer had taken over from me, I would move to Lieutenant Colonel Moore's Regimental Headquarters as the Liaison Officer.

This news shook me to a much greater extent than the true bombshell we had just survived, so much so that I was left near enough speechless. I managed something to the effect that I would be very glad to be allowed to stay with my Troop long enough to complete that particular minefield, with which they immediately agreed.

To show that my mind was not entirely preoccupied with footpaths and little triangles of red painted tin, my letter home written a couple of days before my encounter with the Colonels included:—

> I just haven't had a chance to get at the pheasants. One of our Sappers shot a beautiful cock (just like ours at home) with a .303: lovely clean hole and no damage! They crow like mad when anything like a barrage gets going, and even set off our tripwires.

The weather is still very pleasant, and one gets really hot climbing the hills. My waist is down to 33″, after 37″ when I left England.

We continue to get English beer at 1/9½d (9p) a pint, not too bad, but after next month we won't get it, as the bottles freeze. Ink is the same I hear.

The autumn colours are really lovely.

Soon after we had started the minelaying the next day we finished the stocks of the M3 mines which we had been positioning on the hillside and had to start laying the M2 American bouncing mines instead. These were based on the principle of the much dreaded German "S" mines which were first laid in vast quantities in front of German positions at El Alamein. As with the M3 mines, the tripwires were attached to a form of pull igniter, but on the M2 it was built into a special projection from the base of the mine. Beside it on the base was a steel tube, which contained the fragmenting part of a small mortar bomb. When the tripwire pulled the igniter, instead of it immediately detonating the bomb, a small gunpowder charge threw it straight upwards out of its tube. A wire about four feet long was attached from the mine base to another igniter in the base of the bomb, which exploded as soon as the wire became taut. This was at about head height, and the thoroughly unpleasant concept ensured that no fragments were immediately lost into the ground. A man lying down was just as vulnerable as one standing up.

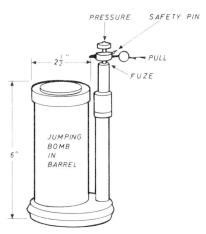

American M2 Mine

The M2 mines were taller than the M3s and needed to be laid upright, or the bomb would not be projected upwards. To fix them on the ground they had to be at least partially buried, and this was easier said than done amongst the large stones and pine roots. However, Sergeant Marshall soon had answers to the problems, and I left him with a party to do the job as I went off with two men rolling out the barbed wire through the trees for the forward fence on the Chinese side of the ridge line. Though there were no friends in front of us, the Chinamen had not been in evidence, but an adequate number of their shells, say one every couple of minutes, were arriving in our area that morning. So long as they cleared the ridge line, I knew we would be unlucky if they did not clear the minelaying party also.

It wasn't long, however, before we heard an explosion with more reverberation than the crack of a shell and knew that another of yesterday's mines had gone off. We assumed that another branch must have fallen on a tripwire, and no messages of anything amiss reached us. I was beginning to understand why the reliability of tripwire minefields was in question, and hoped that not too many more of my mines would go off on their own.

The American C7 canned rations were very good, and we were enjoying the warm lunch that had been sent up to us when Alan James, who was to take over the Troop from me, arrived. He was a good friend from many years before, and I spent most of the afternoon showing him what had been done and what was intended. Meanwhile the minelayers had just topped the hundred mines for the day and I and Sergeant Marshall again stayed after the others had left to remove the safety pins.

The hillside on which those mines had been laid, balanced would be a better word, was much steeper than the gentler slopes of the previous days and the act of arming the mines provided sporting occupation. To approach a mine from uphill, test the tension of the tripwires, very gently remove the safety pins and then climb or crawl up the slope again to regain the comparative safety on the line of the laying tape was quite a feat, of a type to which I was unaccustomed and gymnastically unsuited. Luckily I had foreseen the need not to dislodge stones onto tripwires once the pins had been removed and had taken the precaution of wearing my rubber soled PT shoes.

It was 26th October, 1951, and Alan and I talked late into the night. We had already been back to the Battalion HQ of the King's Own

Scottish Borderers where I had introduced him to Colonel Macdonald and I had said that we hoped to complete the minefield the next day.

In the morning we were off early, and I again started the day on the forward slope with the party setting out the minefield fence. "Why," you might ask, "mark the enemy side of a minefield to show them where it is?" An answer could be "if the battlefield stays static, our own patrols will need to go out into No Man's Land in front of the minefield, so will want to know where they can safely go. If the battle moves, or units take over from each other, then the less doubt there is of where the minefields start and end, the happier for everyone."

No sooner had we started work than there was again the explosion of one of our mines over the brow of the hill. This had happened so soon after our arrival that I sensed something might be wrong, so hastened back down the front minefield fence, reached the end where we had started and stumbled back along the home side fence, a full half mile, to end up only a couple of hundred yards behind where I had left the fencing party. I was soon told that a Sapper had set off a mine and saw that Alan, who had been on that side of the hill, had just found him when I arrived. The injured man was only about fifteen yards inside the minefield, and between us we carried him out, having hastily located the lie of the local tripwires. We did what we could, but he died on the way to the medical post.

Evidently the poor chap had been sent for stores and had taken the shortest route, straight through the edge of the minefield, which was fully fenced and properly marked with its red triangles. A friend had shouted "Stop", but the victim had answered cheerily, "They are not armed," and had gone ahead. It was the more sad because it was such an unnecessary accident, only too typical of the many which were going to occur as the months went by.

In a highly sober mood we continued minelaying at a good speed, the only point of note being that to make up the numbers for the last few mines, we had to use the few of our own British bouncing anit-personnel mines of which we had been the ungrateful recipients. These had a poor reputation at the best of times and, sure enough, I managed to get into difficulties when arming the very last ones. I had the tripwires rather too taut, had pulled out one of the two safety pins with which the mines were fitted and could not budge the other. Nor could I then get the first one back in. Apart from Sergeant Marshall, who was at the other end of our day's work, I was the only United Nations soldier on the Chinese side of that hill, and suddenly felt exceptionally lonely. I was very thankful when Marshall came along the minefield fence a few minutes later to report that he had finished his half of the arming. I told him that I was stuck, and he promptly said he was sure he could put things right. His standards were such that he didn't even suggest that we could leave the mine half armed, a thought that had certainly crossed my mind. He also had no wish to be shown the situation by me, in fact would not approach the mine until I had joined him back at the laying tape. He, too, knew how easy it would be for us both to be killed by trying to deal with one mine. He had the job finished in a matter of seconds and we had the doubtful satisfaction of knowing that we might have laid the last of that particular type of mine ever to be used in anger.

I spent one more day with Alan and 3 Troop, a pleasant change from minelaying and an exciting day in its own right as the General Election results, nearly half a day out of phase, were coming in over the wireless from England. We had known that it was going to be a close thing as, after Labour's vast majority in 1945, they had only had an overall majority of 8 (Labour 315, Conservatives 296 and Liberals 9) in the 1950 election. This had proved to be unmanageably small, and Mr. Attlee had gone back to the country on 26th October, 1951. The Conservatives reversed the position (Conservatives 320, Labour 296 and Liberals 6), a majority which proved rather more solid. I wrote home:—

27 Oct. '51. 12 Squadron

Just heard the election results. Old Winston will certainly have his hands full.

I move to RHQ tomorrow. We finished our minefield, and are really rather proud of it. I think it will shake a great many Chinamen if they are unsociable enough to attack.

This afternoon we all took time off and went to a troops' concert, two women and two men. Ethel Revnell was the star: quite good and, even after nine weeks here, very nice to see something out of khaki.

The nights are definitely cold now, with sharp frost. I wore battledress for the first time all day today, and was none too hot. We have a supply of Guinness, but no champagne! Cambridge seems a long time ago already, and yet the actual weeks seem to fly.

Peace talks are said to be under way again. We all hope they go through, and feel that the object of this last push must have been to show the Chinks that we mean business: it certainly did *not* strengthen our defensive line.

CHAPTER EIGHT

FIRST PHEASANTS

I wouldn't have dreamt of admitting it at the time, but being posted back to Regimental Headquarters, just south of the Imjin and seven miles from my KOSB reserve position, turned out much more pleasantly than I had ever dared to expect. I had been for a short time in an RHQ before, as Assistant Adjutant to Martin Keer in Aldershot. Here we were again, with Martin as Adjutant and me called the Liaison Officer, or odd job man, not much different to the previous occasion, apart from us both being three years older. The only other officers then in RHQ, apart from the Commanding Officer, who was out almost all day but whose presence was ever felt, were the Second-in-Command, Major Bill Woods, another highly able officer, and the Intelligence Officer, Captain Tom Marquis, a splendid ex-prisoner of war of goodly girth and full of wordly wisdom. Peter Leslie, the Signals Officer, was still temporarily commanding 12 Squadron whence I had come, so Tom offered me bedspace in his tent, which could just squeeze in three anyway.

I certainly slept very well my first night, and it wasn't until after another that I realised just how tired I must have been. To be back to the routine of an Officers' Mess, however rustic, seemed almost unbelieveable. Not by any means was all of the day a rush, in fact the real hard work started at dusk when the day's achievements could be assessed, and the CO could plan for the next.

Even to have thought of looking for pheasants during my last few weeks with 3 Troop would have been out of the question, yet, quite unexpectedly, the reason for my volunteering for the Korean War now appeared to have become a reality. Martin made it clear that there was no point in us both hanging around the Command Post on quiet afternoons, the pheasant season was decently open and, if he couldn't get out shooting, then I should. "No better way of getting to know the country," he said, and of course I agreed.

I shot my first Korean pheasant on the afternoon of my first full day with RHQ. We were only a few hundred yards from where I had shared lines with the Canadian gunners only a few weeks before, so I knew that there was a promising piece of marsh land between the road which ran beside us and the Imjin River. It was a pity that a minor airstrip was being built at one end of it, but I hoped that the noise might make any game concentrate at the other. This proved correct, as I first put up a good brood of eight pheasants which rose mainly singly and at which I fired four of the 200 cartridges I had brought with me. Martin had lent me his gun, as mine was still broken with no certainty of repair being possible. After much further walking I put up what I later discovered to be some button quail, game birds between the size of a partridge and a snipe, but hardly worth scarce cartridges. On the way back I fired at a snipe, which continued very happily on his jinking way, saw a deer, rather larger than the little fellow who had frightened me so much on the old Chinese position, and shot a nice young cock pheasant as he crossed me. Considering that I had seen all these in an hour or so with no dog, with the birds put up just by me zigzagging through the long grass, was very encouraging. Yes, there were pheasants in Korea!

The next day aspects of life similar to Aldershot became even more apparent, as I had to sit as a member of a Court Martial. The accused was convicted of desertion, which on active service can be a serious offence, for not turning up with the remainder of his comrades to lay a minefield. I knew what the particular task had been, and that it had not been rated as particularly dangerous, so was surprised that the chap had ever gone absent at the time. There must have been more to the case than I understood.

When I arrived back at RHQ that evening the winter kit, of which we had heard so much, had arrived, to celebrate which the weather turned very warm. There was no doubt though, that most of the clothing was excellent, and that there were many more ways of wearing it than the designers could ever have imagined.

Other than that we were given too much chicken in the rations, very few of us complained about the food in Korea. We, in the Commonwealth Division, undoubtedly had the best of all worlds, with those American fresh rations, meaning meat and veg, coming direct in refrigerated ships from California or Hawaii, and also their excellent combat ration packs, the tinned C rations, and British "dry" rations, meaning everything else, like sugar, tea and butter. Because we were in what could be a very cold place, the sheer size of the authorised rations must have been near to a maximum, so we all did very well indeed. Over and above the issued rations, the British NAAFI canteen system had now had a chance to settle into a fairly efficient routine, and more of most things could be bought if needed.

However, back in England, sugar, and alongside it jam, were still rationed and in very short supply, which vexed my mother intensely. There was our home in North Devon with a large kitchen garden and an excellent gardener, so we had masses of fruit, and a proper cook in the house as well. There also were masses of good jam jars and a splendid storecupboard suitably shelved, but since 1940 it had never been properly laden with jam, all because of no sugar.

Here in Korea I found that I could perfectly legally buy a one hundredweight sack of sugar for no great price and post it back the 11,000 miles to England, from whence it had come. I had been planning this even before I went to 3 Troop and, ever since I had handled ammunition for the Canadian gunners as part of my dinner invitation, had earmarked just the right containers.

Those tins with soldered ends, which drew blood on the unwary and held the cartridge cases for 25 pounder shells, were just what was needed. They were about five inches in diameter by fourteen long and, even when the soldered seal had been removed, the lids still fitted well. Each tin, I discovered, would take six pounds of sugar. The heaviest parcel the Army Post Office would accept was 22lbs, and it was fortuitous that three of the tins, each complete with 6lbs of sugar, could be stuffed in a triangular pattern inside a normal sandbag. Make the end secure and tie on a large label, with the address on one side and a green customs declaration label on the other, and there was your parcel home. The postage charge, so far as I remember, was only moderate, something like half a crown (12½p). My pay, with rather measely allowances, was now about ten times that a day.

I sent off five parcels, totalling ninety pounds of sugar, in the next couple of weeks, and they all arrived home, much to the delight of those concerned, even including our cook. My only worry was for the South Molton postman, as the charming fellow did our beat on foot, three quarters of a mile from the town towards the station, five hundred yards up our drive which crossed the River Mole, then across the fields to two more farms before delivering to the council houses on the Taunton road on his way back into South Molton.

The Command Post of the Headquarters of 28 Engineer Regiment consisted of two 3 ton lorries with special box bodies, and they had been parked with their tailboards about ten feet apart. The gap between the two was covered with a purpose-built, but somewhat cumbersome, tent delighting in the name of "the penthouse". One of the lorries carried the main wirelesses, and they and a couple of operators filled all but about four feet of the box body length. The latter was partitioned off, though there were sliding glass windows to the signallers, and in the remaining four feet there was just room for a desk top and a couple of swivel chairs. In one of them the duty officer would sit with a foolscap

Headquarters 28 Field Engineer Regiment. Winter 1951. Captain Tom Marquis, Major Bill Woods, Sappers and a Dingo.

millboard in front of him, to which log sheets were clipped and on which the day's activities had to be precisely, but concisely, recorded. I soon discovered that when I was not out of the headquarters on a recce or other errand, which included shooting pheasants, I automatically became the duty officer. Down the steps from the wireless vehicle and up those into the other opposite lorry revealed a similar, but larger compartment than mine, in which the Second-in-Command and Adjutant had a table and chairs. Through the dividing wall in their vehicle were the regimental chief clerk, a sergeant, and a couple of clerks.

Tom, the Intelligence Officer, had a table of his own down in the penthouse and walled himself and his draughtsman in with enormous talc (transparent celluloid) covered map boards which tended to divert all but the most inquisitive of visitors. The chair next to the duty officer was sometimes occupied by the signals officer, but was frequently free. I soon discovered why, as it was the commanding officer's habit to enter the vehicle as soon as his jeep brought him back to camp, and, without saying a word, he expected the log board to be placed in front of him.

It took me days to realise how seriously all this was taken. The log sheets had a column for the time a message was received, a column for the gist of the message, another to record those who had been informed, and a further column to show when the action was complete. About ten handwritten serials would fit onto a sheet, and it was then passed across to a clerk for typing. It took me days to realise that action needed to be completed quickly and that, except in exceptional circumstances, the log sheet was not handed out for typing until the action column was complete.

Lieutenant Colonel Peter Moore, who had a dark moustache and was a bachelor aged forty with very little time for small talk when there was a war on, would grab the nearest pencil and avidly scan and digest every item on the log. Occasionally he would address comments to the Second-in-Command or Adjutant in the other vehicle, but most of the time he worked in awe-inspiring silence. The silence was broken quickly enough if the action column of the log was not complete and, if it wasn't, it was usually my fault. To a series of questions starting with "Why hasn't . . .?" my answers of "I thought . . .", or "I couldn't contact them" stood me in no stead at all. "Find out, and show me the log when it is complete" was always the answer. Once I knew that the quickest and only acceptable way was to obtain the answers, the log sheets seemed to be signed off with a speed I would not have imagined possible a few days previously.

Having approved the log, the Commanding Officer would pocket the pencil from the desk, find out what the Second-in-Command, the Adjutant and possibly Tom were doing, then stride away to his next assignment.

In a headquarters not lacking in character, another whose presence was very much felt was Mr. Hacker, the Regimental Sergeant Major. His role as an enforcer of the law was never far below the surface, but he was more popular, and in great demand, for his splendid sense of humour and real ability as a chef. He was a strong squat man, whose leisurely pace belied the speed with which he could move, or chivvy, if necessary. Whilst the rest of us had been awaitini our issue of winter kit, Mr. Hacker had come by a brown woolly jerkin of apparently unique design and very close to his heart. Never did an RSM look more

The Commanding Officer,
Lieutenant Colonel
P. N. M. Moore,
DSO, MC, RE.

Regimental Command Post. Winter 1951/52.

Regimental Sergeant Major Hacker and Sappers.

like a mobile teddy bear, and fortunately mainly a benign teddy at that.

When the CO and RSM prowled together, not every member of the Regiment found them benign. The Colonel carried a copy of the Manual of Military Law in its cheery red covers in his jeep and everyone knew that if an obvious offence were discovered, no justice would be more summary. On one occasion a lance corporal was found to have a dirty rifle. Mr. Hacker carried a sheaf of charge sheets and wrote one out appropriately, backed by its section of the Army Act. The Manual of Military Law was placed on the jeep bonnet and the Colonel stood beside it. Another lance corporal had been detailed to be the escort to the accused, who by now had his hat off. "March him in, Mr. Hacker," and the accused was brought to a crisp halt in front of the jeep's bonnet. "You know what the charge is," said the Colonel, "Have you anything to say?" "No, Sir." "Will you accept my award?" "Yes, Sir." "Reduced to the ranks. March him out please, Mr. Hacker." I never myself saw the likes of this, but that something similar could happen was well known, and the effect on general alertness was dramatic.

My afternoon stroll with Martin's shotgun on 31st October yielded a really fine old cock pheasant but my attentions were then diverted to more military matters, as the Chinese were showing signs of discontent. The time then came for Lieutenant Colonel Moore to take me on one of his outings. There was really only room for three in his jeep, due to the space taken by the wireless and its batteries, but he managed to squash in four, the last man, in addition to his driver and wireless operator, being his bodyguard. Who that was depended on what the Colonel was likely to do. If he thought his day was likely to be warlike, then he usually chose Sergeant Criddle, the Regimental PT Instructor, who was all that such a man should be, fit, intelligent and a good shot as well.

The first day he took me was unlikely to prove exciting, but despite discomfort due to my shape not suiting the space in the back of the vehicle, I found it an interesting and educative occasion. We were due to visit the Canadian Brigade Headquarters, then one of their battalions and the Royal Canadian Engineers Field Squadron commanded by a Major Rochester, whose personal reputation almost outshone Colonel Moore's. My main duties were to read off one or two map references, and I was thankful that the wireless operator was with us to tune the No. 19 set and fiddle with the knobs. The Colonel had been at pains to get it into my head that the only reason for him having a bodyguard with him was to make sure a message could be sent back if he, the Colonel, got hurt.

It was when we approached the battalion that we moved with some caution, as the Chinese just might have been watching, and under such circumstances it was very comforting to know that Lieutenant Colonel Moore was near. I must have sidled up close to him when, for the first of many times I heard, "Go away, Dan! Didn't I tell you to stay well away? There is no point in us both being hurt at the same time." Now I like to think I am a sociable sort of fellow, and felt thoroughly frightened on my own, but that was how it had to be.

As November 1951 started, so did the Chinese Volunteers opposite the First Commonwealth Division show their increasing restlessness. Less than a month before we had knocked them out of the good holes which they had planned as their winter quarters and now, with us on the high ground they had lost, life in their new positions must have been proving thoroughly unpleasant. One thousand 25 pounder shells of harassing fire remained our average daily despatch rate, meaning nearly a shell a minute throughout the twenty-four hours. Lest it be thought that our gunners fired at random into enemy territory, we were assured that much crafty planning went into the expenditure of ammunition. Over and above the harassing fire, all ground in view was scanned by forward observation officers and there were some highly alert tanks with high velocity guns also longing for targets. Add to which an Auster light aircraft was always over our own front line by day and in a position to concentrate the entire divisional artillery, seventy-two 25 pounders, plus any heavier American guns within range, on any selected target. "Impressive firepower" they called it, and there was no need to convince us further.

The result of all this artillery attention was that the Chinese dug and dug, to an extent quite beyond our highest standards at that time. And, of course, the more they dug, the less they feared the harassing fire. The United States Air Force flew frequent sorties to take air photos, and these were avidly and efficiently interpreted by a small section of air photo interpreters, happily answering to APIS, in Divisional Headquarters. Day after day these poor chaps stared through a device like a pair of spectacles on legs to establish a sense of height relief from photos that, when cleverly overlapped were known as stereo pairs. At one time in my training I had cursorily attempted the art, and never ceased to wonder at that those who undertook it professionally, if even for a short time, were not permanently cross-eyed.

To enliven life further for the Chinamen, our own air forces staged air strikes with increasing intensity onto the Chinese held hills just in front of our own. If you happened to be the proud occupant of part of our own front line, you were most keen that your own supporters, often meaning the Royal Australian Air Force with their Meteors, one of the earliest jet aircraft in service, knew where you were. To this end, aircraft identification panels, large oblongs of silk dyed in the most gaudy of colours, were pinned in coded patterns to the ground near the top of our own front hills, but just out of sight of any Chinamen. Like the passwords, the pattern to which these panels were laid changed daily, so that if the enemy attempted to mislead our pilots with their own Dior collection of fine silks, the chances were that a rat would be smelt.

There was no doubt that the United Nations forces had complete air superiority so, when the exception proved the rule, the effect was dramatic. Twice, at night, an unidentified light aircraft with what sounded like a motor cycle engine pop popped over the PINTAIL crossing site, and once it appeared to be firing a machine gun. Nobody ever explained satisfactorily what it was, or from where it came. The only casualty it caused was one American soldier who reached a slit trench first, only to be jumped upon by another.

Perhaps in anticipation of Guy Fawkes Day, the Chinese launched their attack soon after dark on 4th November. As the crow flew, we at Regimental Headquarters were seven miles from our forward positions, but the noise of the Chinese bombardment was very much greater than anything I had dreamt possible. Only two months before I, in good Australian company, had been the recipient of some of the first Chinese gunfire on our front, but now it sounded as if dozens and dozens, if not hundreds, of guns were firing all at once. Every few minutes there would be the distinctive additional roar of ripples of rockets. I had seen and heard our own rockets fired from their trays on Exmoor during training before D Day, hundreds in a few seconds, and this sounded very similar.

The flashes were sufficiently concentrated along the skyline so as to allow us to take a compass bearing, and thus fix on the map which hills were under attack, just before the location came through on the phone. As I had rather feared, they were the KOSB positions, including Hill

317, that were being hammered. Knowing the ground, or at least 317 and the area where I had laid my minefield, all too intimately, made it only too easy to imagine what was happening, all rather awe-inspiring.

Although the Australians and Canadians on either side of them were also heavily attacked, the main Chinese assault fell on the KOSB, and the story of their gallant defence has been told often by others who were much nearer the battle than I. It was on that night that Private Speakman won his VC by leading repeated attacks on the Chinese, remaining undeterred when his ammunition and grenades ran out and continuing the battle with volleys of anything that came to hand, including stones, beer bottles and, eventually, his own kit bag.

Within an hour of the battle starting all communication with the KOSB forward companies was lost but, as the night dragged on we heard that Hill 317, and 217 on its left, had had to be abandoned to the Chinese. Both were commanding features and, in the same way that the Chinese had been reluctant to lose them, so indeed were we.

With this battle in progress, I was immensely proud to be selected by my commanding officer to accompany him with his tactical Headquarters across the Imjin and well to the north. How wrong was my anticipation of action, as perhaps this letter may explain:—

6 Nov. '51

I am with the Regiment's Tactical HQ, consisting of the CO who is out all day in his jeep, the RSM who does most of the cooking, self, wot sits in a rather shabby shooting brake (an old Humber staff car) all day with a wireless and telephone, and three or four drivers. The Chinks started a bit of a battle a couple of days ago, so we moved about five miles nearer, but what I thought might prove interesting has proved dead boring.

I sleep in the car by the phone. Luckily last night was quiet. We are miles from the shooting (not pheasants), or that is to say, I am. I expect we'll be going back to our proper HQ in a couple of days. Having had fireworks on the 5th, it would be appropriate to have Armistice on the 11th!

It has been a quiet poisonous day. Foul drizzle turning to cold rain this afternoon. The only recompense is that a good rum ration has just arrived. It is only issued on shocking days."

What I did not mention in that letter, and possibly just as well, was our counterattack on 5th November. With all telephones to forward companies out of action and with wirelesses delighting in incomprehensible atmospherics at dawn and dusk, it was not until some time after daybreak that the KOSB's state could be truly judged. I had a particular interest, as I knew most of the platoon positions and had built the track that led to them. More important, I had got to know personally quite a few of those who must have been involved.

So far as I could make out, the companies which had each held Hills 317 and 217 were back off them, but the one on the left of my track was still there. So was the covering position on the spur of the hill in front of battalion headquarters held by Alan and my old 3 Troop of 12 Field Squadron. No Chinamen had actually reached them, but I got the impression that Sapper presence had been much appreciated. I also heard indirectly that my minefield on the east slopes of 317 was thought to have done appreciable damage to the Chinese, which, unpleasant though it may sound, was very pleasing at the time.

The other battalions of 28 Commonwealth Brigade, of the Royal Australian Regiment and the King's Shropshire Light Infantry, had also been heavily engaged during the night of the 4th, and the 1st Battalion the Princess Patricia's Canadian Light Infantry, who had only that day relieved their 2nd Battalion, were immediately themselves attacked. I had been led to consider the Chinese as an army of unsophisticated peasants, yet here they were launching an attack supported by a reputed 10,000 rounds of gunfire, complete with ripples of rockets, altogether most unfair.

The Royal Northumberland Fusiliers, who had acquitted themselves magnificently from early in the war until the very end of their tour, had just handed over to 1st Battalion The Royal Leicestershire Regiment. They, for their first action, were selected for the counterattack.

I had always understood that counterattacks to regain ground followed its loss almost immediately. It had never struck me that it must be impossible to foresee the loss of any particular piece of ground, in fact, even to be seen planning, might not be good for the morale of those whose job it was to hold it. I was, though, just beginning to understand what was involved in making a fire-plan for the divisional gunners. The basic requirement was that the enemy should be hit hardest at the right time, yet the supporting fire must remain close, but safe, for the advance of our own troops. All this was much easier said than done, and when friendly airstrikes had to be carefully phased in also, it later seemed surprisingly quick that the Leicesters were allowed to start their attack on Hill 217 at noon, with the Australians making a diversion against 317. Captain John Page, whom I had known from our Supplementary Course at Chatham and who had been with 55 Field

Squadron since their arrival at the end of 1950, was the Sapper supporting the Leicesters. He had taken part in a great variety of actions in his time in Korea, but I gained the impression, when he reported to us in Tac HQ, that there had been none he disliked more than that on 5th November. The Chinese had had time to stock up with ammunition, and our attack, in broad daylight, never really had a chance against their commanding positions.

Hills 317 and 217 were important features, and there must have been much heart searching before the decision was taken not to make further attempts to regain them. 30,000 rounds from our guns and strikes by fifty planes in the previous thirty-six hours had not been enough to dislodge the Chinese, and for those who planned, it must have been all very worrying. It was certainly disturbing for any of our own forces who needed to move in the forward positions, because it was now the turn of the Chinese to overlook us, and their gunnery had made almost unbelieveable progress in the past few weeks. It wasn't until several months later that I realised that the desultory shells which had been fired near us when we were mine laying must actually have been careful registration of targets for the subsequent assault.

PINTAIL pontoon bridge with ice forming.

Martin and Tom seemed surprisingly pleased to see me when Tac HQ returned to our more permanent headquarters behind the Imjin. It took me only a few minutes to discover, though, that it was my presence as a keeper of the log sheets in the command vehicle that was in demand, and not just my charming self.

After the recent battles the Division had a lot of shaking down to do, especially as some of the units which had arrived at the end of 1950 were being relieved by replacements. Luckily the Chinese co-operated and did not further disrupt our already complicated adminstrative arrangements.

To the Royal Engineers, though, there was one administrative problem above all others to surmount, and that was the impending visit of the Engineer-in-Chief from the War Office, Major General Tuck. He was coming for two days, and that was in two days' time. Probably the last thing he expected or wanted was lavish entertainment, but the very fact that we had recently been at war seemed to make it all the more necessary to accentuate the contrast by throwing a peaceful party. A supper cum cocktail party would be given for him, and everybody who was anybody would be asked. Obviously we would not have enough crockery, nor even could the General's Mess in Divisional Headquarters lend us enough. Our Quartermaster, who had his own little tented camp a couple of miles down the road behind us, said that the Rest Camp in Inchon had crockery and cutlery to spare. In no time it was decided that the Liaison Officer should take a vehicle to Inchon to cadge some. I had heard of Inchon, because of the very effective American landing there on their way back up Korea the previous summer. It was reputed to have one of the biggest tide ranges in the world, a good test for any sailor, but I hoped to stick to dry land.

The trip there, down the forty or so miles to Seoul, right through the city itself from east to west and over the Han River, was a great change from our hills by the Imjin, even though I thought our 1 COMWEL countryside much more pleasant. For the further thirty-five miles west of Seoul everything was barren and brown and proving highly uninteresting until the driver I had been allocated, an old sweat who knew the base areas well, said in his most knowledgeable way, "Do you know, Sir, that those hills are full of wolfram?" As he knew perfectly well that I didn't, he added, "That's what this war is all about." I must have looked suitably impressed and stunned, in fact I wished he could have watched the road rather more than my face, as he continued,

"Wolfram is what tungsten comes from, and tools and gun steels use it. Most of the world's wolfram is here." "Really," I said. It was quite a new theory to me and I intended to check it out, but never could find anyone who was much enthused by the subject.

The Rest Camp in Inchon proved remarkably co-operative with my needs. I got the impression that, with leave to Tokyo almost as easily available, Inchon was not overwhelmed with bookings. The lack of holidaymakers made the presence of a few rather dejected British soldiers all too obvious, and my errands were delayed slightly by the arrival of military policemen who had come to pick them up. Evidently they had granted themselves leave of absence from the recent battles and had reached Inchon with indecent haste. It was not a place where I would have wished to stay, so I set off back to the Division with my carefully packed plates, wondering whether the Chinese would show due deference to the E-in-C's visit, or whether they couldn't bear to miss the forthcoming full moon, with the aid of which they loved to mount attacks.

At Cambridge I had been proud of my reputation as the maker of small eats for cocktail parties, also for doing them full justice later, so Mr. Hacker, the RSM, soon demanded my services. Asparagus in bread and butter, anchovies on sliced hard boiled eggs or fried bread, and sardines similarly displayed, must have made our war look unbelieveable to those who had read of the retreats of the previous winter and the fierce subsequent battles. Anyway, the atmosphere was wholly convivial, the main talking point being the excellent heavy woollen khaki jerseys, the first of the British Army's woolly pullies, with which we had all just been issued. Both the Divisional Commander, General Jim Cassels, a fine looking tall man always ready to smile, and his deputy, Brigadier Pike, shorter but highly alert, were in theirs, setting the fashion by wearing no badges of rank. This habit was splendid, providing everyone knew each other. One of my happier memories is of a meeting between my commanding officer and a Battery Sergeant Major of the Royal New Zealand Artillery. Neither wore badges of rank, neither was normally a pompous man, but each was certain that he was senior to the other. As I knew both, I suppose I should have effected introductions, but it seemed a pity to spoil such innocent fun.

The evening of the Engineer-in-Chief's party was just as beautiful and peaceful as the day that preceded it, and General Tuck must have returned home via the Canal Zone thinking that there were worse wars to attend. We suggested, however, that unless the Egyptians cared to behave themselves, 1 COMWEL Div would be delighted to settle their troubles, and we had great confidence in our claims. It was remarkable how quickly a wonderful spirit had been fostered in that very mixed Division, with all the "Colonials" looking about thirty, and all the British about nineteen, which ages they probably were.

Canadian Sappers.

CHAPTER NINE

COUNTER ATTACKS

By mid-November 1951, with winter well on its way, we had hoped that the Chinese would quieten down, but they did not. The most heavily attacked unit was the King's Shropshire Light Infantry on Hill 227, which was the gateway to Hill 355, the craggy and really commanding feature in the sector. I had been on 227 on various occasions and had been impressed by the sheer density of barbed wire, which gained the name "blue haze".

So good were the supplies of that highly unfriendly material, that the normal method of erection of it on pickets in the form of a fence was considered unnecessarily time-consuming. Instead the wire was pulled off the side of the rolls, so that it twisted away like a long and prickly corkscrew. Roll upon roll were dispensed in this way, all building into barbed wire walls, and wall went up behind wall, so that really formidable fortifications appeared to have been achieved. I knew that I had never seen that way of laying barbed wire described in the pamphlets, but assumed that the omission was due to the undoubtedly wasteful aspects of the method. Great efforts had also been made to give overhead protection to individual slit trenches, by decking in most of the top with timber and corrugated iron sheets, then adding a couple of feet of earth.

As the crow flew, Hill 227 was perhaps a mile nearer to us than had been the attack on 317 two weeks before, so the Chinese bombardment could be heard all the more clearly, except when our own guns were superimposed upon it. On the night of 17th November the last message came through that two Vickers water-cooled machine guns were still heard to be firing on 227, but by morning most of the hill had been lost, only to be gallantly retaken the next day. Of the considerable casualties suffered by the KSLI, an appreciable proportion had been due to crushing under the weight of their own overhead cover, which had proved to be insufficiently supported to withstand both intense shell fire and heavy rain. Another sad lesson was that much of the blue haze wire had been blasted from the face of the earth. Whether any form of wiring would have withstood the intensity of the bombardment remained in doubt, but confidence in our field defences was severely dented.

As always, details of the night's battle, abundantly backed by rumours, reached us the next day. One was of personal interest to me as, on the *Empire Fowey* trooping out from England, there had been a particularly meek and mild National Service subaltern amongst fourteen of us young officers destined for Korea. He was called Henry and had been one of the four in my cabin. Being none too tough myself, I had grown to like him, but it was noticeable that in manly pursuits such as drinking, he was not in the same league as most of us. Some of the party considered him incredibly wet, to the extent of deciding to remove all his bedding from the cabin. As this was likely to disrupt cabin

Blue haze barbed wire.

Commanding Officer leaving camp.

life unnecessarily, I joined in a resolute defence against the invaders. Although we beat them off, the intruders still thought Henry wet.

On 227 Henry commanded a platoon of the KSLI with great gallantry and quite early on had his foot nearly severed at the ankle. He then hobbled round pulling up on his boot laces, thus keeping his foot and leg, and also his platoon, together. He was awarded an immediate Military Cross and was, I think, the only officer in our draft to be decorated during the war. The next autumn I heard that Henry had gone up to Cambridge to take his degree, as he had always planned, and was very happy there with his false foot.

Again, a woman in black, waving a pistol and leading the fiercest of the Chinese attacks, was reported so authoritatively that none of us doubted her presence. I wondered whether she was one and the same person as the lady reported near us when we had been supporting the KOSB. The military prowess of these ladies probably gained in the telling, but they must, at least, have been impressive characters.

One of our infantry company commanders when wounded had found himself lying beside a wounded Chinaman. As neither was very mobile, they had spent some time together, with large numbers of other Chinese pursuing their own ends on that very noisy part of the hill. As dawn approached the Chinese decided that it was no place to stay, but before they withdrew shot their wounded comrade, leaving our Major untouched, for which he was grateful. He was then retrieved by his own troops and evacuated.

Meanwhile, my life continued in a manner which, however much I had hoped for it, I had never seriously imagined would come about. My letters home in late November 1951 included:—

> I had another nice cock pheasant three nights ago, and missed a hen. I also know of a grand big brood, but they live right in a minefield and all the noise and handclapping I can make won't make them get up.
>
> We have three bottles of champagne, which will be lucky to last until Christmas: at £1 a bott, much the same as in England. We've also got a bottle of Taylor's Trident port, good value at 8/6d (42½p).
>
> Martin (the Adjutant) and I have found a new bit of pheasant country north of the Imjin. It's a great big valley, mostly paddy and uncut corn, with a smallish river down it. I had two cocks and shot disgracefully to miss five more birds. How I wish we had dogs.
>
> The Chinks continue to be a bloody nuisance, though we aren't affected here, bar hearing the incessant guns. The Canadians describe this as just like knocking down coconuts. One would think the Chinks would get tired of it. 16°F of frost last night, so it is getting colder.

I had volunteered for Korea because of the pheasant shooting, and was achieving my purpose admirably. Lest you think, though, that life in Regimental Headquarters was pure idle joy, it was not. All my companions were able and would have worked hard even without the dominating influence of our commanding officer. Lieutenant Colonel Peter Moore's life was led with such intensity, keeness and dedication, that it was all the more shattering when on occasions out of the blue he unbent. One evening I had just been relieved from my log-keeping in the Command Post and had gone into the Mess for an early supper. The Korean lad who waited on us and answered to "Number One Half" was still fetching it when the Colonel came in saying, "Hello, Dan, let's have a bottle of champagne." That was the kind of order I understood, and few could have complied more quickly or efficiently. The Colonel looked really impressed at the deftness with which I untwisted the wire and gently eased the cork upwards until it emerged with a satisfactory pop, to be followed by the gushing glistening liquid directed into an awaiting glass without the spillage of a drop. I could see him thinking that his Liaison Officer perhaps had hidden depths, even if it had taken him over three months to find them.

I apologise for relating my little triumphs, but my morale needed the odd fillip. Exactly why the Colonel stood me the champagne then, I never discovered. I had taken the precaution of checking when he was due to have a birthday, but had already missed it. Notwithstanding that, you might ask other burning questions, including "What was your Mess like?" and "Why was the boy called Number One Half?" To take the second first, the British forces saw no real reason for learning the Korean language, thinking it better that Korean supporters should learn the necessary rudiments of English. Rather than say something was very good, it seemed simpler to say it was "Number One", by which scale "Number Ten" was very bad. Whether "Number One Half" was so named because he was excellent (he was certainly most helpful), or because he was only half a fellow, I was never sure, but he was proud of his unique name and worked all the better for it.

Our Mess was, in keeping with other preparations for winter, a hole in the ground just deeper than the height of a man and about thirty feet long by eight feet wide. This had been spanned with saplings every foot or so, onto which had been piled a good layer of rice straw to give insulation, then a large tarpaulin had been draped over the lot. One end of the excavation had been screened off as the kitchen, an entrance had been dug from the outer world and there it all was, and very snug too. For furniture we had a couple of six foot folding tables, just what was wanted, but for seating we had nothing better than our camp chairs. These were of the same construction as the rest of our camp kit, with a green canvas top and back supported on a folding frame of wooden struts and steel lattice. What was a good idea, if rather heavy, for beds, was a poor one for chairs. Collapse, accompanied by painful impalement, always seemed imminent and I seldom felt at ease thereon.

Of the specialist tasks in our Regimental Headquarters, that of Tom, the Intelligence Officer, interested me most. He and his two draughtsmen now had a lean-to penthouse off the main tent which enclosed the back doors of the two command vehicles. On every inch of wall space Tom had hung huge map boards, each with its map and covered with a sheet of transparent talc. Map talc was like gold to obtain, but Tom had his own rolls of all necessary dimensions. At the small end of the scale there was the theatre map, which showed the whole of the Korean Peninsula and the part of China beyond the Yalu

River. On the talc the positions of our own known formations and the assumed dispositions of the enemy were shown. The Eighth United States Army Korea, EUSAK, would have about eleven divisions strung across the country on the front line at any time, with a further four in reserve. Apart from the Commonwealth formation, all the divisions were American or South Korean, into which most foreign units had been injected. So far as the enemy went, the Chinese were on the west, facing us, as we well knew, and the North Koreans were on the east.

The medium scaled map showed our I Corps area, with all brigades and battalion sized units being marked, leaving the largest map, both in size and scale, to show our own divisional locations in detail. All the new roads had been added, and Tom was now in the process of adding the minefields. This was proving a nearly impossible task.

As I mentioned when I laid my very own minefield beside Hill 317, officers in charge of laying were expected to take great care in recording what had been done, all on a standard form which was laid out in a reputably foolproof manner. We were following the routine which had apparently stood the British Army in good stead throughout the 1939-45 War, so expected no difficulties. Here in Korea, though, things seemed to be different. We were sitting on an area which had been lost by the South Koreans at the start of the war, regained by the Americans and re-occupied by the South Koreans, lost to the Chinese, who cleared some of the earlier mines, then regained by the Americans and British, who were now laying anti-personnel mines at a previously unprecedented rate.

The minefield records were meant to be filled in and despatched to us in RHQ directly after the completion of each new field. This part of the system worked well, and we were being confronted with an ever-increasing pile of undigested reports. Sometimes four or five new minefields were being laid in the divisional area on the same day, and the more likely it looked that we would be staying in the same area, the more minefields were requested. As routine reliefs of units in the line took place, so came first an urgent request for minefield maps of the area, followed by demands for strengthening the barrier by laying new minefields in front of those existing. The rear edge of the first fields was usually tight up against our own positions, so the newer fields tended to be further out into No Man's Land and nearer and nearer to the Chinese.

The minefield records showed the length and compass bearing of each leg of a minefield, all related to a datum point "which could easily be identified on the map". The six figure grid reference of the datum point had to be given, but at best this meant that it was correct to one hundred yards, and we started to wonder if the maps were as accurate as that anyway. Even our big maps had a scale of only 1:50,000 meaning that quite a large minefield, and five hundred yards was quite long, only made a very small mark when plotted on the map. Providing that no other minefields were near, all this was of no great consequence, as the barbed wire perimeter fence with its red painted tin triangles would show where the field lay on the ground, and that was what mattered. However, once one minefield was laid close to another existing one, the problems of foolproof recording increased tremendously. Allowing for only a little human error, the records as plotted on the map could relate quite differently when compared with the true position of the minefields on the ground.

All these technicalities may now sound tedious, but knowing at the time that I was likely to personally become involved in some of our minefields, I realised that their correct recording might then make a difference of life or death.

As if to prove the point, I soon saw another minefield accident. I was crammed in the back of my commanding officer's jeep with his radio operator, the set and batteries, and he and his driver were in front. The road, actually a two way earth and gravel track, had almost continuous old minefield fences along its sides, so the overgrown paddy fields were empty and ominous. Suddenly, though, a man stood up about sixty yards on our left. The CO said, "Stop, that man is in the minefield!" He sprang from the jeep, again shouting "Stop!" to the American signaller, as he turned out to be.

The soldier looked towards us, rather as if he were unused to being spoken to in that manner, or in that accent, took his next step and set off a mine. He fell down, but was obviously alive, so there was an immediate need to rescue him. The CO ordered me to go back to regimental headquarters to fetch the minefield record whilst he attended to the casualty. I was almost certain that we did not hold useful records for that particular minefield, and I also knew the risks involved in minefield rescues, especially if tripwires had been laid.

It was with very mixed feelings that I sped back in the jeep to Tom and the minefield records. Like me, he knew that it was hardly worth wasting time searching. We were lucky, though, and almost immediately found the record, neatly written in Korean with "Note: Possible Chinese interference subsequent to laying" written across the top in English.

Although I was back on the scene within half an hour of the accident, the signaller was already on his way to hospital and the CO was waiting for his jeep. As I had expected, he was more concerned that our organization could not produce good minefield records than with the task he had just undertaken. As time went by, drills were established for the rescue of minefield casualties, but at that time we had none.

Five newly commissioned officers, not long out of Sandhurst, arrived and spent a few days with us in regimental headquarters before being sent out to join their squadrons. They promised well as congenial company, but made me realise that I was now an elderly, even if not obviously senior, subaltern. The newcomers soon found themselves trying to identify positively on the ground minefields over which we had doubts. One of them, who had made an excellent first impression, was sent back to Seoul Airfield to check a suspect field, where most unfortunately he was almost immediately killed. Evidently the mines had been laid under a barbed wire fence, making it hopeless to use a mine detector which identified metal objects. We could only surmise that he had prodded one too hard.

Our General was known to have been concerned that, because his Division was holding a wide front, he needed to put too many battalions in the front line and was left with very few in reserve to cope with any Chinese breakthrough. The American general who commanded I Corps took the point by side stepping our front slightly to the left, which meant that we handed over the areas of our right-hand two battalions to the Americans, and these included Hill 355, the only really dominating feature remaining in our hands. In the last week in November, soon after the handover, the Chinese took this minor mountain. A main problem for the Americans had been shortage of ammunition, as the .303, much of which we had left on the positions was useless to them, with their weapons only firing rounds of the .30-06 ammunition.

With the Chinese back on 355, and with their Forward Observation Officers commanding an excellent view of most of our area, life north of the Imjin became even less attractive than of late. I knew that our CO would be going to see what had happened, but was not as keen as usual to offer my services as his companion. Perhaps because he expected trouble, he took another officer in his jeep. I did, in fact, have to take a vehicle forward later in the day but, although many of our roads were receiving unaccustomed and unwelcome attention, I was not personally selected as a target. The Americans were also finding the situation intolerable and mounted a massive and brave counterattack, regaining Hill 355 at a severe cost. Both sides had now learnt that any form of attack, in the face of massive artillery support, was likely to prove a very costly undertaking.

CHAPTER TEN

THE SPIRIT OF CHRISTMAS

Apparently the continued Chinese pressure, as with our own earlier, had been a form of jockeying for position with a view to holding a convenient line if, and when, peace could be arranged. The two sides were still meeting daily at Panmunjon, only fifteen miles to the west of our positions and within sound of our guns and, on 28th November 1951, it looked as if matters had been settled when I wrote home:—

> It looks as if there really may be peace here. We all got orders last night not to shoot unless provoked, and there was quite a bit of hopeful peace drinking. Evidently the negotiators have argued as much about this part of the line as anywhere. Everything is very quiet today, so perhaps the Chinks are going to behave too.
>
> We have had a couple of inches of snow and for the last three nights more than 20° of frost, 25 last night, but we haven't suffered from it yet. The Imjin is frozen, they say it stays frozen for ninety days, but our office trucks and Mess are good and warm. However, at lunch today with 12 Squadron, our Second-in-Command was given a bottle of solid frozen Guinness!

Colonel Eddie Myers, our Commander Royal Engineers, came to dinner in our Mess whilst we were still in a jubilant mood at the peace prospects; little did we know that the Korean War was then only at its half-way point, eighteen months had gone and nineteen to go. We ate the last brace of cock pheasants that I had shot, and the CRE was more appreciative than we had ever expected, saying that the General's Mess never aspired to such luxuries. He was much too polite a man to drop hints, but Martin and I thought it would be a nice gesture if we tried to get them the four birds that would be needed to cover their numbers. As the next morning was lovely, we set about the task immediately, though we admitted to a twinge of conscience lest some operation should crop up. However, the Second-in-Command, Major Bill Woods, wished us well and I was able to report:—

> *30 Nov. '51*
>
> Well, we did get the four birds we wanted yesterday, though only just. Martin and I crossed the river to the hopeful spot. I had the CO's gun, which is shockingly heavy in the barrel and has various idiosyncrasies, one being that the right barrel doesn't cock unless one breaks the gun with all one's might.
>
> We started well, by me putting up a hen which made a beautiful shot for Martin. Then a cock got up and I missed him clean. Then another, but I heaved at the right trigger which wasn't cocked and missed again. We walked along a hillside and a hen got up and I did the same thing, but at last tried the left barrel and got a very nice long shot. Then we walked for an hour and saw nothing, but when Martin went back to bring the Dingo (Daimler scout car) round, I found a very wild brood of about ten. I should have had a right and left, but somehow missed a huge cock with my right barrel, then got a hen with the left. As Martin arrived the most beautiful cock I've ever seen, a four-year-old bird I think settled a hundred yards in front of him, and he made no mistake when it got up. So that was a cock and three hens in an hour and a half.
>
> In the afternoon the Second-in-Command and Peter Leslie, who is back in HQRE from 12 Squadron, wanted to go for a potter, so I took them onto the local marsh and said that I'd drive the far end for them. I only saw a cock and a hen, and had them both, the only shots fired: the cock was a most unexpected kill, straight into the sun, so that was a cock and three hens for me for the day, and ten birds to date.

I had not thought it worth mentioning that it had taken me some time to find the cock, who had fallen stone dead into a particularly thick bush. The two birds I shot would, of course, not have flown near my companions, or so I told them.

My next duty of note was to go down to Seoul railway station to meet the platoon of mine dogs which had been requested from England two months previously because we had no means of finding wooden mines. The fact that, since they left England, we had lost most of the ground that was likely to have contained some hidden Chinese wooden mines, was unfortunate, but it was not with a view to commiserating that I had been keen to meet them. What I was looking for was a gundog.

I found the dogs, sixteen of the them, to be very nice fellows, but it was soon made plain to me that only their masters were allowed to be friendly with them. Each handler had two dog, all of which were crosses, though one obviously had a lot of spaniel in it and was the one I would have picked.

After I had welcomed the platoon on behalf of the CRE, I guided them to their tents, a few miles back behind our headquarters and under the wing of our Quartermaster's empire. Such a to-do had been made about the speedy arrival of the dogs that there was some embarrassment in wondering how now to use them.

Another arrival was Peter Duckworth, who had married a cousin of mine, with the "Skins", the Fifth Royal Inniskilling Dragoon Guards, who were taking over from the Eighth Hussars. It was apparent that both Peter and his brother officers appreciated the better sides of life, as had their predecessors, but with a kinsman as a Captain in a Squadron, I was likely to know the Skins better.

It was openly known that before he left Korea, Colonel Sir Guy Lowther, Commanding Officer of the 8th Hussars, had been asked by

Peter Duckworth.

General Cassels to write him an appreciation of the situation regarding the use of tanks in Korea under the static conditions into which the war had slipped. As with the war in France from 1915 onwards, where there had been little use for cavalry, so in Korea were the conventional uses of tanks not obviously in demand. In France they had had Flanders mud, in Korea we had paddy fields, specially sited to catch all the water and soft enough for a man in bare feet to sink above his ankles.

A military appreciation took a precisely prescribed form, and the writing thereof was a well known form of torture at staff colleges. Without a doubt a serious paper was expected to result, whatever the subject and whoever the writer. What Sir Guy proposed we were never told, though some ideas which subsequently emerged were probably due to him. All we did hear was that the appreciation included "and, what is more, I will bet you a bottle of champagne that . . .", thus proving that the subject was of an important nature.

By early December we had all been issued with our full winter kit, all with the exception of those with size 12 feet, of whom an unexpected number were found. Overall, we considered the quality excellent. The form of over garment known as a middle parkha was a source of endless fun: it had a splendid nylon fur lining and an enormous hood with a soft wire edge that could be bent to keep any required shape. It also had a large frock tail, which could either be worn like a morning coat, or buttoned up between the legs to ensure full bodily warmth. The parkhas were made by "Windsmoor", who had an attractive line of advertising in fashionable glossy periodicals. Seeing us looking like great green Father Christmasses would not have helped their normal markets, but we would have regarded the excellent garments even more highly had they been accompanied by the young ladies who normally modelled the firm's produce.

Our boots, with their composite plastic soles and their removable nylon net insoles, were considered a real advance. We were beseeched to remember to rinse the insoles as well as our socks. The few British reporters who visited Korea during that autumn had mainly attempted to dramatise the poor provision that was being made for our troops' needs, thus certainly worrying the families of those at home. Now that all was nearly well, very few reports reached the British papers.

By December, most of the British units which had been in Korea the previous winter had gone home and those of us who had come out in the summer suddenly found ourselves to have been in Korea longer than most. The Royal Engineers had chosen, however, not to replace units with units, but to replace officers and soldiers on an individual basis. With reservists and national servicemen to be demobilised, there was a constant stream of men both ways, so the Sapper system had its merits, though it meant that some individuals spent longer than others in the country. The maximum time had been agreed at eighteen months, and it had also been agreed that time spent in Korea would count double towards a full overseas tour of three years, so I saw every advantage in staying in Korea the full eighteen months if possible, then going directly home.

The first Royal Engineers unit in Korea had been 55 Field Squadron, which had arrived in December 1950 and quickly made their presence felt. By December 1951 their signwriter was preparing a sign for New Year's Day 1952 saying "Third Year in Korea". Every large military bridge built by the American Army Engineers was normally named after some comrade who had recently been killed, and was adorned with an elaborate sign giving full credit to those who had done the work. 55 themselves built a large bridge, but the only sign it carried was "This bridge was built by 55 Field Squadron Royal Engineers in the normal course of duty". It was perhaps unfortunate that a unit of the American 2nd Infantry Division which was supporting us had to be quartered just along the road from 55. 2 Div's motto was "Second to None", which was bill boarded along the road. 55 then added the word "None" under their normal sign board.

Two reinforcement officers for 55 whom I was delighted to see were Angus McKay Forbes and Peter Park, with both of whom I had helped keep the local public houses solvent at Chatham before we had been sent off to get our degrees. I knew that Angus, in particular, had come to Korea with pheasant shooting in mind, and my local knowledge was soon in demand.

Even if we now had good clothing, there was still the need to heat our living accommodation, meaning dug outs and tents. Although various standard patterns of tent heaters came later, none were on issue to us in 1951, so improvisation was the answer, and remarkably ingenious were some of the solutions.

To make the stoves, the only commonly available materials were steel ammunition boxes, brass shell cases, and the round tin cans in which the 25 pounder cartridges were packed, the same horrid items on which I had ripped my fingers when put to work by the Canadian gunners and the same splendid containers in which I had sent home the sugar for my mother's jam. The stoves were usually fashioned from the steel boxes, and the flues from the cartridge cans with the bottoms cut out and many pushed into each other, end to end, to make an adequate, if wobbly flue pipe of the required length. For solid fuel there was initially wood from local trees, a few packing cases and the waxed paper cones which were used to protect the curved noses of the 25 pounder shells in their steel boxes. These lumps of unusual fuel were, like the other items, freely available in large quantities from any gun site, and we quickly realised their importance.

For those who were not near trees and gunsites, though, the only answer to fuel was petrol, or diesel. Both were available in almost unlimited quantities, as very little was being used in motoring, and it wasn't long before rubber tubing and small stop cocks, or taps, were obtained, presumably from Japan. It was with the liquid fuels that large shell cases, like the 20 pounder cases from our Centurion tanks, came into their own as stoves. Prizes were on offer for good designs, and many of the designs worked splendidly. As may just have struck you, even if prizes for effectiveness were being awarded, safety certificates were not. Some of the stoves burnt as much as fifteen gallons of petrol a day, and even if the piping connections were sound, the stove pipes generally poked through a roughly cut hole in the canvas tent roof and easily became red hot, all very dangerous.

Before and after Christmas 1951 probably the greatest cause of casualties in 1 Commonwealth Division was tent fires, but with care and common sense, comfortable warmth could be achieved. Just how stupid some folk could be was unbelieveable, until it happened. One soldier managed to heat a bowl of petrol on his tent stove instead of his shaving water. Both liquids came in four and a half gallon jerry cans, but usually smelt different.

Although tent fires took a seasonal toll, accidents in our minefields continued all the year round. As Sappers had laid them, Sappers felt a responsibility for preventing casualties to our own side, but however much we tried we could suggest no easy answers. With a view to analysing what went wrong, we kept a tally of all accidents, a task in which I soon became involved. Very soon it became evident that about half of the casualties were due to warlike circumstances, such as a shell splinter cutting the minefield fence, and a returning patrol walking in by mistake, and half due to plain stupidity. We had soldiers running into minefields and shouting to military police, "Come and get me," sensitive souls who were determined to get behind a bush or bank before spending a penny, and soldiers chasing deer. All set off mines.

I was wondering how I might myself be classified if I wandered into a minefield when pheasant shooting, when into our command post strolled a soldier from the airstrip on the marsh opposite our headquarters asking, "Please could you tell me, is this a mine?" Our visitor proudly, but luckily very gently, passed across his trophy, and a paper clip made a speedy and adequate substitute for a safety pin. It was one of the anti-personnel mines formed from a block of cast iron filled with high explosive, the American M3, and a short length of trip wire still dangled from the pull igniter which was screwed into it. Who had cut the trip wire, and when, we never asked.

We did ask, though, just where the mine had come from. Our visitor's description of the place precisely fitted my favourite pheasant shooting area but, before accompanying him to the spot, I found the old minefield record with what I considered to be commendable speed. It was one I had looked at with interest before, laid by the South Koreans the previous winter. I had even had it translated and had been relieved to find "Lifted by the Chinese, Spring 1951" written on it. I had worked with Chinamen in Sumatra and had always found them very thorough in their work, so had perhaps had too great a faith in their minefield clearance. If they had taken the minefield fence away, as they had, then surely, I had thought, they would have cleared all the mines. Here, in front of us, was an extremely live mine of the type noted on the record, so it seemed that I had been wrong, a point which officers senior to me and who had been shooting on the same ground found distinctly indigestible. For those who remember that the title of my earlier book was *Wrong Again Dan!*, may I assure you that by now I considered myself a reformed and trustworthy character.

Across the marsh we went to see where the mine had been found, and it was uncanny how our guide took us directly to the bush under which I had had some trouble finding the last cock pheasant I had shot. "Did you *really* find it there?" I asked, only for my informant to look slightly pained because he couldn't understand why I might think he was telling me untruths. It was just as well, I thought to myself, that the mine had been fitted with a pull igniter and not a push one, a type which was also commonly used.

There was no point in hushing up this incident, and some were quite pleased to hear of it, as the old minefield would again have to be thoroughly searched, this time with the aid of the record, and that should make an appropriate job for the newly arrived and under-employed mine finding dogs. They had arrived with a sergeant in charge, but an officer was considered to be necessary and Alec Jackson accepted the appointment with, I understood, mixed feelings. On first acquaintance he told us what charming animals he found them to be, but on the next day one bit him.

A greater worry than their teeth, though, was whether the dogs could find mines, not just some mines, but every single mine. One anti-personnel mine missed would be quite enough to reduce the attraction of canine friends, and the handlers took this point also. Dogs might be fine for finding anti-tank mines, upon which a man could usually walk without much danger of breaking the shear rod and killing himself, but anti-personnel mines actuated by trip wires were another matter. Alec and his dog handlers completed the unpleasant task on the marsh, though more reliance was put on men to find trip wires, and on mine detectors to find metallic mines, than on dogs.

With the Imjin frozen we had hoped that life south of the PINTAIL crossing where we lived would become quieter. The cause of the noise previously had been of the firing of four Sherman tanks with 17 pounder guns, which had been permanently employed on the bank just upstream of the bridge, shooting at large lumps of debris floating down the Imjin before they damaged the rubber floating bridge. True, the noisiest time had been during the floods when parts of other bridges upstream and complete dwellings had come careering down the river, but some firing had continued on most days. What had surprised many of us was just how difficult it had proved for the extremely accurate high velocity guns manned by experienced tank crews to hit the moving debris. With only a very small angle between the trajectory of the gun and the surface of the water, and with most of the debris below the surface, the problem soon became apparent. High explosive shells set off by a fuze in the nose were used and, if these hit anything solid, off they went. Often, though, the curved ogive of the front of the shell skipped off the water as a splendid richochet, to land and explode some miles to the east in our neighbouring American Division's sector. Yes,

Raft site with Imjin ice.

Bleak midwinter. Major Howard Stephens, Lieutenant Colonel Peter Moore and driver.

they did complain, but perhaps did so too politely, as the firing continued whenever the bridge was endangered.

Now, with the ice growing thicker daily, there was no queston of anything floating down the Imjin, but the bridge itself, being a floating bridge, went up and down vertically under the load of anything crossing it; a few inches under a jeep, over a foot under a tank. With water under and around the pontoons, each of which was kept in position against the flow of the stream by a cable leading to an anchor on the river bed many yards upstream, all was fine, but with jagged ice rubbing on the inflated black rubber pontoons, punctures quickly followed. To cope with this problem, the American Engineers who tended the bridge at first swirled the water upstream with icebreaking boats. Soon, though, this was not enough and an amphibious tracked vehicle, known as a BUFFALO, was used to churn its way across, dropping explosive charges in its wake which, by their lifting action, broke up the ice effectively. On cold nights this had to be done every half hour. The charges were large and the noise, even from the underwater explosions, loud. How many tons of explosive were used in keeping that bridge ice free that winter would have been an interesting statistic, but what mattered was that the method worked.

For most of December 1951 an end to the Korean War at any minute appeared possible, but on the 12th I wrote home:—

> The peace talks now sound bad. There are still a lot of small patrols out and our guns keep fairly busy, but otherwise it's the phoney war again.

And, on the 15th:—

> We have just got an order to work as usual (meaning wage war), but everything possible is being done to keep things quiet. All the Infantry in slit trenches have been promised a Christmas dinner, and the Chinamen are going in for Christmas in a big way in the propaganda world. They've printed some excellent cards, free and much better than our Division's effort which are on sale for tuppence, and yesterday sent across a messenger with a sack of them and some junk "sample" presents. He was only a lad of about seventeen and was sent home (with some good advice in his ear). Meanwhile, the guns continue to thump and it doesn't sound a bit peaceful. Terrible bad luck on our prisoners, supposing that they know that the talks are on.

At that time there were nearly 1,000 prisoners from the Commonwealth alone in North Korea.

However great, or disappointing, were the prospects of peace, we had some exceptionally busy days. One evening I was told that a South Korean soldier had been killed in one of the old minefields behind us and that everyone would be much obliged if I would please get him out. "Tomorrow will do" had been the Adjutant's final words and, with a lot on my mind, I did not sleep too soundly. As the officer holding the minefield record, again a South Korean one, I was not in a position to suggest anyone more appropriate for the task.

The next morning, from the track beside the minefield off which the soldier had strayed, the poor chap's friends pointed out to me in which direction he lay. Although, luckily from my point of view, he was not very far into the field from the fence, only about twenty-five yards, the undergrowth confirmed my worst fears. The field had been laid with trip wires over unharvested rice the previous winter, then the summer growth had swamped the evidence and died off in the frost, to leave a tangled mat of what looked like long dead grass. Even without the weed tangle, there was obviously no chance of identifying the location of individual mines from the information on the record.

There was no point in hurrying, and I didn't. Having set the Koreans away in one direction and my driver and jeep in the other down the track, I crawled under the fence and into the field. Never have I concentrated so continuously, as every piece of very cold dead rice had to be combed with my fingers to find any trip wires. If the rules for laying minefields were obeyed, no mine or trip wire should have been nearer than five yards from the fence, but I was in no mind to trust those who had laid the field during a retreat.

I never was the best shape for elegant crawling, and it was a relief to stand up every few yards, stretch and attempt to see the casualty. On the second occasion I did, and luckily was not far off the shortest route to him. I pegged a tape beside me as I went, and had some safety pins with me in case I came upon a mine actually on my route, which I did not. I only found two trip wires, both slack, so it would have been safe to cut them, but I had a fear of jerking them in so doing, so laid a white handkerchief on top. I then had to stand up, take a step over the handkerchief, kneel, and start combing the foliage again with all too numb fingers before continuing again at the crawl.

It took me nearly two hours to reach the poor little Korean, who was so small that I could carry him under one arm. Being of no great strength, one of my worries had been whether I could use the prescribed fireman's lift. Back down my marking tape I walked, again stepping with great care and considerable fear of wobble over my hankies on the trip wires, and was back at the minefield fence and onto the track in next to no time.

I called the Koreans, who tried to thank me but gave the impression that such incidents were a matter of course, walked down to my vehicle and was very glad to be back in the Mess for lunch. Getting folk out of minefields was, indeed, becoming a matter of course; many of us had to do it, often more than once, and no Sapper thought it an unusually hazardous task.

Evidently some infiltrators had been making their presence felt somewhere near the rear edge of the boundaries of responsibility of our Division. These boundaries coincided with the front boundary of the formations further to the rear, including the headquarters of I Corps. Quietly most of us wished those infiltrators a little luck, as there was much to be said for anyone who kept the rear areas on their toes. The Commander I Corps and his staff did not agree, and, a week before Christmas, mounted a guerilla hunt by every unit not actually on the front line.

Luckily the operation only lasted one day, as I found myself expected to participate actively. What the overall plan was, I was never sure, but my role with Corporal Landimore, our RHQ Royal Signals NCO, was to carry a very heavy wireless set, a No. 62, and its battery for the day. We climbed a total of over 3,000 feet up various hills in the morning, Landimore carrying the set and me the smaller battery, with a cable about ten feet long dangling between us. To keep the right distance with the lead not pulling itself unplugged was a matter of great skill, particularly going downhill, but mercifully, when we reached a hilltop, our set worked perfectly and everyone seemed delighted with the very dull messages we managed to relay.

We lunched there and only then realised how chilly the wind was, as our water bottles were frozen solid, and we were thankful that we had taken our parkhas up with us, tied to our belts. It wasn't until we were reloading after lunch that I realised that the battery was considerably heavier than the wireless, and Corporal Landimore, an excellent fellow, also realised that it would be tactful to offer to swap loads. My six weeks back in RHQ had done nothing for my fitness, and I was still very stiff a week later. When I sat the next morning outside our

Mess dugout in lovely winter sunshine, having my hair cut by a visiting Korean barber and sipping a glass of sherry, I mused that the Korean War did not lack variety.

By 20th December the Peace/War see-saw had swung firmly down in favour of peace and some leave to Tokyo was cancelled so that the planes would be available in case our prisoners were released. Again, nothing came of it all.

The best entertainment in Christmas week 1951, however unintentional, was the initiation of the Regiment's own telephone exchange. Previously, as subscribers to the Div HQ exchange, we evidently had, through our exemplary keeness, been blocking most other telephone traffic. Our new exchange was known by the codename NATION, and lines which had been laid to each of the four Squadrons, to the Quartermaster and to others were connected. The initial result was a hideous shambles and, with no particular Signals responsibility, I was in the happy position of watching the teething troubles.

An officer rang and wished to speak to the commanding officer urgently. The NATION operator thought he had seen the CO go to the Command Post, where I answered the phone to say they were wrong, so they tried to transfer the call to his tent, only to be connected with an irate QM three miles away. A runner was then sent to find the CO, who arrived at the CP steaming, to be told that the call had been lost and the operator had not been able to reconnect it. The CO was very angry and, as was his wont, pocketed the CP log-keeping pencil as he left. That happened to be the day that I had decided to discourage this habit, by securing the pencil to a long length of springy wire, a system which retrieved it well, but it was a real pity about my timing. By this time the Adjutant personally had taken over the manning of the exchange from the operator and achieved a further muddle on the lines to an extent which none would believe. The immediate answer was to revert to using the wireless, which meant encoding all messages which were at all secret, and involved great delay.

With Christmas just coming, it really must have been an accident, but our Quartermaster then lost his entire store tent in a fire, including, in classic fashion, every ledger. The loss which caused most general concern was of two complete crates of Guinness (the broken bottles had to be produced as proof), which were being kept for the great day. Of less concern to others was that my only pair of battledress trousers were amongst the items burnt, and battledress was worn for leave in Japan.

Although the weather did its best to dampen spirits, going from sleet to snow to solid rain which soused most of the dugouts, Christmas 1951 was happy and memorable. The officers spent the evening of Christmas Eve in the Sergeants Mess, then we all went to the midnight service in the church tent over the hill in Div HQ. It was packed, some of the congregation swayed, but all were orderly.

The next morning I was involved in the ritual serving of early morning tea by jolly officers to sleeping soldiers. After breakfast my task was making the brandy butter for the plum pudding, one of my more popular occupations. The brandy provided by the NAAFI was labelled "Louis Desroches". Its quality may well have been better than we imagined, but few were convinced, and "Uncle Louis" was only usually mentioned in humorous vein. Humorous or not, it was just the stuff for brandy butter and there was no cause to stint the mixture as I poured the brandy into the caster sugar. Tom was supervising the dinner preparations and demanded first taste of my produce. He sampled a good spoonful, pulled a very pained face and spat in a most unappreciative manner. He was normally the politest of souls, and I have seldom been more shocked or pained. Tom then spluttered, amongst other things, "You've made it with salt, not sugar." Luckily there was plenty more of Uncle Louis to come to the rescue and I made no mistake with the second mix.

We had a soup and sandwich lunch, then I went for such a long walk north of the river that I had some trouble hitching lifts home. The dinner, as arranged by Tom, was traditional, turkey and/or roast pork and a good plum pudding, and it was my job to open the champagne, of which sufficient supplies had been conserved. Parcels from home had produced crystallised fruits and ginger, chocolates and marons glacées. We drank the King's health in port, and stayed commendably sober. It was hard to remember that there was a war on: perhaps they felt much the same at the Duchess of Richmond's ball before Waterloo.

Fortunately there was no battle waiting for us the next day, but I did go to visit some of the forward battalions with the CO. Sporadic, but considerable harassing fire from our 25 pounders was going overhead as usual, some falling out of earshot behind the Chinese forward positions and some raising spouts of earth on the forward slopes of their front line positions under a mile away. The compliment was being returned in a much more sparing manner, but there were just enough Chinese shells to suggest that the greeting on my father's card "Happy Christmas, and may everything go your way in 1952" might have been ambiguous.

I spent New Year's Eve healthily and pleasantly axeing down some small larch trees with which to line another bunker. I had had a good chance to gain proficiency under the expert guidance of our gardener in North Devon who had been a woodsman, but I never quite mastered the art. However, I had obviously had more opportunity to use an axe than some of my contemporaries and it was an unusual experience to find others, including the RSM, praising my efforts.

CHAPTER ELEVEN

NEW YEAR 1952

Whether the average Chinese volunteer in Korea realised the significance of midnight on 31st December was doubtful, but the several rounds of "celebration" fire which each of our guns then fired must have left them in no doubt that something out of the ordinary was happening. Although intense gunfire was commonplace, there was something special about that New Year salute, perhaps based on the hope that peace might really come soon. Our morale was definitely raised by it, and hopefully it frightened a few Chinamen.

Thought was still being given to the useful occupation of our excellent tanks in the static war. Many were employed as mobile pillboxes on the forward hills, the rear slopes of which were scarred with trackmarks leading up what looked impossibly steep gradients to precarious firing points on the hill crests. However useful, this was a dull and static occupation of the Royal Armoured Corps. Experience the previous winter had shown that real cold could make movement of tanks possible over frozen paddy, whereas they would have sunk into the mud in summer. The question was, could this capability be harnessed?

On the left of our divisional sector the River Samichon came down into the Imjin from the north. Either side of it there was a wide flat expanse of paddy fields stretching over our front line, then over No Man's Land and up between the Chinese held hills a mile on either side. Three further miles up the valley lay a village called KU-WAH-RI, which the airphotos showed to be a place of importance in the Chinese organisation and the location of a considerable supply dump, which our air and artillery attacks had failed to disrupt effectively.

The plan for the tanks was quite simple. Wait until the paddy was sufficiently frozen to support them, then stage a bold raid up the valley onto Kuwahri. The codeword DRAGON was allocated to the operation and the Skins were keen to undertake it as their first regimental task in the war.

The possibility of the Samichon Valley proving suitable for tanks had not eluded the Chinese, who had dug a substantial anti-tank ditch across it. With the frost, the walls of the ditch would be as hard as concrete, so there wasn't a hope of the Skins' Centurion tanks crossing it unless it were bridged or broken down. In Korea we had none of the assault engineer equipment which had proved of such benefit during the invasion of Europe seven years before, so back we went to improvisation. A small party of Sappers under an officer would be needed, and Angus McKay Forbes, my potential pheasant shooting friend, had been selected as the officer. The idea was that he and his assistants would travel in a turretless Centurion, known as a tug because, having more power to spare than a normal tank, it was literally used for tugging stuck or damaged tanks. On arrival at the ditch, they

Planning operation "DRAGON". Lieutenant Colonel Peter Moore, DSO, MC, Colonel Eddie Myers, CBE, DSO, Major Derek Fletcher, DSO, Major The Hon. Gilbert Monckton, MC.

would then nip out of the hatches of their tug, blow down the walls and get back to their tug to await their next task.

All this sounded most dangerous to me. Angus could have felt proud to have been selected for the task, but I did not envy him. For reasons which I never fully understood, except that I had let it be known that I liked using explosives, Lieutenant Colonel Moore appointed me as his observer of the trials which Angus and a representative troop of tanks were to undertake; blowing down a short length of ditch which had been specially dug for the purpose with bulldozers. I felt honoured to be involved in any way, as Operation DRAGON was considered to be highly important, and was also highly secret. Security, in the sense that the whole population had understood it in the 1939-45 War, when all overseas letters had been censored and the keeping of diaries was not encouraged, did not seem generally to apply in Korea, but DRAGON was in a special category.

I spent a very happy series of sunny January days with Angus and the Skins, which were followed by nights which went down to zero Fahrenheit and froze the ditch walls very satisfactorily. Our methods for blowing them down gradually improved through trial and error, though there seemed to be no way of doing the job in a single blast. A two stage procedure evolved, whereby a large special charge was propped against the far wall of the ditch and fired with the Sappers back by the tank. This drilled a deep hole, which was then stuffed full of further explosive and fired. The agility and physical fitness required to nip out of, and back into, the tug appalled me, but Angus was a fit fellow.

Camouflaged dumps in the open, like those at Kuwahri, tended to be dull and featureless, and to destroy them would be much easier said than done. Both Colonel Eddie Myers and Lieutenant Colonel Peter Moore had spent a good part of the 1939-45 War with guerillas, the one in Greece and the other in Yugoslavia, and they knew from personal experience that to blow up an ammunition dump was remarkably difficult. Angus was therefore told to practise, and various boxes of ammunition and explosives that could be spared were assembled and attacked with a variety of explosive devices. All most entertaining, except that most of the stack usually remained apparently undamaged, but probably in a highly dangerous state. Just to prove the cussedness of explosives, one of the blasts, initiated by carefully placed charges, detonated very little of its intended target of munitions, but lobbed a mortar bomb from it over the hill and into the next valley, where stood a much prized stack of ammunition, which was certainly not available for destruction. The mortar bomb, falling entirely at random in this stack, set the lot off, causing considerable consternation.

The lovely warm days were thawing the iced paddy fields upon which the whole feasibility of Operation DRAGON depended. Day after day the "not before . . ." date for the operation had to be put back. However, after a fortnight, both the days and nights stayed cold, but at the same time an officer on the staff of our Divisional Headquarters returned from leave in Tokyo and reported that DRAGON was being discussed openly in his hotel. Even with complete secrecy it would have been a very dangerous undertaking, and we understood that his report clinched the decision to cancel. Years later Angus was best man at my wedding: had Operation DRAGON materialised, I doubt if he would have been available.

One evening in early January our Divisional Commander, Major General Jim Cassels, walked over the hill from his headquarters to have dinner with us. What might have proved to be a rather formal evening turned out to be entirely the reverse: he fully confirmed his reputation for being a truly charming man, as well as an outstanding soldier. He and our CO were old friends, as Peter Moore had been his CRE when the General had commanded 6 Airborne Division in Palestine only three years before they both came to Korea.

As might be expected, we ate pheasant, followed by a plum pudding which had survived Christmas. After dinner we played poker. Now, when teaching me the rudiments of the game as part of my education, my father had advised, "Never play poker with anyone who is much richer than you." I had already learnt what excellent sense this made as, without some form of artificial limits which immediately destroyed the subtlety of the game, it seemed to be only too easy for a rich man to outbid a poor one, whatever the cards. I expressed my concern to Colonel Peter, who fully took the point, but promised that the General had a way round the problem.

His rules, though simple, would take time to divulge, but ensured that our powers of deception were fully exercised. My evening ended with a very satisfactory win of two shillings.

There were very few evenings, though, when many of us could gather for long in the Mess. From dusk onwards reports on the day's achievements and disasters, and requests for new work, would be coming in. All information on the day's work and operations had to be available and collated in time for the Colonel's order ("O") group. Normally orders were held at seven in the evening, which gave the Squadron Commanders time to assess progress, then drive in, often half an hour's motoring on the rippling earth roads where the speed limit remained at 20 mph.

For the "O" Group meeting we all stood in a fixed order in a semicircle in the tented penthouse between the vehicles. Second-in-Command, Adjutant, then the majors commanding the three Field Squadrons, two British and one Canadian, and the British Field Park Squadron. Next stood the Intelligence Officer, Liaison officers, usually just me, the Quartermaster and the RSM. Someone normally stayed on duty in the command vehicle as messages continued to come in, and that was usually the Signals Officer.

The Colonel stood facing us, within easy access of the maps, which Tom would have brought up-to-date just before the meeting started. Each officer was then expected to speak in turn, and brevity was demanded. I soon learnt that this was not the time for merry quips or idle reminiscing, and managed to cut the reports of my own activities to a degree which, to my mind, in no way did them justice. Colonel Peter was positively disinterested in whether I had personally shot any pheasants that day, or had made startling new discoveries of areas abounding with birds. He had certainly been interested about the progress of Angus' demolition trials, but brushed over the fact that Angus had most gallantly run to retrieve my ancient camera when I happened to have left it near a large charge on which he then lit the fuse.

By New Year 1952, when we had been static for three months, the complexity of the codewords and codenames which had been adopted was sufficient to confuse newcomers for weeks. Normally codewords are used for security purposes and, like the password, changed frequently. The Commonwealth Division password was disseminated with close attention to security, usually in sealed envelopes either by vehicle or hand, or, if the transmission had been overtaken by events, by complex and tedious encoded signals. At the end of all this, no one could see much point to the system, as the average Commonwealth member of the Division was likely to be able to make it abundantly plain in a few short words that he was neither Chinese nor Korean, and it was unlikely that the locals could do the same. There was a nice tale of a particularly tough Australian challenging a shape in the dark with the word "WILLIAM". He who was challenged knew that it would be highly dangerous to do anything other than stand perfectly still and, having never been told the password for that night, kept shouting "FRIEND" loudly. Eventually the Aussie yelled, "Don't you know the ....ing answer?" and received, "You know I ....ing don't." "Say SHAKESPEARE, and I'll let you pass." He did, and the incident concluded satisfactorily for everyone except the young officer in Div HQ who still had faith in passwords.

When the Imjin River was behaving itself, the reports on the day's work usually concentrated on mine laying and road building. Again, the codewords dominated the conversation. Every minefield had a number, if laid since the formation of the Commonwealth Division, preceded with the number of the Squadron that laid it. The trip wire minefield I had laid near Hill 317 was 12/8. Now, three months later, the minefield number was up to over 60, and a great deal that I had never imagined had been learnt about laying minefields.

The road network was also growing impressively. We always called them roads, unsurfaced tracks though they were. From next to nothing north of the river when we had recrossed, we now had more than fifty miles of roads on the map, with the main routes stemming from the PINTAIL and TEAL bridges, liberally laced together by laterals. Roads in a certain area were known by a colour, but this was never enough, as spurs were promptly built, so GREEN ONE begat GREEN TWO, THREE and FOUR with indecent haste, whereas the PURPLE routes were never so prolific.

After hearing the length of minefields laid and the number of mines they contained, the matter of greatest interest to the commanding officer was the state of our engineer plant, particularly the bulldozers. In all we had about a dozen of these, two of which had been procured from our allies during the last "bug-out" by the simple recourse of pouring fuel into the fuel tanks. In turn, each piece of plant had its own codename, the main theme being the titles of the British nobility. We had Duke, Duchess, Earl, Countess and Baron. Tom, the Intelligence Officer, whose surname was Marquis, had vetoed any use of that title, as he considered the muddles we were achieving were bad enough without involving him personally. Such names were of no great attraction to the Canadians, whose bulldozer operators considered it their right to name their machines after their girl friends, amongst whom DONNA and RAMONA proved to be ladies of character.

Whereas it would have been highly insecure on the wireless to admit that a Caterpillar D7 dozer was at a certain location, it was considered perfectly fair to say that "BARON is on PURPLE TWO". Had any Chinamen had the slightest wish to break the code, he easily could have done so, though his confusion would then have been complete. We were however, slightly worried of what our adversaries must have thought of our moral decadence on hearing, "COUNTESS is spending the night at DUKE'S location and DONNA is joining him later."

After the "O" Group, the Squadron Commanders were always invited into the Mess for a drink, but seldom stayed, as they had to get back to their own folk to detail off the next day's work. Before going to bed themselves, they might sometimes go to visit a Troop that was minelaying, usually out in front of our lines but, however commendable in intent, visits in the dark usually proved to be a mixed blessing. All this went on, of course, seven days a week, every week.

The prospects of peace, which really had seemed very hopeful before Christmas, had petered out by mid January and we were back to war as usual, except that both sides were better defended and the prospects of major movement seemed less and less. I certainly could see no reason why we should not be on the same ground in under nine months' time when the new pheasant season would open, and suggested that we should keep to "cocks only" to preserve the breeding stock. However, some who were due home shortly thought that this would be stretching sportsmanship excessively. Nevertheless, "cocks only" became the rule.

Even if no major battles were raging, a new cause of casualties had been detected, at least on the west of the Korean line, where we were: rats, though none were sure it wasn't mice. Some form of nastiness, akin to the plague, was striking down a worrying number of the visiting soldiery and, once down, many stayed down. Hard frost, static war and an over-generous ration scale which resulted in much waste had turned into piles of rubbish which could not be buried and became a rich resort for rodents. Where the rats came from was not explained, but presumably the old villages had been full of them. Anyway, the way in which they gathered and multiplied was impressive.

The extent of the epidemic became a matter of severe embarrassment and, apart from OP DRAGON, seemed to be on a more confidential basis than any other topic in Korea. The secrecy led to rumours, to the extent of a slight worry of how and when the dreaded disease might strike me, but I never encountered a case in the flesh. That did not, however, prevent me being sent on a one day, officers only, rat catching course. John Page, who had taken over from Martin Keer as Adjutant, told me that I could be proud to have been selected, so great was the demand for places.

Off I went, therefore, with my jeep and driver back down the main supply route with its old minefields and ever increasing festoons of telephone cables on either side, past Rear Divisional Headquarters where the administrative staff were based, past the massive ammunition dump with its lines of pre-loaded lorries and past the fuel and ration dumps, besieged by trucks from every quartermaster. Then came the NAAFI and the Intelligence Unit intended for the interrogation of Chinese prisoners but, as the latter were scarce, kept itself moderately busy checking on any doubtful Koreans who were drafted in to work for us.

All this stretched over only about eight miles, but at 20 mph maximum and with no lack of other traffic, it took the full half hour. Once out of the rear of the Division, there were nothing but odd American and South Korean units until one reached I Corps Headquarters and UIJONGBU, half way between the Imjin and Seoul.

I had imagined that the Rodent Course would teach me practical rat catching. Ever since having a rat up my trousers in our potting shed in Devonshire, I had had a genuine interest in the subject. I doubted if they'd have terriers, but perhaps there would be something better than the old break back traps, on which the rather soapy tinned cheese on issue tended not to adhere. Not a bit of it, we were to be trained as poisoners. Our instructor, an American captain, who doubtless had Borgia ancestry, delighted in making all but a literal meal of what I think I could have understood over the telephone.

What I had always known as "rat poison" was referred to with reverence and handled much like I imagined had been the case with frankincense and myrrh. In so doing, Captain Borgia certainly expected to be considered a Very Wise Man. If he found his British audience rather unappreciative, our Commonwealth friends left him in no doubt of his popularity rating. Anyway, what it all came down to was that if a good teaspoonful of the recommended mixture were wrapped in silver paper, it became known as a "sweet". So appropriate was the name, that we had another long lecture on not giving them to children. Apart from "Number One Half", our Mess boy, whose voice had broken, I couldn't think of a single child still in the Commonwealth Division area. Lay a "sweet" where there might be a rodent and, Lo and Behold, it might be nibbled and, if so, death should follow within a week.

Our prizes for attending the course were a small tub of the mixture and a small roll of an early form of aluminium foil. So armed, I returned to Regimental HQ, where my arrival was rated as the anti-climax of the campaign. Nothing loth, I made up some sweets and left some near the Mess, some near the Sergeants Mess, and a goodly cupful near the other ranks' cookhouse.

A busy week followed, so my thoughts quickly wandered away from mice and rats. Nearing the end of a tiring day, I had returned to the Mess dugout to read the English newspapers which had arrived that evening. No one else was there, the light was brighter than normal, indicating that a recharged battery had been "borrowed" from a vehicle, and the atmosphere was cosy, or fuggy, depending upon one's personal taste. The rice straw ceiling, laid on the logs which spanned the hole, and kept dry by the superimposed tarpaulin, provided wonderful insulation. We had a bottle of port, and I stood myself a glass as I settled with what comfort was possible on one of the collapsible

The Royal Engineers Officers Mess dug in for the winter 1951/52. The airstrip and cliffs on the north bank of the Imjin are in the background.

camp chairs beside the table. Moments later there was a thud or, more precisely, a heavy plop, on the table behind my paper. There, not more than two feet from me, lay a writhing rat and, with incredible timing, down came another out of the staw, but this one never moved on the table.

Whatever the limitations of my physique, I have always had fairly quick reactions, and now I was electrified. I had never tried before, and have no intention of repeating that particular gymnastic feat, but I was in no time standing on the collapsible chair in a manner which its designer could never have imagined. I then shouted "HELP" loudly. This coincided with the entrance to the Mess of Lieutenant Colonel Peter Moore, my commanding officer. He never commented on my behaviour, but after a short pause during which Number One Half was summoned with the equivalent of a dustpan and brush, said, "Well done, Dan, you seem to be putting your Course to good effect."

If the first results of my efforts had been dramatic, the sequel was equally repulsive. The stench of dead rodents in the rice staw roof grew so frightful that, in the middle of winter, the tarpaulin had to come off and the rice straw had to be replaced. "Sweets" forsooth!

Luckily our tents seemed to be free of rats, and we were now thankful that we had not taken our food up to them. I say up because the Command Post and Mess were in a small valley, with our sleeping tents through a couple of barbed wire fences just over the rise. Tom and I, and Dick Sullivan, who had recently taken over as Signals Officer, were comfortably settled into our ridge tent, which was dug in and allowed room for our camp beds and for a good home made stove, for which the preferred fuel remained the waxed paper cones from the 25 pounder ammunition boxes. Early morning was, naturally, the worst part of the day, but was made much more reasonable by Number One Half, who slept in the Mess and brought us a cup of Gunfire tea and a jug of shaving water.

The tea was great, but the temptation to stay in our excellent sleeping bags remained. Tom, whose experience as a prisoner of war after Dunkirk had given him the edge on Dick and me, would show the first leg with his ritual remark, "Up in the morning feeling rosy," to which we replied, "Good old Rosie!" A positive indicator of the day being cold was when one's fingers stuck to one's razor, in which case the milk would be frozen at breakfast and the ink would be frozen in the office truck. On really cold nights, below zero Fahrenheit, there was a routine whereby the guard started all engines periodically and tracked vehicles were moved slightly, lest their tracks became frozen down.

Tom now went off for his five days' leave in Tokyo, so I acted as Intelligence Officer, just as I had hoped. I enjoyed trying to glean information from scarce material and recording what we knew in a manner that could quickly be retrieved. Much of it went on the huge talc covered maps, but marking them up was the part of the job at which I was initially hopeless and knew that I would never become good. Tom was artistic by nature and appeared to mark the maps with ease, achieving accurate and pleasing results. When I took the same wax pencils, chinagraphs, and pressed on the map, nothing happened. Tom had shown me that the way to achieve results was first to rub the talc hard to warm it, then draw on the same spot immediately. Luckily I had, as my assistants, two very good NCOs who were draughtsmen and literally held my hand.

My only trip with the CO that week was to a lumber camp which our Canadian Squadron had opened up twenty-five miles away. Since losing our hard won hills in November, there had been some deep thinking on field defences, the main conclusion being that overhead cover on a slit trench needed to be properly constructed, or omitted. It was now evident, that, with the materials available locally on the hills, that the Infantry had not had the wherewithall to build properly supported roofs on which to pile earth over their trenches. Good strong timber was required, and that was what some forty Canadians were cutting, at the rate of 1,500 lengths a day. They were certainly the right men for the job, but, with weeks of logging in front of them, some suggested that their war lacked glamour.

With the main airstrip for our Division now built on the marsh opposite our Regimental HQ, it was not difficult to make friends with the Royal Artillery officers who were the pilots. Their Auster aircraft had two seats, one behind the other, yet they normally flew only with a pilot, whose job was to act as an Aerial Observation Post and direct the guns on the ground by radio. I had met Air O P officers in Sumatra seven years before, and had admired the manoeuvrability of their little planes and been amazed at the short distance in which they could take off and land. I was by no means the first to think of it, but most of our intelligence was being gleaned from air photos and here was I, an Intelligence Officer, with the chance of going up in the air and gaining

An Auster.

the information first hand. All I needed to do was to ask the Air O P
Flight, and they would surely take me up.

I did ask, and the response was not overwhelmingly enthusiastic. It
was explained to me that quite a lot of the space behind the pilot was
taken up with wireless sets and batteries and that even the weight of a
second man made a difference to the rate of climb of the plane. No,
parachutes were not carried! Rate of climb was apparently a very topical
point, as not long before one of the five Air O P officers had come home
from his two hours over the Chinese lines with faulty steering. We had
all seen and heard him circle the strip many times, then, when at last he
tried to land the Auster, it had veered off into the cliff on the Imjin bank
and he had been killed. When later the plane had been examined it had
been found that the steering control had been cut by a bullet.

Until then the pilots had flown at almost any height they chose, often
very low even over the Chinese lines. Now the rule had been made that
before crossing our front line the aircraft must be higher than the height
at which small arms fire might be effective. This was considered to be
7,000 feet, or just over 2,000 metres, which turned out to be higher
than I had imagined.

I was sure, however, that if only I could ascend with an Air O P, all would be revealed, and I must have been so pressing in my demands that a kindly Captain eventually agreed to take me on his afternoon duty. It was just as well that I had forgotten that flying made me sick. I certainly felt very sick, but cold was my greater worry, as, of course, there was neither pressurisation nor heating.

It took us twenty minutes of circling over our lines to gain the height of 7,000 feet. I had my map board on my knee, also a large brown envelope, just in case, and an intercom microphone fixed to my headset and projecting in front of my mouth. I had assumed that with landmarks like the Imjin River, with its distinctive junctions and bends, the land would be laid out before me just like the map. For the first ten minutes it was, then I think the pilot must have become bored with climbing in left-handed circles and changed to right-handed ones without me realising. I was thoroughly lost, and can't have helped his concentration by questioning him on the intercom and pointing vaguely

The author prior to an Auster flight.

at the map I could just see on his knee. Before we had started he had said, "Remember that the north facing hills have snow on them. It has thawed on most of the south facing slopes." This was very valuable advice, I was sure, but somehow the north-east, and north-west, slopes seemed to have snow too, as did some of the south facing valleys.

I grew so embarrassed at admitting that I had no idea where we were that I reassured the pilot that all was well. It wasn't, but as we had now reached our height, he could go the normal five miles over the Chinese lines, which coincided with the maximum arcs of fire of our 25 pounder guns. Once there, we again started circling. I peered through my binoculars, but could identify precisely nothing of engineer intelligence interest. The pilot pointed out a Korean village being shelled by the American artillery on the right of our Division, and reported to the ground that he could see about thirty Chinamen. I was blessed if I could! Anyway, they were unfortunately out of range of our guns, so I was denied the satisfaction of seeing an Air O P actually landing shells on the ground.

When our ninety minutes over the Chinese Volunteers, who appeared not to have acknowledged our presence above them, were up, my host showed that, although it had taken him twenty minutes to reach 7,000 feet, an Auster could come down much quicker. This proved very painful on my ears, so that, all in all, my excursion had not proved to be one of my happier experiences in Korea. If the intention had been to dissuade me from pressing too strongly to fly with the Air O P Flight again, the aim had been achieved. Fortuitously, the need for an aerial reconnaissance-cum-taxi service separate from the Air O P, whose sole job was to direct gunfire, had been noted and, within days, a flight of a further five Austers, known as the Light Liaison Flight arrived. I liaised with them at once.

After morning church in the tent in Div HQ on Sunday, 20th January, 1952, the Commander Royal Artillery, Brigadier Pike, who was generally known as "Willie", beckoned me across. I had met him many times, and he had always had a kind word for me since the day we had tried to push his Dingo up the forward slope of a road I had been building during Op COMMANDO. "Please could you tell me," he asked, "can I take a gun across the river at JIMMY?" JIMMY was a point which had been used for crossing the Imjin ice the previous winter, but because of the cliff on the home bank, had since been

disregarded as a crossing place, so had never been graced with a duck's
name when the codewords had been changed to PINTAIL, TEAL,
WIDGEON, etc. I had always had a high regard for the CRA, but it
was immediately evident to me that he either didn't know JIMMY, or
was badly off form, perhaps due to the sermon. A 25 pounder gun
weighed over two tons, and, even if it could be swung down the cliff,
would almost certainly fall through the ice, which had never thickened
quite as expected. "Not a hope, Sir," I said. It then transpired that he
meant a shotgun, and invited me to join him. As all days were working
days, we in Korea had waived the English law that no game may be shot
of Sundays. The CRA said that it would be nice if I could advise him
where the minefields lay.

Earlier it had just passed through me mind that he who kept the
minefield records might be in demand as a guide for shooting parties,
but as Tom didn't shoot, he had not been invited on that score. My
letter home that evening included:—

> We were six of us, the CRA, the Commanding Officer and Second-in-
> Command of the British Field Regiment RA, another Gunner officer, a
> New Zealand Signals officer and me. For beaters we had the Brigade
> Major RA and five batmen. The bag was ten pheasants, of which I had
> five and lost another. The standard of shooting was very poor, and I
> should have had twice as many, but it was a most enjoyable afternoon.
> Because the ice was only just thick enough for us on foot, others had not
> been to the spot before, and we must have seen fifty birds. None of the
> corn on the north side of the Imjin has been cut, so an army of pheasants
> could live there very happily.

Not far to the west of us the peace talks were continuing at Pan-Mun-
Jon, but nothing was being achieved and those on the front line were
back at war, static though it was. By day no one expected to see a
Chinaman, so it was all the more surprising when one gentleman
emerged on a forward slope not many hundreds of yards from our
positions and undertook what many pairs of binoculars agreed was the
Chinese equivalent of a formal kit layout. I did not see it, and only wish
that I had, but understood that the actor, for so he must have been, went
through the motions with deliberate care, laying down his mat, then his
few belongings, carefully upon it. Then, with equal precision he packed
everything up again and departed with great dignity. Noboby dreamt of
shooting at him. Perhaps he was drunk, or perhaps he had done it for a
bet, but our opponent had provided excellent entertainment.

Back at the Regiment, I heard that the NAAFI had run out of port. Things were indeed getting rugged!

February started very cold, with the ink frozen at night and well into the next morning. Tom was back from his leave in Japan, upon which he reported favourably, but almost immediately was required to take over as Adjutant, as John Page was going home. This meant that I was given the Intelligence Officer's job permanently and was delighted, not only because I knew I would enjoy it, but also because I would be a Captain at last.

The last day of pheasant shooting according to British law is 1st February and so we, officially at any rate, observed it in the second pheasant season of the Korean War. On that day I felt myself very lucky again to be invited to join the CRA's party. It was certainly not on account of my shooting ability and, had it been understood how little I really knew about the minefields in the Divisional area, it would not have been on that count either. Such minefields as there were near the north bank of the Imjin were of South Korean origin, with which the Chinese had probably tinkered. Unless the fence, with its red triangles, was still up and apparent above the crops and weeds, it would have taken a better man than me to say exactly where a minefield lay.

Our party of six guns consisted of the General and his ADC, the CRA, two other officers and me, plus some batmen to beat. With the General Officer Commanding and his Deputy both rather off the beaten track, some special arrangements had been made with a wireless link, lest they were needed, but these formalities had no adverse effect upon our plans. General Cassels said that he was very glad to see a Sapper, as on a previous excursion he had found himself against a minefield fence and wasn't sure if he was coming out of a field or going into it. Sensibly, he then walked along the fence until he was sure where he was, but had found the experience detracted from the pleasures of his sport.

We shot nine lovely pheasants: seven cocks and two hens, and regrettably lost several others due to the absence of dogs. I also remember that the General had very little shooting, but remained first rate company, and that my own shooting was back to a very poor level.

On 6th February we heard that King George VI had died. We had known that he was very ill, but had never expected his sudden death. There can have been few such mixed groups of his subjects at the time as in the Commonwealth Division, and there was no doubt that we were genuinely sad at the news, also rather worried that Princess Elizabeth was still so young. It took the Gunners very little time to arrange a salute of 101 guns at intervals of one minute in memory of the King and another to salute the new Queen, and there was a certain satisfaction in knowing that there was no need to fire special blank for ceremonial purposes. The soldierly banter near where the shells landed might have included, "Just our luck to be opposite the British Division at this time." Actually, the Chinese probably never noticed anything different from the normal routine, as our harassing fire alone often exceeded the ceremonial rate. Whatever else our gunfire achieved, it did ensure that the Chinese dug magnificient trench and tunnel systems. It may have been intentional, or just due to shortage of ammunition, but the Chinese reluctance to return our harassing fire reduced the incentive for us to dig as deeply as them.

With the peace talks having, until recently, been so promising, the tempo of the war had slackened greatly for several weeks and, pleasant though this had been for some of us, the pause had given the enemy a wonderful opportunity to re-group and prepare for an attack. The Chinese had swept the United Nations forces down the country the previous winter, and there was no reason to doubt that they and the North Koreans might try again now.

The EUSAK (Eighth United States Army Korea) intelligence summaries, which I now saw daily, threw very little light upon enemy intentions. The North Koreans certainly had spies in the South, as we knew from the regular stream of infiltrators who strayed into our minefields, but the converse did not appear to be true. Anyway, it was the Chinese, not the North Koreans, who had made the running for the past year, and the chances of infiltrating the Chinese command structure must have been slim. The only routine sources of information were, therefore, air photos and prisoners. The snags were that cloudy days cut down the air photos, and prisoners were as scarce as the bottles of port which I had found so reassuring on a cold winter's evening. The quest for prisoners was again pursued, I guess with mixed feelings, as our previous efforts "just to pop over to a Chinese hill, pick up a few prisoners and pop back again" had proved a costly failure.

New ideas in the prisoner catching game were few and far between but, with the frost still in the ground, the chance of using tanks in an attack was reconsidered. The Skins, for whom there had been no opportunity to use their tanks except as static pillboxes, were delighted to have the chance of an outing, particularly because the cancellation of Op DRAGON had been a great disappointment for them.

The new operation was planned to start with two troops of four tanks going out through our own lines, then into the Chinese side of No Man's Land, one on the right and one of the left of the Divisional boundaries. Lieutenant Peter Park, who had arrived with Angus, had been selected to accompany the right-hand probe. The task was out of the ordinary and interesting, so in my new capacity as Intelligence Officer I made sure of seeing Peter and briefing him on items for which it would be nice if he looked. With a cheery remark on the lines of "see you soon" I left with a nostalgic hankering to be back in a Field Troop, but knowing that life on the staff had its compensations.

The main trouble about taking tanks out on those tracks was that we had, the previous autumn, dug holes in them and laid anti-tank mines. These mines were now frozen into the ground just as firmly as if they were set in concrete, so there was no chance of lifting them and every chance of a tank still setting them off.

I was one of a diminishing populaton of old timers who could remember why the tracks had been mined in the first place. When we advanced north of the Imjin in September, we had been unsure how far we would be going, so had left the tracks open. As I myself had then discovered, it was possible to go further along an open road than perhaps was intended, and that was just what Captain Blue of the American Artillery had unfortunately achieved with more lasting effect than my own small excursion. Blue was with a very popular unit, the "Persuaders", a Regiment of eight inch guns, which could throw their shells, each weighing 200lbs, onto "a tennis court at ten miles", or so we believed.

Captain Blue, whom I remembered as a friendly and apparently able fellow, received an urgent fire task for one of his guns, including a grid reference. He then made the unfortunate, but to me understandable, error of thinking the location referred to the place he should position his gun, whereas it was actually the designated target. For those manning our front line at the time, it was a real surprise to see an American officer in a jeep drive fast through it towards the Chinese, and even more of a surprise to find that he was being closely followed by an eight inch gun, an unwieldy brute even on a decent road. The gun had been stopped, but Captain Blue had gone, seemingly for ever, though later we heard that he had been taken prisoner. It was at that stage that it was thought prudent to block the road, lest the enemy should motor through our front lines in the opposite direction with equal carefree abandon.

On Peter Park's route the anti-tank mines had only been laid in the hard road, and the sides, which were boggy paddy, had been left free. However, as an afterthought, these sides had been sown with anti-personnel mines actuated by trip wires. Now a tank's armour is specifically designed to keep out shell fragments, and mines are usually smaller than shells, so Peter's plan was to take his tanks off the road at the point where it was covered with anti-tank mines, churn over the frozen ground to the side, then steer back onto the road. An anti-personnel mine or two would probably go off, but that should do no harm.

We soon heard that the tank excursion had not been successful, then, later, that Peter Park had been hurt and evacuated by helicopter. Soon, the CO came back to RHQ and told us what had happened. Peter Park and his Sergeant had travelled in the front tank and, to make quite sure that the tank took the right route round the anti-tank mines, Peter had bravely kept his head out of the turret, so that he could direct the driver on the intercom. A fragment from one of the anti-personnel mines had badly wounded him, and an American helicopter had taken him to hospital. The Colonel ended with, "Dan, I want you to find him." I was told of the most likely MASH (Mobile Army Surgical Hospital), twenty miles away to the east, to which the helicopter should have taken him.

My driver took me by jeep right across the next Divisional area, 1 ROK (Republic of Korea) Div, where it was soon apparent that Commonwealth vehicles were seldom seen, then into the American Infantry Divisional area on its right. We found the MASH and I asked if they had any British officers, and received a friendly but definite "No". I then asked if they had had any cas-evac helicopters that morning, and was told that a Belgian soldier had been brought in, and was still in the operating theatre.

I asked if I might see the Belgian, and had to press firmly to gain permission. Nor were the two surgeons best pleased when an unknown officer wearing a face mask was shown into the theatre tent. There was no doubt that the patient was Peter, and I managed to beckon to one of the staff to come outside to talk to me. I told them who Peter was (the identity discs which should have been on a string round his neck were missing), and, in turn, was told that although they were doing their best, Peter was very severely wounded and would be unlikely to regain consciousness. I obtained some phone numbers and returned very sadly to the Regiment.

We managed to get through to the MASH later that evening and heard that Peter had died. I was then sent to find the American Graves Unit to which he would be despatched, which I did early the next morning and managed to ring the Regiment. The Colonel brought a padré across with him, and the congregation for the brief funeral service consisted of the Colonel, the American Second Lieutenant who commanded the all negro Graves Unit, and me.

Three days of thaw set in that day, and the slush was shocking as we drove home.

CHAPTER TWELVE

REST AND RECUPERATION

By now all those who had arrived in Korea when the Division had been formed had been on leave to Japan, or at least had been offered it. One officer, who had been a prisoner of the Japanese in the war, had refused the kind invitation. Our commanding officer had himself taken a little persuading that he would be all the better for the change, before he eventually and reluctantly departed for Tokyo. I wouldn't suggest that the mice actually played whilst he was away, but the conduct of the war was pursued with rather less intensity. He then discovered that he could not fly back on the prescribed day, so chose to return to us a day early rather than a day late. As always, his sense of timing was dramatic, and it was not just the Sappers who knew that he was back.

Those who had arrived as recently as me were now due to go on leave in a week or two, but the CO was keen to regain any touch he had lost during his four days away, so took me off the next afternoon to call once more on the Canadian Brigade, whose battalions were on the front line. First we "did" the Royal Canadian Regiment, proudly proclaimed as "Canada's First and Finest" though the other units of the Brigade were themselves not lacking in good reputation, then moved to the Princess Patricia's Canadian Light Infantry. We called in at their Command Post, and were lucky to find the Commanding Officer in. He and his Adjutant briefed us on the disposition of the companies, and made a special point of thanking Colonel Peter for the splendid minefields which had been laid for the battalion. As an afterthought, the PPCLI Colonel wondered if we could lift one of the fields laid for his predecessor, as it covered just the piece of ground on which he wished to position a platoon.

This was not the first time we had been asked to lift our own minefields, and my Colonel made no promises. Even with the minefield records available, lifting anti-personnel mines and their associated trip wires was a lengthy and skilled task, sufficiently hazardous as usually to require the presence of an already busy officer.

We moved to a forward company headquarters, where we were offered a guide to the most forward platoon. Colonel Peter had been there before, so declined the escort, saying that the fewer we were, the less likely we were to attract attention. He had made this point to me often. Visitors to forward units could do real good for morale if it became apparent that they could offer practical help. However, if they were just there for the swan and, as likely as not, attracted fire onto the heads of the locals who would have to stay there long after their visitors had left, great was the unpopularity that could be generated.

That walk forward was much like any other visit on which I had accompanied Lieutenant Colonel Peter Moore. I suppose the really surprising aspect was that the Chinese permitted us to undertake it in broad daylight. True, there was a spur along the side of which we could shelter for most of the quarter of a mile or so we had to cover, but for at least a hundred yards we were on the Chinese side of the hill, and they were less than a mile away. The Colonel was the first to use any form of cover that was available, be it a communication trench or a fold in the ground, and I was very thankful that he did so, particularly as a single Chinese field gun was dropping a shell on, or near, the platoon every two or three minutes.

I found those Chinese shells peculiarly disturbing, as no sooner had the dust from one settled than listening for the whine of the next became my main preoccupation, so much so that I was soon tagging along nearly touching the Colonel. Every time I started to feel reassured, "Go away Dan!" was his predictable order. "Ten yards. Go away, at least ten yards!" "Sorry Sir," I would mutter, then wait feeling very lonely, as he strode away to a "safe" distance.

From the trenches of the forward platoon we could look down into the valley between us and the Chinamen, from which a solitary and elderly Korean civilian had recently been rescued by the Australians. He had chosen to stay there after our advance into the area and, whereas all other civilians had been evacuated, he alone had been allowed to remain. Although nobody considered the old boy to be a security risk, there was no doubt that he was proving to be a great nuisance, as his presence had to be considered when any patrol went out or when any fireplan was made. Whether or not the Chinese were equally considerate we weren't sure, but eventually it was decided that his continued presence in No Man's Land could not be tolerated. One night a small patrol was sent to bring him in and, although the Australians had behaved in their normal gentle manner, the shock had been too much for the poor fellow and he died on the way into our lines.

Our main talk that afternoon, however, was of minefields and of the minefield gaps through which every patrol in front of our lines had to make a hazardous passage. If the single strand wire fence stayed up, there was no problem, but once it had been cut, and just one shell or mortar fragment was all that was needed, the chances of straying into the trip wires at night became so high as to be better not pursued.

The Chinese gun, which we surmised to be probably an American 105mm throwing a 30lb shell, landed a further half dozen in our vicinity whilst we were talking. No harm was done, but my questions dried up rapidly when the Colonel suggested that we should retrace our steps. We booked out with company and battalion headquarters in the same manner as we had booked in and left the Princess Pat's, thinking what a splendid unit they were. With so many different nationalities in the Commonwealth Division, it would have been easy to compare the units of one country with those of another, but I never heard it done. So far as the British were concerned, the Australians, Canadians and Kiwis, not forgetting the Indians in their medical unit, were all very good folk to have around.

I certainly did not realise that the Chinese gun had been registering the forward platoon, so that later many other guns could be accurately trained upon it. That very evening a heavy barrage fell upon the platoon and for a few hours the position was lost, only to be regained before dawn. In terms of warfare, these attacks on outpost positions, which became common later, were very minor actions, but none the less terrible for those involved. My respect for the infantry, who had to stay on the forward positions day after day, night after night and week after week, grew ever higher.

In the same way that our visit to the PPCLI followed standard procedures, so did the use of the No. 19 wireless set in the CO's jeep. Quite rightly he expected to remain in contact with his headquarters and squadrons but, even in good daylight, this was easier said than done in the Korean valleys, and many messages had to be relaid through other stations, a tedious business. Lieutenant Colonel Peter Moore expected wars to be waged fast and efficiently, but sometimes the rules for security of speech made this almost impossible.

I may have given the impression that some aspects of our wireless security were less tight than Fougasse's wartime "Walls have Ears" campaign would have demanded, but the level seemed to meet the needs of our sector of Korea.

The form of code which was used for anything that was secret was the well known SLIDEX, which consisted of a series of printed cards divided into lines and columns, with each space filled with words in common military usage, such as BRIDGE, GUN, RATIONS, GRENADES, and over a hundred of them on each card. The clever bit lay in the sliding cursors (plastic strips), on which a series of jumbled code letters were written. These letters were changed at least weekly, when all concerned were informed by secret letter delivered by road. Sending a SLIDEX message was indeed a slow means of passing information, and to encode and decode successfully when travelling in the back of a jeep was beyond me, and often beyond the Colonel himself. His tendency, in common with other senior officers to whisper on the air, with a view to maintaining secrecy, when he should have sent a SLIDEX message, might have been questioned by purist communicators.

A purist might also have been shocked by our method of reopening the wireless net when almost everyone was out of contact. This situation was usually related to terrible weather, resulting in atmospherics and all that. Another inference of terrible weather was that a rum ration could be issued on the personal authorisation of commanding officers. The rum was sitting in store at each location, and our CO's discretion was easily stretched into deciding that the weather was terrible and that the rum could thus be authorised. Armed with this trump card, the poor soul controlling our regimental net, who had become completely exasperated by none of the out stations answering his calls, looked a new man. "Hello all stations," he would say, "rum ration authorised tonight." It always worked, with the immediate answers of "Two Zero roger, out", "Three Zero roger, out", and so on coming through loud and clear. "Roger" meant that the message had been received and understood, in fact the action of cork pulling followed so rapidly that the pops might have been included in the transmission. Once everyone was in contact again, the net usually stayed open for the night without further difficulty.

Of all the messages passed from the CO's jeep when he was out and about for the day, the one considered the most important was that giving his estimated time of arrival back at regimental headquarters. So great was his influence, that precise warning of his time of arrival could make all the difference to the subsequent course of the evening's planning. It was the bodyguard's duty to pass the estimated time of arrival message, so this often fell to me, and woe betide if we arrived earlier than expected, lest certain actions on the log sheet should be found to be incomplete when the Colonel strode into the Command Post.

The end of the pheasant shooting season had been observed with good faith after 1st February, though it is true that I suffered a temporary lapse when a cock pheasant presented himself just outside our Mess a few days later. It was known that the General himself was keen that the pheasants should not be disturbed during the breeding season, so the chances of moving camp seemed slight. Had this information been passed to the Chinese, it could have been of real interest to them. However, they, like the Koreans, seemed not to be interested in eating pheasants and would, if they had known, probably have rated the British odder than ever.

I was finding work as the Intelligence Officer harder than I had imagined, due mainly to a further review of the records of the 350 minefields we now had in the divisional area. The number of casualties we were suffering from them made our task all the more urgent, so I was going to bed later and later, and I am a chap who needs his beauty sleep. After six and a half months in Korea I was very ready for my five days' R & R, which officially stood for Rest and Recuperation. Two other Sapper officers were going to Tokyo at the same time, both called Peter and both likely to prove congenial companions. We soon accomplished the illegal but necessary action of swapping English pounds for American dollars, and Korean won for Japanese yen. The pound was officially worth 2 dollars 80 cents, or 1,008 yen, or 16,800 won, which meant that 100 won were worth about a penny farthing.

The two Peters and I spent the night on our way to Tokyo in the officers' transit building in Seoul which, like everything else we saw there, was grim. The next day we flew the 800 miles to Tokyo Haneda airport in an American four-engined Skymaster, and from there we had forty-five minutes in an Army bus, mostly through very old fashioned and broken down suburbs, to the British transit camp. Documentation there was delightfully brisk and was accompanied, for the first ten officers, by an invitation to attend a "large, unofficial, cocktail party" at the British Embassy to meet Countess Mountbatten. The "unofficial" was explained by the official mourning which was being observed following the King's recent death. We three Sappers, and also three New Zealand Artillery officers with whom we were on good terms, all received invitations. They then asked, "What do we call a real live Countess?" I replied nonchalantly, "Oh, just call her Lady Mountbatten." I was to be reminded of this later.

From the transit camp we were taken by taxi at the Queen's expense to the Marounouchi Hotel, which had already become quite an institution. It was run for Commonwealth personnel of officer status, which included a lot of girls from the Embassy, and proved to be a rare good place. If we had a complaint, it was that, after living in our tents in many degrees of frost, it was a trifle overheated. The Marounouchi cost us sixteen shillings a day, and the Government were said to be paying another guinea on our behalf. The dining room food was thrown in and was good, but there was also an excellent grill room to which, after a bath, we soon repaired. A prodigous meal, for which we had plenty of money to pay, was backed by a Porterhouse steak and washed down with champagne.

The next morning we began a tour of the shops, starting with the American Post Exchange, or PX, which was huge and appeared to sell everything. It gave us a good idea of prices and confirmed, as we had been told, that the items most worth buying were china and silk, also pearls, about which I luckily realised that I knew nothing. We then went to, and did most of our shopping at, Takashimayas, which liked to be considered the Japanese equivalent of Harrods.

Peter Francis and I both searched for most of the afternoon, then each bought ninety-three piece Noritake dinner services, twelve of everything and a few oddments besides. We then checked what we had chosen and it turned out that we had both selected precisely the same pattern, a sort of blue on a primrose background. The shop had them beautifully packed and boxed up, but unfortunately the boxes were too heavy for the 22lbs maximum of the British Post Office, so off we had to go back to the PX and have the whole lot, including additional tea sets for six, reboxed into no less than eight 20lb boxes for each of us. For postage, American stamps then had to be used. The china cost me £17, with £4 extra for the repacking and postage, all representing wonderful value.

The next morning I bought silk, which proved very difficult to choose, and some water colours painted on silk which, whatever else, were bright. That evening two of us were given some tickets for the American GHQ Club. We found an enormus gathering of everything except British officers. Their absence in no way detracted from our enjoyment, but we thought it sufficiently strange as to enquire the reason the next day. "Mourning, you fools" we were told. Apparently we should never have been there at all, let alone in uniform.

Uniform for my R & R had been a problem, as the only battledress trousers of mine had been burnt in the Quartermaster's fire. The answer had been to borrow Tom's, although his girth was even larger than mine. My hips had always been smaller than my waist, making belts of little use, so, as usual, braces had to be the answer: my battledress top luckily covered these. I would have liked to add the ribbons of the British Korea medal, of yellow and blue stripes, and the first ever United Nations medal, of thin white and blue stripes, to the uniform, but couldn't obtain them. For both medals one needed to have been in Korea for a month, but, pleased though we were to qualify, many of us thought that to be given two for the same job was hardly British.

The Embassy cocktail party was on the Wednesday evening, and prior to our departure from the Marounouchi the two Peters, I and our Kiwi friends had gathered in the bar with the purpose of assuring each other how well we intended to behave.

We, the British contingent, were given a lift to the Ambassador's house by the Indian Brigadier who was their Military Attaché in Tokyo. At the Embassy we were met at the door by a shower of girls who took our hats, then introduced us to His Excellency the Ambassador, who was a bachelor, his sister who acted as hostess for him, and Lady Mountbatten, all absolutely charming. There weren't more than about a hundred people in all, but, with sufficient distractions to divert my attentions, I missed the Japanese Prime Minister, Yoshida, though it was said that he was there.

Lady Mountbatten made a point of talking to us in a most informal manner and seemed to be amused when I reminded her of our previous meeting when, at the Bangalore Hunt Ball with General Telfer-Smollett as Master, I and other young officers acted as barmen and drank the profits. She also took interest in Tom's trousers, the lack of fit of which I had explained to her. We were taking full advantage of the limitless dry martinis on offer, and my friends later told me that I had not acted with the decorum that might be expected when addressing an ex-Vicereine, but that she took it in the best of heart.

As the guests started to thin out, so did I feel that I needed to make a quick visit without delay. A small chap was standing alone in the hall, so I asked him, "Where's the Gents?" and was given precise and polite instructions. Back in the room, I felt like continuing the party, but my friends urged me towards the door and to thank HM Ambassador. He was the same little fellow whom I had just befriended, and I thanked him very much indeed.

A couple of the Embassy girls had asked us how we were getting back to the Marounouchi. We had answered, "With you," and they obviously had our interests at heart as they ushered us to the Embassy door. Standing there was a large staff car with the Turkish Military Attaché, himself a handsome Brigadier, by the door waving the girls into the car saying, "Charmed, my dears, charmed!" We went round the far side of the car, opened the door, pulled them out, and went home by taxi.

Our last day of leave was potentially a very long one, as we were not due to fly out until 4.00 a.m. the following night. However, the Peters and I were tired, so devoted most of the day to gentle sightseeing. We noted that Tokyo had many big modern buildings, but that most of them were uninteresting. 1952 seemed a long while after the war, towards the end of which Tokyo had been severely bombed, but to expect to find much of great architectural repute was probably asking too much.

Later that day, we decided to walk around the Imperial Palace, a praiseworthy but not very profitable outing, though it was reputed to be the one show place of the capital. It had an enormous moat that reminded us of the Suez Canal, except that the moat had vast grass banks which someone must have had to scythe in summer. Other than impressive stone walls, we could see nothing of the inside and had to believe the picture postcards, that truly the place was marvellous. As regards our views on the centre of Tokyo, we judged it as nothing like as dirty as London, but were quite certain that to cross a road was much more dangerous than being at war in Korea. We assessed the Japanese people as "very polite and civilised", and that was without even seeing a geisha girl.

On the way to the airport that night our New Zealand friends persisted in asking me how I thought I had addressed Lady Mountbatten the previous evening. I came all over non-committal, but eventually the truth was out; that I had only called her "My dear girl".

The excellent organisation of our leave lapsed slightly as we searched for our plane back to Seoul on a dark night on Haneda. Eventually we were directed onto an American freight plane and settled with relief, but no great comfort, on the floor. It was as the engines started to run up that a crewman asked us, "Youse for Guam?" I had always prided myself on that sort of geography, putting the right name to the right dot on the map, and doubtful though I was on the precise location of the island of Guam in the Pacific, remembered that the island had featured during the Pacific War. I also doubted if I wanted to go there now. We piled out onto the tarmac again, and in due course found another aircraft of the same type to take us back to Seoul. It had on board a father and son, both from the Canadian Brigade and both looking so unwell that we felt, relatively, better.

We eventually took off at 5.40 a.m. and the flight to Seoul against a strong head wind took a full five hours. We arrived back in the Divisional area on 18th March, 1952 to find that the thaw had really set in. The mud was literally heaving, like jam boiling in a saucepan, and our beautiful roads were a very sorry sight.

Although it had been the last thing which we went to Japan for, that few days away from Korea had brought us back into touch with what the rest of the world was doing. The French war in Indo-China under General de Lattre de Tessigny, who we all rated an excellent fellow, seemed to be rising to a crescendo, and none of us doubted that he would win. Sir Winston Churchill was apparently not finding Prime Ministering in peacetime to be all joy, though his move away from rationing and controls was proving most welcome. Mr. Harry Truman was in his seventh year as President of the United States and, as the man who had removed the legendary General MacArthur from Japan, was himself regarded with awe in those parts: it appeared, though, as if he, too, had his problems at home. Relations with the Russians over Germany were still very sensitive, and Malaya and the Canal Zone were actively military and both on our own British plate. All in all, the world around didn't sound very attractive and I, for one, was quite glad to be going back to Korea.

CHAPTER THIRTEEN

FLOODS AND FALSE ALARMS

Back with the Division, the main rumours were of the impending Chinese "Sixth Phase" Offensive, based on some intelligence of substance, and of "germ warfare", based on absolutely nothing, other than perhaps than the aftermath of the rats.

My first job, the very morning I arrived back in Regimental Headquarters was to fly over the roads in our area in one of the Light Liaison Flight Austers. This was done at low level, very low indeed. With concentration, and complete disregard for my queasy tummy, I found I could see most of what was wanted. I'm not sure that my report, that our roads were in a terrible mess, was of any real value, but I was graciously thanked for the unwelcome, but obvious, news.

Lady Mountbatten visited the Division for only a few days, but left everyone the happier for meeting her. I only saw her from a distance, very trim in her Red Cross uniform with matching cap, but later, when a bubble fronted helicopter carried her over us, she waved. I liked to think she had recognised me.

Spring must have been in the air, as I had brought some cheap packets of seeds back from Japan and my parents had managed to include some nasturtium seeds in one of their letters. Major Bill Woods, the Second-in-Command, had his own lettuce seeds, and horticulture became such a topical subject that we thought the war effort would justify the employment of a Korean as a gardener. However, with the soil around RHQ being highly eroded and of doubtful fertility, we planted our seeds at random and let them take their chance. We did so with mixed feelings, as their presence was almost sure to tempt the fates into moving us, and the longer we were static, the less we wanted to move.

Lieutenant Colonel Moore took me with him to visit the Australians the next day. It was the 3rd Battalion of the Royal Australian Regiment, the unit with which I had served six months before, but many of the officers had now been replaced from home. 3 RAR had just been joined in the same Brigade by the 1st Battalion of the same Regiment, making ten infantry units in the Division; five British, three Canadian and two Australian, an excellent mixture. I wrote home:—

> *23 March '52*
>
> The Australians are absolutely wonderful and never seem to worry about anything. Things were incredibly quiet when we visited them, just the odd tank firing occasionally, with a shocking crack, at nothing in particular. The Gunners are now averaging over 1,500 rounds a day of harassing fire too. When we were with the Austs we saw three skeins of geese going over very high, and I wanted to frighten them with my rifle, but was warned that unnecessary shooting might rouse even an Australian!
>
> It still just freezes at night, but we have taken to playing cricket on the "square" in the evenings: we need a new bat and won't get one in a hurry.

Whilst I had been in Japan, one of the Canadian Engineer officers had come into Regimental Headquarters to lend a hand. Sheriff Cooke, to which he answered, had tried to put the aerial reconnaissance of our road system on a less random basis and, out of his ingenious mind, had devised a route plan that covered every mile of our roads north of the Imjin. This became known as the Flight of the Bumble Bee, and a great help it was, though some of the turns to avoid going low over the Chinese or, possibly worse, over our neighbouring allies, were extremely tight.

I flew the Flight of the Bumble Bee three times in the next five days. It took just over an hour, which fitted with the average speed of the Austers of about 80 mph. The method of navigation was for me to sit behind the pilot and tap him on the relevant shoulder each time we needed to turn up the next road to right or left. This worked admirably, but of course we couldn't precisely fly over the road all the time, and our gun areas lay close to the roads. We all agreed that the chances of being hit by an outgoing shell were tiny, but on occasion the thump of the gun firing almost directly underneath was disturbing. The Light Liaison Flight, known as Downward's Devils after their commander, Captain Peter Downward, were out to provide a service and nothing was too much to ask. Only once did a pilot complain, saying, after we had landed, "Dan, you seem to have infinite faith that I can get out of any valley you put me into. Well, you stretched it today, and if you are thinking of changing the route, please tell me another time before we take off."

The spring weather was, by day, really hot and we were soon working in our shirt sleeves. The birds got the message quickly enough and there was soon a fine magpie's nest in the Officers' Mess larch trees. I hadn't the heart to shoot them: pheasant preservation could go too far!

A side effect of the hot weather was the "forest" fires. The three months of intense frost had killed off all the grass, rice and weeds, and the scrub oak and chestnuts, with their undergrowth of creepers and wild azaleas, must have been parched dry too. Before the sap rose the fires started, we never knew how, though there was the usual talk of broken bottles acting as magnifying glasses, and very pretty an uninhabited hillside could be if it blazed at night.

When there was a fire in a minefield beside a road, matters became less attractive. If the rules of minefield laying had been obeyed, no mine should have been nearer than five yards from the perimeter fence, but no one would answer for what the South Koreans might have done when retreating the previous winter. Some of the mines exploded in the flames, but I never heard of anyone being hurt by one as they motored past. As the proud custodian of the minefield records, I did know that more and more of the old minefilds had become of questionable danger to the enemy, but remained a perishing nuisance to ourselves.

A slight diversion from our routine arose when a parcel for me was delivered. Had it not been clearly addressed by my mother, the mutters of "germ warfare" which accompanied its arrival would have resulted in its being dumped before opening. It turned out that my father had remembered that I fancied a morsel of cheese and had sent me one of Danish Blue and one of the round, red skinned Dutch type. The latter remained in excellent condition, but the Red Sea, even in March, had proved too much for the former. It might seem strange to post perishable items to Korea from Britain, but some regiments even received hampers from Fortnums, of which I was sometimes fortunate enough to partake.

Lest life would appear to have been all beer and skittles, the Chinese continued to make their presence felt, though never in sufficient strength to worry others than the units under attack. The Canadians repulsed an onslaught by about 100 Chinamen, and attacks of this size seemed to be the standard for a while, almost as if certain units were being tested against others as part of their final training. My next letters gave the background:—

7 Apr '52

No tremendous excitements, but the Chinaman has been very ill mannered, then caught a very bloody nose, with the KOSB again, who inflicted casualties of over 15-1 in some Company attacks. All we hear back here is a certain amount of thumping.

My old Troop, 3 Troop 12 Field Squadron, had a tragedy last night when some "schu" mines exploded on a lorry, killing five and wounding two. A terrible cut, and more than the Squadron had lost in nine months here.

I've been for one walk this week with the Colonel, seeing how difficult it would be to build a new road, and one more flight round the countryside. I like to think that I am getting my air legs, as it was very bumpy and the pilot looked worse than me.

There is just the odd sprout of new grass, and the larch trees which support the Mess roof are sprouting too. The dust on the roads is already frightful, as bad as mid-summer.

Sun, 20 Apr '52

As a Captain I now get 32/- (£1.60) a day, which is very fair beer money, plus what should be about a £50 Korean gratuity when we leave here. My nasturtiums are doing fine, there are at least ten good plants and I expect some more will come through. The Jap seeds aren't doing too well. I'm afraid I put them in too deep.

One of our major troubles here, as at home, is with breaking sledge hammer handles. This road work just eats them up, as does knocking in pickets for barbed wire, especially with lots of unskilled users. I believe something of the tubular steel type, like a golf club, might pay, as the carpenters can't keep up with fitting new helves.

Tom Marquis, who has been Adjutant since I took over from him as Intelligence Officer, left here for home yesterday, and we were very sorry to see him go. Peter Leslie has come from the CRE's HQ to take on the job. The place continues to get green: Oliver Keef, who is the new Liaison Officer, even found a japonica bush, and the Colonel heard a cuckoo yesterday morning: we think we ought to write to *The Times*. Meanwhile, all the dead leaves are still clinging to the scrub oak and chestnut.

Yesterday we had snow again and, like a chump, I chose to climb that particularly evil hill (355) which we have now been given back by the Americans. It has been well and truly fought over since we first took it last October, and I'm afraid it will be again if the Chinks ever want to advance in this part of the world: just stiff with booby traps and very unpleasant. All the same, there was a wonderful view from the top, but I certainly felt very sorry for the Infantry, with their trenches running with water like streams. Everything seems exceptionally quiet. I hope that the Chinese will get fed up with it all. On average they haven't gained any ground for a year.

I flew only once this week on a lovely day, all very pleasant.

28 Apr '52

It is pouring with rain here, so I've no dobut that the day's troubles are not over. Very soon we will get endless calls saying that, "The culverts have washed out and the roads are under water, and *What* are *You* going to do about it?" I suppose the Chinaman has his own road problems, but he could certainly shake us on these rainy days. To have a go now, though, he would have to be enormously strong to dislodge us, and anyone who stays in the open gets hurt, as both sides have so much artillery.

However, I've been out with the Colonel once, going right out in front of the Infantry in broad daylight without the slightest enemy reaction: all very queer. I also went for a walk down a splendid new road which 12 Squadron are building. I found some miniature iris two or three inches high, and I'll try to get a few bulbs. My nasturtiums can't stop laughing at this rain, but the frost caught Major Woods' cucumbers, truly tragic!

Our infantry battalions used to spend about two months in front line positions, then one month in reserve a couple of miles back. Each time a new battalion went into the line there was a demand for new anti-personnel minefields between the forward platoons and the opposition, usually supported by a request to move, or remove, some of the existing fields which failed to fit into the tactical plan of the new unit on the old ground. As all the convenient ground had already been sown with mines, the new fields had to be well out into No Man's Land and ever nearer to the Chinese, who, hardly surprisingly were none too keen on the activities of the Commonwealth engineers. As the fields were laid, so the report forms came into my office for marking on the master map and for safekeeping. It was up to me to ensure that the standard of reporting was uniformly good, and it was only too easy, from the comfort of my warm chair miles back, to demand training field precision and classroom neatness in every report. It was when Jock Cormack, a red headed and robust Troop Commander, submitted a report with the heading "Laid in the presence of the enemy. Accuracy cannot be guaranteed." that I realised that allowance needed to be made. In fact, it was very seldom that the reports were not full and excellent. Every officer knew that he might well be asked to lift a similar field later, and there was no doubt that being in possession of the relevant record made this task quicker and safer.

There was an occasion when one of the Australian battalions had just gone back into the line and wanted part of a minefield lifted in a hurry so that a platoon could be positioned there that night. The Sapper officer whose Troop supported them undertook to do the task without waiting to obtain the minefield record from us at RHQ, which would have involved a delay of at least two hours. He could see that the trip wire mines were laid to a pattern which could be established from outside the minefield fence, so he went in and neutralised them in no time. He then told the delighted Australians that they could go back onto the ground, which had the added attraction of some good trenches remaining in existence from the occupants before last. Quite unknown to our officer and quite outside our normal minelaying habits, those who had mined the area when it was vacated had, for good measure, mined the slit trenches as well. The first Australian who jumped in one of the trenches consequently blew off his foot.

The Sapper officer, a conscientious and able fellow, could well have been shaken completely off balance by this. However, without further to do, he took the minefield record, which had by now been sent forward, and set about clearing the "schu" mines from the bottom of the trenches, and a nastier task would be difficult to devise.

"Schu" mines were made of wood, so could not be detected with our mine detectors, and very little pressure was needed to set them off. Slit trenches were narrow holes, not much wider than a man and about four feet deep. To climb down into the trench without dislodging a clod of earth onto a mine, or then stepping on one, must have been the most difficult part of the job and I would have liked to have known how it was done, but the subject was not one to pursue. The officer involved was just so sorry about the previous accident that he certainly did not expect praise for his subsequent action, but what he did was as brave as anything I heard of in Korea.

With the spring growth starting to entangle even the newest of trip wires, faith in our minefields as stoppers of Chinamen had all but evaporated. Now we were told that mines were in such plentiful supply that fields with the mines sown much more densely could be laid. After seeing that train load of anti-personnel mines soon after I arrived in

Korea I had always wondered why there was a supply problem, but was surprised just how far the pendulum had now swung. It was decided that no more mines would be laid with trip wires and that, instead, twenty would be laid with pressure fuzes to cover the same frontage as one mine with its trip wires had previously. This would mean about one mine every nine inches along the length of a minefield and, as a man had two feet each about four and a half inches wide, it appeared at first sight that every man would be almost certain to step on a mine.

I should explain that, both to make the mines difficult to find and to stop them setting each other off, they were well spaced out in the minefield, but the overall pattern resulted in four mines to every yard of front, which sounded nigh on impenetrable. Nobody claimed that the new proposals were based on deep mathematics, but we had been taught enough statistics at Cambridge to make me question whether just the width of a fellow's foot was the only dimension we needed to consider. I felt that length of stride might have something to do with it as well, and was stupid enough to mention my doubts in the presence of my seniors. "The easiest way to find out if they'll tread on them or not, Dan, is to stage a trial. You go and stage one!" Once I had understood that the trial was not to be with live mines, but with little markers on the ground to represent them, I was attracted by the idea.

I took the two NCOs who helped me in the intelligence section and a driver, and we set off to a typical hillside to lay our typical minefield. With little squares of paper fixed on the ground by nails, it didn't take us long to lay a representative panel of six rows of mines, with a cluster of four mines every six yards on each of the rows. We assumed that our hypothetical Chinamen would be moving through the minefield by night, without having made any attempt to clear a path through it. That seemed to fit their tactics, so, to play the game properly, it was agreed that our representative enemy must be blindfolded. The Corporal and the Lance Corporal had already, unknown to me, allocated the morning's duties. I was to be the Chinaman, the Corporal would go backwards and forwards through the minefield with me, watching for every time I put a foot on one of the squares of paper, and the Lance Corporal would note the results. They seemed to take great pleasure in blindfolding me most effectively, with the driver taking little part, except for saying, "Now I've seen everything."

I really was blind, and had in no way assessed the hazards to which I was being submitted. I tripped and stumbled, usually painfully, on every traverse of the field, to the extent that I had to insist that I was warned of impending danger. To cut a long and tiring morning short, I went through the minefield twenty times, about sixty yards on each occasion, walking at various speeds and at various angles. At the end of it all I had only trodden, or fallen, on four mines.

Back we went to RHQ, where I announced that the chance of a man standing on a mine when crossing one of our new minefields would only be one in five. "That confirms what we have now worked out," I was told, "so, when possible we are going to lay M2 bouncing mines." Most of the minefields laid in our Divisional area after that, and there were many of them, were laid to the new pattern, and the total number of anti-personnel mines in the ground soared, from about twenty thousand through thirty, forty to fifty thousand within a few months. The problem was how to attract the Chinese into them, but it was also pleasing to assure ourselves that the minefields had deterred them from coming.

With it now being virtually certain that, so far as the United Nations were concerned, the Korean War was likely to remain static, it was obviously undesirable to leave the front line soldiers entirely dependent upon supplies that had to cross the unpredictable and often unfriendly River Imjin. The American Engineers had done splendidly to keep the floating bridges open throughout the winter ice, but now floods were again probable, and no floating bridge could survive the Imjin floods. However, based on recent experience, no fixed bridge could either, and the Koreans delighted in telling us their old legend "Bridge the Imjin, and die".

Undeterred by the legends, Colonel Myers, our Commander Royal Engineers, asked the Americans to build us two permanent high level bridges, and their specialist construction units had these well under way before mid-summer. Both bridges were to have the roadway fifty feet above the ice level of the river, the one at PINTAIL to be of concrete and steel, the other at TEAL to have the steel girders carrying the roadway supported on enormous timber trestles. Both were interesting projects in their own right, but military engineers are concerned not just with construction, but destruction as well, and it was the latter that had always tended to attract me. To have a bridge is delightful so long as your own forces are on the far side, but highly dangerous if the enemy suddenly arrive.

High level PINTAIL bridge being built.

With our enemy only six miles north of PINTAIL, we would have very little time to prepare the big new bridges for demolition, if that were ever needed. A way of reducing the time required would be to build boxes to hold explosives onto the girders beforehand, and I was sent to ask the Major commanding the US Army Engineers building at PINTAIL to do this. To me it seemed an entirely reasonable request, but it didn't take me long to discover that he thought otherwise. I knew him to be normally a polite and co-operative man, but there was something about his new bridge that had got into him. It had taken him and his men a lot of trouble, it had tested their skill to the full and it had proved a dangerous task, to the extent that one poor fellow had already fallen off and broken his neck: the Korean legend was proving all too correct.

It took much longer than I had expected to convince my ally that it was in all our interests to prevent hordes of Chinese pouring over the bridge, especially as his own unit's camp was not many miles back down the same road. The demolition boxes were duly welded on, and I learnt to appreciate the sense of creative artistry that bridge building can inspire.

By early May the hot weather was back, the flies were pestilential and
the wild azaleas were giving whole hillsides a beautiful purple tinge. To
celebrate the end of winter we moved our Command Post, both the 3
tonners and their associated tenting, out of its hole and into "summer
quarters". There was strong talk of moving the Mess out of its much
deeper hole but, as that would mean moving my nasturtiums which
were doing so well, I managed to change the conversation.

Nasturtiums, however, were not my main concern when, on 19th
May, 1952, I wrote:—

> I went out with the Colonel early today and just missed seeing a real
> live Chinaman through a telescope.

What I didn't mention was that another one, whom we never saw and
who must have been a lot closer, just missed us with an unknown
explosive projectile. We thought that perhaps it came from a rocket
launcher.

I spent the same afternoon looking at minefields on Hill 355 with my
old friend Angus, which gave us a chance to discuss shooting plans for
the next season. Martin Keer would have gone home by then, so
another keen shot would be needed, and Angus was just the man.

355 felt, as usual, a thoroughly unfriendly hill, and the feeling was
not helped by knowing that Colin Carr who, like Angus, commanded a
Troop in 55 Field Squadron, had lost a foot when laying a particularly
dangerous minefield there earlier in the week. He had been awarded an
immediate MC, but that made the place feel no more pleasant. Even as
Angus and I strolled over the gentler slopes an ill mannered Chinaman
kept dropping small mortar bombs near us. We heard the pop of the
mortar, so knew a bomb was coming, but only the slightest of rustles
just before it landed announced its arrival. We couldn't imagine what
had made him object to us so personally.

The following night I went to see some night minelaying on real
ankle twisting country in front of our infantry positions. The night was
excessively quiet, and the party tapping in the steel fence pickets with
their sledge hammers were not our most popular brethren, but the
Chinese did not react. There was some artillery harassing fire in front of
the next battalion, but the startling noise came from the Besa machine
gun on a Centurion tank up the hill behind us. It fired occasional long
bursts well over our heads, and each time I was not alone in nearly
jumping out of my skin.

By the end of May I had been in Korea nine months, or half the maximum length of a tour there. A lot could happen in that time but, meanwhile, life had many compensations, as I reported home:—

Sun, 25 May '52

Everyone from the UK in the Division has received an individual parcel from Australia this week, and jolly good parcels too! Awfully kind of them. The Aussies here say they reckon they've been sent to try and make us emigrate. They also say that, if so, their people at home must be very misguided!

We haven't had more than a couple of drops of rain all the month and it has been really lovely with temperatures up to 94°, though nearly a frost last night.

There's talk of those who were here last winter being moved before next. As I'd probably only get a shocking transit job in Japan, I reckon I'd rather stay here.

No excitements. We still build endless roads and are trying to ditch and culvert the others properly, to beat the rains. I've now got to get down to the ghastly job of writing the Regiment's official "War Diary", which I always leave to the end of the month."

30 May '52

Peter Duckworth was slightly wounded three days ago with a shell splinter in the muscle of his leg. His Squadron caught some unpleasant shelling in their harbour area. Peter's quite all right: I went down to the Norwegian Hospital expecting to find him in bed, instead of which he was walking easily and has now been sent back as good as new. Peter says he was lying under a tank, so that was not the best of places to be!

Otherwise, nothing very fierce. The Infantry are patrolling and, as usual, some of it isn't very pleasant. Here we still sit in the same Officers' Mess hole we've been in for eight months, and are rather attached to it."

My visit to NORMASH, the Norwegian Mobile Army Surgical Hospital that supported our Division, had not been entirely with a view to seeing Peter. There were reputed to be some very pretty nurses there, but if that were the case, I unfortunately did not come upon them.

June 1952 started with all the intelligence sources, such as they were, telling of an impending Chinese offensive. The air photo interpreters added joy to their predictions by suggesting that large holes which had been dug near the front line must be for use as mass graves. We sat and waited, hoping that not just our defences but also our roads and bridges would hold if the attack came.

I made my next "Bumble Bee" recce flight of the roads at dawn after a rainy night. The Auster pilot had one of the wirelesses tuned to our

Regimental net, which should have speeded transmissions considerably. As it was, those who knew my normal leisurely transmissions from a jeep could not believe that I was covering the ground so fast, and kept blocking the air by asking me to, "Say again your location." Luckily our Signals Officer, Dick Sullivan, was in contact and managed to restore sense before I landed.

For the next few days our small airstrip was unusually busy, as Field Marshal Lord Alexander, the Defence Minister, came on 14th June accompanied by thirteen light aircraft which carried, in addition to a vast staff, General Mark Clark from Japan, General Van Fleet, who commanded in Korea, and General O'Daniell, our Army Corps Commander. We only saw them through binoculars, and they looked a very happy travelling circus. Thankfully there was no thought in our Division of staging a special attack as a spectacle for the visitors, but others further along our line would not have been beyond it.

It was at this time that I was one of a few officers selected for the doubtful honour of attending a course on "escape and evasion", or "what to do if you are taken prisoner". I never claimed to be the Commonwealth Division's greatest asset, but had hoped that it would

Engineer Mess Garden. Summer 1952. Captain Roy Gout, Major Joe Black and Asahi beer.

never be hinted so publicly that I was expendable. None of us, needless to say, had the slightest intention of becoming prisoners but the theme, just in case we were, was that it would be much appreciated if we could please escape and then tell our friends where the thousand or so Britons already in captivity were. It was not explained why none of them had escaped previously, nor with what super powers we were to be gifted to waft us back to our own lines. Our lecturer was a much decorated and tough airman, who had made various escapes, the last one successful, in the German war. It took little imagination to see him in the part, especially as he had blue eyes and admitted that he spoke fluent German. None of us thought that we looked like Koreans, nor did we speak the language and, if the prison camps turned out to be in Manchuria, as was possible, nor did we speak Chinese. They were an interesting couple of days and made a change from our routine duties, but none of us came away convinced that we were born Houdinis. The one fact that I remembered later was that, if one had to live on vegetables and greenstuff alone, it needed a tremendous quantity to keep a chap's energy up. Luckily I have never had to put this to the test.

An unexpected aftermath to that course, and certainly a matter of pure chance, was that two of our small number were the next two officers not to return from patrol. Unfortunately neither of them returned at the end of the war either.

I had an unusual morning on 17th June watching one of the Inniskilling Dragoon Guards' tank Squadrons setting out across the No Man's Land valley and onto the hills on the enemy side. Colonel Moore took me with him and, to be there at dawn, we had to get up at 3.30 a.m. As we left our jeep on a steep reverse slope, before climbing up to the observation post on top of the hill, I was so bold as to ask the Colonel if he thought the hill was really steep enough to protect the jeep from incoming shells. He said he thought it was.

The static tanks covering the sortie started firing their 20 pounder guns at 5 o'clock, and it was a memorable sight to see the frequent flashes along the hill tops in the half light. That tanks could climb to such perches seemed unbelievable: the tremendous crack of their high velocity guns was soon joined by the crackle of the machine guns of the dozen or so tanks crossing the valley. Chatter, chatter, chatter went their 7.92mm Besas, we were blessed if we knew at what. We were later told that every bush that might have held a nasty man with a bazooka or other anti-tank weapon had been anointed, but that no one had been at home. As it turned out, all the Chinese opposite had very sensibly gone to the bottom of their bottomless holes, and stayed there.

In the meanwhile I had left Colonel Peter in the Observation Post trench, which was uncomfortably crowded, and had found myself a short tunnel through the hilltop to a small trench with a perfect view over the valley. I was delighted and surprised that no one else had found it, until I discovered that I was directly under the gun of a well camouflaged Centurion tank, which luckily didn't fire whilst I was there, though my stay was not prolonged. Had it done so, the blast would certainly have knocked my head off.

Exactly what our tanks were trying to achieve was not clear to me, though the main aim may have been to disrupt any Chinese attack plans. With the exception of one tank which got stuck early on, the others in the Squadron reached the bottom of the enemy hills, found nothing of interest, drew no anti-tank fire, and retired home in good order. With them back, the covering tanks reversed off the skyline over our heads and it was not until then that the Chinese gunners started to shell us very precisely with biggish guns, and then kept it up slowly but steadily for forty-five minutes.

By this time I was in a Canadian dugout on the reverse slope of the hill, as were the CO and Major Derek Fletcher, the officer commanding 55 Field Squadron. I counted the shells falling locally and tried to read a truly terrible book on film stars belonging to my host, who was not the most prepossessing member of our Division. Through the open doorway we could see one of the Skins' Centurions which had motored through a major barbed wire fence and ended up with hundreds of pounds of wire wrapped around one of its track sprockets. Even a tank can be stopped by too much wire, so a member of the crew, whom I later discovered was a national serviceman named Trooper Manners, emerged with an enormous pair of wire cutters and, completely unperturbed, set about freeing the tangle. The shells, we reckoned they were Russian 122mm, continued to arrive, several of them going off in the air immediately over the pinioned tank. Each time, as the dust and smoke cleared, we expected to see Manners lying wounded or dead, and each time there he was happily clipping away as if topiary were his hobby. Another tank drew alongside to help, and it turned out to be commanded by Peter Duckworth, who had apparently been on the ridgeline over our heads all morning. One meets one's family in the strangest places.

Peter asked us back for a gin with his Squadron, we all felt that we deserved one, but at that moment a message requested Lieutenant Colonel Moore to visit Hill 159, an exposed feature just to the north of us. The Chinese gunners had just transferred their attention to it, so I suggested that Peter's gin would be better for us. Off we went though to 159, but later managed to accept a good lunch at the Skins' Regimental Headquarters, where we filled in the details of the morning's outing. Like me, Lieutenant Colonel Moore noticed that our jeep had been slightly peppered by shell fragments in the "safe" location where we had left it, but I did not pursue the subject.

The tank that was stuck out in the open valley caused, as we expected, plenty of problems. It was in full view of the Chinese artillery observers and on nasty soft ground that made towing difficult. At nightfall it also provided a centre of attraction for rival patrols, and its retrieval resulted in more British casualties than did the whole of the rest of the sortie.

The reason for the tank's breakdown was later established. It and its companions had intentionally motored through some of our own beastly little "schu" mines, knowing that they shouldn't be hurt by them, they being the best tanks in the world, and 50 tons of steel at that. By bad chance the damaged tank had touched its belly on a paddy bund as it crossed it and, "Pop", or so the explosion sounded when muffled by the bulk of the tank, went the half pound charge of TNT in one of the mines. This happened to have been precisely under the mounting of the tank's gear box, and the thump had been enough to stop the tank. Luckily we, the Royal Engineers, were in no way blamed for the hidden powers of our mines, and the Skins continued to invite us to some very congenial parties.

My letter home that evening showed the contrast between our life, south of the Imjin and six or seven miles from the front line, and that of those who had to stay on the forward hills where we had spent the morning:—

17 June '52

Tomorrow I'm off to Seoul to scrounge for the Guest Night we're giving the Signals next week. (The Royal Signals had been formed from the Royal Engineers in the 1914-18 War and it had become traditional for each to make the other their guests on alternate years.) I've got to see an American gunner about ice cream, the ice factory for ice, the Canadians for dozens of things which they get in there rations which we don't and, to cap it all, a Major in Seoul to get a sack of spuds! Fresh potatoes are, in the words of the country "Hav-a-no", but we just must have them to go with the meat. We've got Australian hock at 4/6d (22½p) a bottle: hope it's not too sweet.

What we think may be wild orchids, but more likely are lilies, are out at present with great big orange trumpets. Some of my nasturtiums have flowered, much too small, but there are some good ones yet to come. We are down on rainfall for the year, but are preparing for the old Imjin to flood. Last year it rose 36 feet in 24 hours, which is no good for bridging.

The party went well, as my sequel letter told:—

25 June '52

Well, this was meant to be the day for the big Chinese attack and it hasn't come yet, so, as is frequent, poor old Intelligence have had their leg pulled.

Here, in what is meant to be the rainy season, it's a red hot drought. The humidity was almost like Calcutta yesterday, and I've never seen a thirstier bunch of rogues assemble for the Guest Night we gave the Signals.

We had a huge marquee 70 feet long, with a big kitchen tent and a cloakroom off it as wings. We sat down to dinner with General Cassels as the Guest of Honour and 73 officers in all. I was in charge of food, and by good chance found a catering warrant officer who was a real master and produced a rare good meal. Iced clear soup (he'd used two turkeys in it), some excellent beef steak with tinned asparagus in cheese sauce, peas and two types of spud, then ice cream, fruit, and angels on horseback. It really did go awfully well, and our quite untrained waiters (mainly volunteers from the Canadian Field Squadron) were wonderful. We drank *"The Queen"* for the first time, and £44 of drink was drunk which, with gin at 7/9d (38p) a bottle, is quite something. Beer alone worked out at half a gallon a head, so we were pretty rowdy and the breakages bill is also fairly heavy. The Australian hock was excellent.

At the beginning, nothing looked like arriving. The ice melted, but we got more and more and, eventually two lots of ice cream, which we British never see, one from an American and one from the Canadians. Yes. What a War!

Our Division has had quite an active week, as have most of the others. Both sides are so firmly dug in that anything in the way of an attack proves very costly. Rather like the First War, I should think, but No Man's Land here is a valley.

John Dunn, the subaltern who is meant to help me with my Intelligence Officer job has been slightly wounded by a mine. Someone had tied a tripwire to the perimeter fence, instead of five yards clear of it:

thoroughly bad form. I'm going to see him in hospital tomorrow. He has been out marking minefields most of his time, so him being away luckily won't give me more work in the Command Post.

A couple of days ago I got up at 3 a.m. to watch one of our raids across the valley and to debrief our Sapper officer who was on it. As usual nothing was achieved, as the Infantry could not even reach the Chinese positions due to the gunfire, let alone get into them. I did my debriefing at the Regimental Aid Post, where about fifteen wounded men were waiting their turn to see the doctor. They answered my questions remarkably politely!

I've had a wisdom tooth taken out in the back of a 3 ton dental wagon. Painless, but I thought I was brave.

We have a lovely pair of swallows nesting on a guy rope of our tent. We were intending to move the tent, which is only temporary, but now it'll have to stay. The RSM is building us a lovely log hut, which should be the best in the Division!

Life remained relatively uneventful, but I always had more than enough to do. About once a fortnight I would try to call on the Intelligence officers of the forward infantry battalions, and also on their Brigade Headquarters. Such occasions involved meeting many folk who were becoming good friends, and the problem always was to leave them

Tent for Royal Engineers/Royal Signals Guest Night. Seven miles from the front line.

and complete the day's task. Whenever I had the chance I used to call upon my friend "Stew", the Gunner, and his Troop of 4.2 inch mortars. Because their range was so short, they had to be positioned well forward with the Infantry. The mortars had been having trouble with what were known as "creepers", meaning that rather than going to their prescribed range, the bombs fell drastically short. The Infantry, over whose heads the mortars always fired, tended not to appreciate this, but some thought that matters were being rather over dramatised. There had even been talk of taking the mortars out of action. It was on an occasion when I was taking tea with Stew's Troop that he, from his observation post, called for fire, and not just as a demonstration to please his friend. A single mortar was firing, and it and its crew treated me to a classic "creeper" exhibition.

The first bomb left the mortar and presumably cleared the Infantry as intended, as we never heard its explosion. Those of us behind the mortar could see the second bomb going up much more slowly, and it fell half a mile in front of us, just short of the ridgeline where the infantry positions were. The third bomb halved that distance to about 400 yards, and the crack as it exploded was decidedly unfriendly: the greatest advantage claimed for the 4.2 inch mortar was the punch that its 20lb bomb packed. A few strong words were addressed to the mortar before the next bomb was fired, but they must have fallen upon deaf ears as the bomb crept to just one hundred yards in front of us, sufficiently close for prudence to dictate evasive action. We then felt foolish, as it did not go off, presumably because the fuze had not been given a sufficient enough thump to arm it. Stew was then informed that that particular mortar was being taken out of action for a while.

It took years before the cause of "creeper" bombs was understood and the fault rectified, but there were some fatal accidents before then, one of them unfortunately in Stew's Troop.

Our Divisional Engineers had plenty of British and Canadian representatives, with a few New Zealanders to add tone, but, despite their strong presence in the Infantry, there were no Royal Australian Engineers until Captain Ian Gilmore arrived. He was given command of a British Field Troop and fitted in so well that, apart from his wide brimmed bush hat, it was hard to remember his origin. Now, with several of the Regiment's original officers from Tripoli due to go home, there was a general shuffle, and Ian joined us in Regimental Headquarters. I was delighted, as he took a great interest in my intelligence duties and quickly knew as much about the task as I did. With the shooting season only three months off, and with the chance of another short leave in Japan, it was most reassuring to know that an efficient stand-in was already on the spot.

Quite soon after Ian's arrival with us, a second Australian Sapper, Captain Philip Greville, arrived and was attached to the First Battalion of the Royal Australian Regiment as their Pioneer Officer. He and Ian were old friends, so Phil managed to call on us frequently, usually when suitable beverages were being served. Much too soon, though, he was ambushed and reported missing from a party checking the minefield fences in front of his battalion positions. After the end of the War, thirteen months later when I was back in England, it was a very great pleasure to see Phil's name amongst the prisoners of the Chinese who had been repatriated.

When Angus, too, arrived in our Headquarters as Adjutant, I began to think that my plans for pheasant shooting in Korea had gone unbelievably well. In war, the post of Adjutant was considered highly important and that Angus, who was one of the more junior Captains in the Regiment, had been selected for the job was a great compliment to his ability: I was much too junior to have had an influence on his posting, but that didn't stop some folk suggesting that I had. His arrival set me worrying because, nearly a year after my arrival in the country, the wooden stock of my shotgun remained broken. I had ever sent it back to Japan, hoping that a Japanese armourer of repute could mend it, but it must have gone to the wrong man, as it came back untouched. In the meanwhile, Angus had purchased an American shotgun from the PX in Seoul. When I saw what was on offer, I was all the more keen to have my own repaired.

We were told that the Peace Talks in Pan Mun Jon were continuing, but so was the Korean War. Considerable international consternation had recently been caused by the American bombing of the North Korean power stations, although we who were on the spot could see no harm in it: any way of knocking some sense into our enemies would be welcome. The peace talks had, in our opinion, gone entirely the Chinese way, by giving them time to regain their balance after we had knocked them off their winter positions, without us learning anything useful about the prisoners they held. There was nothing obvious for us to gain by advancing up North Korea again, but the Chinese still might try to knock us out of the South.

Although there had been no major attacks by, or onto, our Division for several months, neither side allowed the other to take liberties. The war reverted to the old sport of trying to catch prisoners, in the hope that they would tell all and, if this could not be done on patrol in No Man's Land, the next best hope was to bite off a protruding outpost.

The American system of defence consisted of a Main Line of Resistance, the MLR, forward of which was the outpost line, each outpost comprising about half a company of infantry, or sixty men. It was intended that the outposts should hold out whilst the MLR was strengthened to prevent a Chinese breakthrough. The concept was based on a breakthrough being planned, but it seldom was: instead, the Chinese made the overwhelming of outposts their main speciality. They learnt how to complete the task in depressingly short time, then departed with their prisoners, leaving the small patch of ground invitingly empty again.

The Chinese had no outpost line, so their forward positions formed part of their MLR, which was hard to penetrate. We, the Commonwealth Division, didn't have outposts either, but we often kept small pockets of men forward of our defences, and called them standing patrols, or listening posts. It was not difficult to locate these on a static battlefield, and the Chinese delighted in nipping them off too. The First Battalion of the Royal Norfolk Regiment, to whom Angus McKay Forbes and his Troop had been affiliated, had been having trouble in this respect on a feature known as Crete, quite close to where I had been with the King's Own Scottish Borderers the year before.

Each time the Norfolks put out a listening post on Crete, the Chinese either captured the hillock on which they sat, or sent the small patrol home with scant dignity. This vexed the Norfolks, who lit fires on the hill by day, then withdrew by night, forlornly hoping to fox the Chinese into thinking the feature was still occupied. We had been hearing of all this back in Regimental Headquarters, and I had become increasingly attached to the idea of an explosive device which, if it could be fired through electric wires from a distance, might lead the Chinamen into thinking that the hill was still held. These devices became known as battle blankets, and consisted of a selection of the small explosive stores that were easily available to us, pinned, sewn, or clipped to an old blanket. We were sure that the idea must have been tried before, but none of us had heard of it in the form in which it eventualy evolved.

In addition to the blanket, the stores required were a length of black coloured safety fuse, which burnt at the slow rate of two feet in one minute, a longer length of so-called instantaneous fuse, which was orange in colour and burnt fast and violently, some detonators and a few one ounce guncotton primers which, if set off by a burning fuse and a detonator, made much the same noise as a hand grenade. By carefully cutting a nick in both types of fuse, their trains of powder could be exposed and then bound together with sticky tape. By making these joins every few inches along the main length of safety fuse, new pops and bangs could be initiated every few seconds, even including simulated machine gun fire from a series of knots tied in the instantaneous fuse.

We tested the first of our battle blankets in private, and thought it had potential. I now wanted to try it on those who had no idea of its origin, and could think of none better than the staff of Divisional Headquarters, just over the rise from us. I told my friends in the Operations tent of what I had planned and obtained their approval, but first they warned some of the more senior, or potentially trigger happy, officers.

There was no doubt that the blanket achieved its aim. I lit the safety fuse just before dusk with the blanket a hundred yards away from the main command area, and no one would have believed the invigorating effect its explosions had on staff officers and clerks not normally accustomed to warlike diversions. It all took a bit of explaining, but we remained encouraged.

Corporal Ford, an able and steady NCO from Angus' old Troop, now took over and built the battle blanket he would leave on the hillock at the far end of Crete. The Chinese had again been there the night before, so the Royal Norfolks had made great play of occupying it again the next day. Corporal Ford laid nearly a quarter of a mile of electric cable to the hillock, then unfolded his battle blanket and, at dusk, connected up is initiator. After dark the small party with Corporal Ford withdrew with great stealth from the feature, but two platoons of the Norfolks remained in ambush nearby.

Sure enough, well into the night, the arrival of the Chinese was reported. Corporal Ford then pushed down the handle of his electric exploder to ignite the safety fuse of his battle blanket up on the hill. Within seconds there was the first bang of a guncotton primer, just like a grenade, then another, then crack, crack, as a couple of detonators represented rifle shots, then further bangs, and automatic fire, all overlapping. As had been hoped, this proved too much for the Chinese, who promptly attacked the top of the hill. The two platoons of Royal Norfolks came up behind them and found their enemy looking into empty holes. The Norfolks killed twelve Chinese and took six hearty prisoners, at relatively small loss to themselves.

Those six prisoners posed, for me, one of the most interesting questions of the War. None had been badly wounded and one was quite untouched, but they were all taken back through the Norfolk's Regimental Aid Post and given any necessary medical attention. Before morning all six had managed to die, the very last thing that had been wanted. Prisoners were difficult enough to take without disasters like that and, as an Intelligence Officer, I felt it part of my duty to establish the facts. I can only record that I got nowhere. None of the dead men was found to have carried any means of committing suicide, so all we could conclude was that they had each, and individually, willed themselves to die, all within a few hours of each other. Kipling, I thought, was on the right lines with his "East is East, and West is West, and never the twain shall meet."

An immediate award of the Military Medal was made to Corporal Ford for his part in this successful and unusual action, but sadly he was killed only a few weeks later when a motor grader on which he was travelling went off the road and rolled over.

Our minefields certainly affected our daily lives, so it was pleasing to hear that the Chinese took note of them. We heard that their trainees were expected to make their way through a live anti-personnel minefield during their eighth one hour period of mines training. It sounded a most effective way of separating good and bad recruits.

I had an unwelcome refresher in minefield breaching myself, when I had to retrieve another dead Korean from one of our rear area minefields. The body lay on a steep slope and I had to work my way down to it. The undergrowth was nothing like as thick as when I had previously been confronted with a similar task, so the trip wires were easier to find. The problem lay in carrying the victim up the hillside and out of the minefield.

Whatever else our mines achieved, they proved a real hazard to the North Korean infiltrators who must have been passing in quite large numbers through our lines. Oliver Keef, one of my companions in Regimental Headquarters, undertook many more than his share of rescues or retrievals, always with no fuss. Those of us who thus avoided some of this very unpleasant work were most grateful, though we didn't tell Oliver too strongly, lest he volunteered for it less frequently.

The wet heat of Korea in July was much nastier than I had expected, so much so that when I accompanied Colonel Moore up to a company position on a steep, but not very high, hill, neither of us could ever remember feeling hotter. Luckily, though, the nights were much cooler than in the sticky tropics, and there was no doubt that much of the countryside was beautiful, if viewed in a favourable spirit. On 11th July, 1952 my letter home reported:—

> Angus and I went for a bathe (which combines with a bath) this afternoon, and the beautiful silver sands by the Imjin were hot enough to burn our feet. There are a mass of wild raspberries: in fact the most common weed, as we thought, has turned out to be a sort of raspberry (they taste like blackberries, and are awfully good too). There are also masses of yellowy-orange lilies growing wild everywhere.
>
> I walked across to look at a plane which had made a false landing on our airstrip after an air strike (pilot OK), and put up a hen pheasant and five very well grown cheepers. I think the birds survive despite the crows and magpies, as the vermin seem to emigrate out, though big bunches are now back. There are also plenty of foxes, and the rats must play hell too.
>
> The most beautiful emerald green moth has just landed on my writing paper. It has gold wing tips. This is a great country for queer insects!

The July rains very considerably waited until our new permanent bridges over the Imjin were open. The first rise of the river for the summer was nineteen feet, including eight of them in one hour. Although we knew that very much worse would come, the sense of "all right so far" was reassuring. This didn't last long as, within the week, the Imjin achieved a thirty-nine feet rise. TEAL, the high trestle bridge, was cleanly washed out in the middle, leaving an unbridgable gap. Luckily, the steel piers of the PINTAIL bridge near our headquarters held, though the build up of debris, as usual including complete wooden houses and parts of bridges from upstream, had fluttered many hearts.

One of our Sappers had been near the middle of TEAL when he felt the pier under him tilt. He started to run and, every seventy feet along the bridge, as he went over each pier, felt it toppling. He kept on

Teal bridge soon after building.

running until he reached dry land. At Bideford in Devon the locals used to hold an annual competition to see if anyone could run the length of the bridge whilst the church clock struck twelve. Spectators considered that our Sapper could have taught those fine folk from the banks of the River Torridge several lessons. They also observed that, once the first pier had toppled, it had not been the weight of water that had pulled down four more, but the vast numbers of strong telephone cables laid along the side of the roadway which had the strength to pull over each of the next piers, before themselves breaking.

The rain also proved destructive to many of the infantry bunkers, to the extent that our Canadian Field Squadron again had to open up a lumber camp in the rear areas and the Commanding Officer, knowing that I enjoyed using an axe, took me to see them. We were invited to test our skill, and I was thankful that, due to seniority, the Colonel was allocated a much larger tree to cut down than me.

In the middle of August, nearly a year after my arrival in Korea, I was, at short notice, offered another few days' leave in Japan, this time to the British base at Kure. As Peter Francis, one of my companions from R & R in Tokyo could also come, I accepted, and we flew from

Seoul the next day. The airport for Kure, Iwa Kuni, was twenty miles away, which meant a journey of two and a half hours in a launch along the beautiful fjord-like coastline of the Inland Sea.

We stayed in the Britcom Engineer Regiment's Mess, which had been built for Japanese naval officers, and they had done themselves proud, with even a huge ballroom. Most of our hosts were very generous Australians and, by sheer coincidence, the three New Zealand officers who had been with us in Tokyo turned up again as our companions.

My boxes of china from our last leave had arrived home safely and my parents had said they approved of the pattern. "What a pity, though," wrote my mother, "that the ninety-three pieces did not include any vegetable dishes." The most worthy quest of my leave in Kure was to find those dishes, and Peter was only too keen to join me in it, as he had bought china of the same pattern. We went up and down the many china shops, remembering less and less exactly what we had bought before. Eventually we saw just the vegetable dishes we wanted, and convinced ourselves that they were of the right pattern. We asked their price. "Gentlemen, do you realise that it is nearly as cheap to buy them in a sixty-six piece set for eight people as to buy them alone?" We bought a sixty-six piece set each, also a separate tea set and some coffee cups for good measure. Their arrival home in due course roused my father to take up his pen. "Delighted to report that your second batch of china has arrived safely. We like the blue in the new pattern even better than the yellow on the previous load. Are you intending to open an hotel when you come back?"

Our next duty was to visit the Base Hospital to see any Sappers who were there. These included Jock Cormack, for whom we smuggled in a bottle of whisky. We also met a very friendly dog outside and took it in too, and got hell from a sister. It provided a good diversion from the smuggled whisky.

Another letter home told enough of that very happy leave:—

18 Aug '52

We got back from our really excellent leave yesterday. This time we went by jeep to the airfield, two hours with a speed crazed driver, including through Hiroshima. We arrived at 0555 hrs., only to be told that our plane had left an hour before, but we hitched a lift on an American freight plane and were in Seoul by midday. We were the only passengers and, to put us at our ease, they made us wear Mae West lifejackets and parachutes throughout the trip for "when (not if) we ditch".

On Friday, Major Don Cooper, the Australian Second-in-Command of the Britcom Engr Regt, who is like a fairy godmother to visiting Brits, arranged for a launch to take us to the holy island of Miya Jima, about fifteen miles from Kure. We were liberally provided with iced beer, and got there in an hour and a quarter. It's certainly a lovely spot, with a couple of good big hills and a really beautiful forest of what looks like Scots pine.

It is one of those places where no one is meant to kill anything. In fact, you're not even allowed to die there, and if your family don't manage to heave you into a boat before you pop off, then the whole family is expelled from the island. Evidently the suicide pilots in the war used to spend their last leave there. There is a beautiful hotel, which is the COMWEL convalescent centre, where we had lunch.

In the afternoon I set my heart on climbing one of the hills (about 1,200 feet) whilst the others went bathing. I got completely lost and only just made it back to the launch in time, nor could I see anything from the top, due to the dense jungle! I had a quick bathe before we left, as seldom have I been hotter or dirtier, having slid quite a way down the hill on my backside in my haste to return.

Back in Kure we had a quiet supper (mostly of shrimps, with some excellent smoked oysters before) at the Club, then met Major Cooper and

Miya Jima. The ancient Torri.

another couple of Sapper majors. We were all desperately tired and just off to bed, but Major C was determined that we should see Hiroshima, and so the seven of us went out in his magnificent new Buick.

We arrived just in time to see the last half hour of the theatre strip show. Very good value, but not much better than the Chatham Empire. The Japs don't applaud at all: nothing to the Navy!

We then proceeded to a nightclub called PRINTEMP -N, which we supposed was meant to be Printemps. One is greeted at the door by a mass of Japanese dance hostesses who can't speak a word of English, some of whom are quite pretty, and some quite frightful. We all danced keenly, and I can still manage to get round the floor. Between dances we sipped beer out of minute glasses and the girls insisted in mopping our faces with scented ice flannels, pretty horrible, but quite pleasant!

We left there about midnight, but one of the Majors then saw another nightclub called BESSOS of which we had heard tell, so we all piled out of the car again for the same routine. The bands were quite good, and the Jap music very like the normal American. We eventually got home at 0330. Hiroshima is certainly a great big city, and nobody would ever imagine they'd had an atom bomb. The street lighting is quite wonderful, thousands and thousands of globe lanterns and enormous neon signs that would make Piccadilly Circus look pathetic.

It may have been the discomfort of sitting on the floor of that freight plane, but for the first time I doubted if I wished to stay in Korea for much longer. With twelve months gone and the routine in RHQ very well established, it looked as if the next six months to complete my overseas tour could even become dull. The saving grace was the prospect of the pheasant season opening in October. It was for the pheasants that I had volunteered for the War, and, in this respect, I was maintaining my aim (in the Clausewitz sense) commendably.

On arrival back in the Regiment I found that, although I had not had any inkling of the change, I was to be moved a couple of hundred yards over the hill into Divisional Headquarters to take up a post entitled SORE 3 (Int). This stood for Staff Officer Royal Engineers grade 3, meaning a captain's job and specialising in intelligence. My thoughts on the plane had apparently borne immediate fruit and, apart from the change, an added advantage would be that the duties should interfere even less than before with my pheasant shooting.

Lieutenant Colonel Peter Moore explained to me that, now Colonel Eddie Myers and his staff officer, Major Abbott, had just left, there was going to be a lack of continuity in Headquarters Royal Engineers. True, the fourth officer in the tiny staff was my old friend Roy Gout from 12 Squadron, but he, too, was due to go home shortly. The new

Commander Royal Engineers, Colonel Paddy Hill, and his new Canadian Major, Joe Black, needed someone who knew the countryside and, whatever else, I ought by now to fall into that category.

Colonel Peter was himself due to go home in a month's time and we had been at him for ages that, whatever his posting, his next job was to get married. As a 41-year-old bachelor we thought that he might find this task more difficult than coping so naturally with the nastiest of military situations. How wrong we were: he was married within a year and Mr. Hacker, our Regimental Sergeant Major, and I were amongst the many guests at his and Rosemary's wedding at Latimer.

We were delighted, but not surprised, when Lieutenant Colonel Peter Moore was awarded a second bar to his Distinguished Service Order when he left Korea. Few awards in that War can have given more pleasure to more people, and we were immensely proud to be associated with him.

CHAPTER FOURTEEN

SEND PORT AND PYJAMAS!

As SORE (Int) I took over, in name, from Captain Philip Crofton. Philip had been posted directly into the job on arrival in Korea which, with no background knowledge of our static war, had not made it easy for him. He had asked if he could soon go out to a Field Squadron to discover the form, but then had had a short spell in hospital, which accounted for my rather hurried move to HQRE. It was a pleasant experience to be actually wanted where I was going. Previous moves at similar speed had been because those who had me already on their strength were keen that I should go elsewhere.

Roy Gout, whose speciality was the procurement of stores, made a splendid job of introducing me around the Divisional Headquarters in my new capacity, though in the main I was meeting old friends. In the same way that Ian Gilmore, the Australian, well knew the Regimental Intelligence task which he took over from me, so I had been liaising daily with Philip Crofton before he had become ill. The difference between my old and new jobs would mainly be that, whereas as the Regimental Intelligence Officer I had been liaising with the units in our own Division, now as the RE Intelligence Staff Officer I would be dealing with the Headquarters of the American I Corps, of which we were a part, and with the allied Divisions on either side of us in the line. This would give me plenty of scope to travel around the countryside, swanning others called it, all very pleasing, especially as I would have my own jeep again, complete with driver.

The Transport Platoon of the Headquarters of 1st Commonwealth Division was the only unit, apart from their Gunner Regiment, provided by New Zealand and was, if anything even more full of characters. All the drivers were Maoris of fine Polynesian stock, and they provided a splendid service in a rather unorthodox manner. My own driver was called Pohibi, and a great experience it was to be with him.

The close comradeship between the Australian and New Zealand Armies, as immortalised by the ANZACs at Gallipoli, is well known, but perhaps the banter between individual soldiers of the two nations has been less widely reported. Because of their privileged position driving the staff all over the Divisional area, the HQ Transport Platoon saw, and were seen by, everybody. The custom had become established that if a Kiwi driver passed an Australian driver, greetings would be exchanged, in the phrasing of which much forethought and individuality was shown. All of us who knew the Maoris took this as a matter of course, but explanations had to be made to senior visiting officers, a few of whom did not fully appreciate the oratory, some of which lacked subtlety. The word went round that only polite greetings were in future to be tolerated, and both sides immediately complied. "Good Day, my Kiwi (usually KAY ONE DOUBLE YOU ONE) cousin" would be answered with "Felicitations, my Antipodean brother", or words on those lines, all of which meant that the vehicles had to slow to a tedious crawl to complete their exchanges, which became so cloying as to induce sickness. It wasn't long before the old, and much healthier, form of address was again permitted. Pohibi's vocabulary was fully up to standard, and he was a good driver as well.

Within three days of changing to my new job I injured myself in innocent circumstances which not all would believe. Officers of the rank of Captain and below used a tent as their Mess, known as "C" Mess. It lay just over the brow of a hill from the command vehicles and tents where the work was done and, as a gesture to warlike circumstances, one had to wend one's way through a couple of barbed wire fences between the two. On a dark night after supper I had negotiated the fences and gone into the G Ops tent to get the latest news before returning to my own table to tackle the paperwork that had accumulated in Philip's absence. The operations tent was the heart of the Division, and those who worked there, although only captains, were considered to be officers of the highest quality. Currently they comprised a South African, Sunny Schumann; a Kiwi, Brian Poananga; and a lone Englishman. Their boss was a Canadian, and their intelligence associates were an Australian and another Briton. The lighting in the Ops tent was unusually good and probably caused my downfall as, on going out into the dark night I was completely blind and soon stumbled over a steel picket, the end of which removed a small part of my thigh.

I picked myself up and went back into the Ops tent to view the damage. It was not extensive but, so far as I know, that was the only blood seen in Divisional Headquarters in the entire conflict. We all carried first aid field dressings, a little packet with a bandage in it, and, here at last was cause to use the thing, which normally proved a confounded nuisance every time I changed my clothes.

My companions were full of good advice on the medical channels I should now pursue. We were fortunate in being supported by a splendid choice, so the only problem was to select the best among the good. On balance the Indian Field Ambulance won, as they provided a magnificient curry lunch on Sundays, and this was Saturday evening. First, though, it would be polite to call on the Div HQ medical officer in the next valley, where I was driven by jeep.

The MO was more interested in my wound than I had expected and was keen to send me to the British Field Ambulance for attention. I had to lay my background with the old Indian Army on rather thickly before he changed his mind and allowed me to route myself that way. My leg was hardly hurting and had stopped bleeding, so the whole incident was proving highly inconvenient, and I was already wondering how many would believe that I was chilly sober, as indeed I had been, on my way back from the Mess. I asked the MO if he would mind if I called in at the Engineer Regiment on my way to the Indians, so that they knew the form and, as he lent me his jeep, he agreed.

In RHQ the Colonel had finished his orders and returned to his log hut, but all except the duty officer were in the Mess, full of commiseration and pleased to have a diversion from routine. I was known to be partial to port, so my glass was filled quite frequently in the hour before they eventually thought that I should not be further delayed. So far as they could see, I was a big sham and most unlikely to be kept by the Indians.

They were right. I arrived at the Indian Field Ambulance, north of the Imjin and much nearer to the Chinese than to Div HQ, at 11 p.m. The reception NCO was charming, but firm, and even at that hour of the night smart in every detail of his dress. Every man in that unit was a paratrooper, and theirs was the only unit in the Division that had achieved the grading "excellent" even for its vehicle maintenance.

Apart from having a splendid medical reputation also, the unit was the best possible advertisement for India five years after the departure of the British. "No, Sir, I am most sorry, but you cannot stay here. Our surgery is being reorganised and it is our policy not to keep officers here overnight." I knew that I had met my match, and that if I muttered "curry lunch", it would be likely to fall on deaf ears. "No, Sir, you must go to 8055 MASH. I will call for an ambulance jeep."

The ambulance took no time to come, but I gained permission to sit beside the driver and enjoyed chatting to him in the hour and a half it took us to get to the MASH (which certainly came off the tongue quicker than Mobile Army Surgical Hospital), as 20mph was still a sensible speed limit on our roads. We had to cross our Divisional boundary to the east, then go right across 1 ROK Div's area, a hair raising experience at night, as the South Koreans took the war very seriously, and just into the American 3rd Division on the far side. I expected it to be the same MASH where I had found Peter Park, but it was another. We arrived at 1 a.m., and I was very kindly greeted.

By 2 a.m. I was on an operating table, about to be dealt with by an American Captain. With him he had a Korean whom he explained to me was learning surgery, so he hoped I wouldn't mind if his friend helped. I had no choice, and I'm sure both of them were excellent doctors but, with only a local anaesthetic in my thigh, the temptation to move my leg when the American said to the Korean, "No! No! The other way!" was great. I only had six stitches and, again, nothing hurt. What interested us all was that, although I knew I had fallen over a steel picket, the surgeons had extracted a piece of wood from the wound.

I was put in a bed in the main ward and took no further interest, as I wanted to sleep off my port. The next morning a glance around confirmed that MASHes did not practise officer segregation. In the bed on my left was a French Canadian, and on my right was an American Private, with some very amusing Koreans against the opposite wall. Breakfast was quite passable, and I managed to prevent them mixing my puffed wheat with my sausage and toast.

The male staff were helpful and pleasant, but two females, who were very fat indeed (somebody ought to have told them that trousers did not suit them), taxed my sense of chivalry. The third was more attractive, and I addressed her as "Sister" in my most polite manner. Now, I had never before been in hospital in the Army, but remembered visiting others there and always pleasing the nurses by calling them "Sister".

That was evidently not the form in America, though. "You call me Noice," she said. "Sister" was evidently altogether too fresh.

I asked, now that my leg had been repaired, "Please may I go back to my job?" The answer was firmly negative, now I was in the medical system I would have to stay in it. I would probably be sent to the Canadian hospital in Seoul the next day. For good measure and to ensure that I knew my place, one of the fat nurses then gave me the most enormous penicillin jab in my bottom.

My companions proved most congenial and I spent a thoroughly interesting morning, once I had managed to stop every passer-by asking, "Where did you get hit?" My reply of, "Well, actually, I fell over a picket in the dark," proved downright embarrassing when compared to their answers to the same question.

Time magazine that week had a map of the United States on the front, with every state named. The American in the next bed, whom I immediately liked once I discovered that his combat wound had been the removal of his appendix, thought my accent amazing and my pronounciation of the state names very funny indeed. With his tummy all stitched up though, he had not to laugh, which made everything worse. I was genuinely surprised to discover that AR-KANSAS was called AR-KEN-SAW.

I pottered down to the end of the ward and was delighted to be able to route a short telephone call through to the Commonwealth Division. I got our Engineer clerk. I told him where I was, and asked him to send port and pyjamas. My shopping list was not questioned and, with amazing efficiency, a pair of my pyjamas and a bottle of port were delivered early that evening. Luckily they had had the sense to disguise the port in a parcel, but unluckily had not thought of sending a corkscrew.

I chanced letting my American friend in on my secret, and gained the impression that alcohol was *not* allowed in a MASH, nor elsewhere in the chain. I had feared as much, so refrained from requesting a corkscrew from the nurses. To broach the bottle I pushed the cork in, but the problem of where to secrete a fairly full bottle with no cork remained. I practised pushing my thumb in the neck, then very gently laying the bottle under the bedclothes. It worked.

Despite my ungentlemanly remarks about the ladies of 8055 MASH, I enjoyed my two day stay and would have preferred to remain there rather than going on to the Canadian hospital unit in Seoul. I had visited other patients there before, and knew it to be not the jolliest of places. It wasn't the staff's fault, but with good Field Ambulances and MASHes in front and the excellent Base Hospital in Japan behind, there really wasn't a need for an extra link in the chain.

I had to spend three days in Seoul, and had plenty of time to think of what I should have been doing instead of resting in hospital. I had spent one of my first days in Divisional Headquarters showing Colonel Hill, the new CRE, around one of our reserve defensive lines. He had proved to be a good walker and a keen botanist, and between us we had collected thirty-seven different types of wild flowers in the day. We had also seen seven broods of pheasants, all very heartening. Since then I had heard that the Imjin had achieved a rise of forty-two feet, and also that the new PINTAIL bridge had passed that severe test. I kept wondering whether the Chinese ever realised how dependent we were upon our bridges, and hoped they did not. There were we with absolute air superiority and able to see anything from on top, and there were they presumably dependent for their intelligence upon the few infiltrators who achieved the desperately dangerous trip through our lines and back again. If we ran similar spies, and I assumed that we did, the value of what they achieved was not obvious at my level.

I returned to my trestle table in Div HQ to find that the prodigious piles of paper had not been touched, other than that more had been added. On top was an official accident report form, which the chief clerk asked me to fill in without delay. Against the question demanding details of the circumstances of the accident I just wrote "I was sober", a statement which someone up the chain must have corroborated. Many years later, with that statement sitting on my personal file in the Ministry of Defence, the fact that my being sober was so notable may have raised a few eyebrows.

Sitting down to all the paperwork fitted quite well with my leg demanding that I did not move too much. As it was, it turned out that the Canadians had been right and I should have stayed with them a little longer. I had to go back to bed for a couple of days, after which all was well.

September 1952 started in Divisional Headquarters with a really excellent buffet luncheon party to mark the departure of General Jim Cassels. The Black Watch pipers set the scene, managing to march and countermarch most effectively on the very limited level ground.

General Cassels had been an inspired choice to be the first commander of the Commonwealth Division, and none of us who knew him were surprised when he later became a Field Marshal.

Meanwhile, the Korean War continued, with our earlier thoughts of peace nearly out of mind.

6 Sept '52

I am getting the hang of my job, and like it. Quite a lot of my time is spent visiting. Yesterday I flew down to Corps HQ and back, saving a three hour bumpy jeep drive. Light aircraft are nearly as easy to get as jeeps and, if there is an airfield near where one is going, it saves ages.

Today I've been to the US Marine Div on our left. They sprawl out over miles and miles to the west coast and travel isn't helped by their only good bridge being right the other end from us, so to cross the river one has to go to come back. I went in a very old Humber staff car, with a most amusing Kiwi driver. The car is the 1935 model, with a lovely engine, but next to no brakes. We can't get new brake linings for it, as there are so few cars out here, so it's a case of careful gear changing or giving the vehicle up, which we can't afford, as transport is always short. Two Marines we gave a lift to were so impressed with our car that they said, "Say, youse guys, you get out and have your photos taken," which, after some argument, we did! To them our proud possession is an object from the past.

The Marines are an excellent bunch and fight splendidly. The worst thing one can call them is "Army", as, of course, they are a Service on their own. We had lunch (chow) with their engineers: stew and ice cream. They keep a very lively war going over at Bunker Hill and have lost a lot of men, though of course the Chinks have had it harder.

Yesterday evening I went to give a lecture to officers of the Durham Light Infantry, who have just arrived, on mines and bunker construction. A very dull lecture, but they still gave me a good dinner.

It's getting cooler and the scrub oak is starting to change colour. The pheasants are thriving, even on our beastly Hill 355, but it must have been a noisy nesting season for them. The Workshops Troop of the Field Park Squadron now have someone who they think really can mend my gun.

One of my first impressions from my contacts outside the Division was the contrast between the relative quietness of operations in our area and the pugnacity of the Chinese in attacking those on either side of us. With the Marine Division under pressure on our left, I asked for a flight in an Auster to see what was going on. From 7,000 feet above the Chinese front we were in the front row of the dress circle and saw two air strikes, each of four planes, attack the KELLY outpost which had been lost two nights previously. The great red flames followed by dense black smoke from the napalm provided a better display than the flash and brown smoke of the high explosive bombs. The fact that in the plane we could hear nothing from the ground still left little to the imagination.

The Americans had apparently decided that, so long as the peace talks continued, not one hill would be lost, and the South Koreans dutifully followed American doctrine. This attitude was most praiseworthy, but we often wondered if the great cost it involved was justified. Some hills had to be held, but the value of some others would have been very difficult to argue in our way of thinking, and it was a mercy that we were not put to the test on such matters.

My twenty-seventh birthday on 24th September was much happier than I expected, starting the evening before with what used to be called an ENSA show led by Carole Carr, of whom we had all heard and who turned out to be a very pleasant, pretty and chatty girl. She had a very amusing pianist and a good Australian comedian with her, and they put on a wonderful show, which was much appreciated. We all had supper afterwards in the Field Park Squadron Mess.

The morning was hectic in my office, but in the afternoon I drove round the divisional area with one of the Canadian staff officers. We naturally visited his own Regiment, the Royal Canadian Regiment, where we were slipped a goodly cup of rum and coca-cola by an elderly canteen sergeant. Thus fortified, we set about an excellent tea of flap-jacks and treacle and were joined by a very meek looking officer called Russ Gardner. Russ had caught a real live Chinese prisoner the night before, so would have been well worth meeting even had the capture proved easy.

The RCR had not captured anyone for five months, so new ideas had been wearing a bit thin, but Russ had noted that the Chinese relied greatly on telephones for communications. His plan had been to get behind a Chinese position, find a phone cable, cut it, and then wait for a linesman to come and mend it. That is exactly what he did.

Russ had taken a sergeant and two soldiers with him, and they had gone out stealthily through one of our own minefield gaps. For many people the possibility of a Chinese ambush waiting at the far end would have been enough, but Russ' small party then had to cross No Man's Land and infiltrate the tightly co-ordinated Chinese positions. This had been done before, but not often. Even to find a telephone cable on the ground in the dark had not proved easy, but their luck had been in and, after selecting a suitable spot for their ambush, they cut the wire and waited. It had been nearly dawn, just as they thought they could wait no longer, than along came the linesman. He bent over to start mending the cable, and Russ and his companions jumped on him. Their plan had been to knock their quarry insensible, then carry him home on a stretcher, but they had reckoned without his reactions to the proposal. Little did they know that they had chosen the thickest-skulled, loudest-mouthed, member of the opposing forces, who had no intention whatever of lying placidly on a stretcher.

Even with a sack over his head the prisoner had managed to emit a remarkable quantity of noise, to the extent that the entire Chinese Army stood to and started shooting. Russ and his companions decided that life was going to be dangerous with or without their Chinaman, so they hustled him along with them, managed to find another gap further along the minefield, got through their own sentries (no mean feat) and were home.

Despite the buffeting he had received, the prisoner was not seriously injured and proved unexpectedly co-operative when questioned. "If you are happy to be so helpful now, why did you raise such a din last night?" asked the questioner. "All I was trying to say," answered the Chinaman, "was that if they would stop hitting me, I would come quietly."

That evening the CRE asked me to his caravan for a gin, then I went over to the Regiment for dinner where Angus and others helped me to deal with a couple of bottles of birthday champagne.

My best birthday present was the return of my old 12 bore shotgun, repaired with a new stock that looked as if it really would last. The carpenter had first made one in beech, but found it very hard to get the wood to grip. He had then found a piece of mahogany, and had achieved a real gunsmith's job with it, even though walnut would be the normal timber to use. To gild the lily, he had added a colossal brass butt plate, which he had filed down from a large shell case. It looked unusual, and might prove cold in winter, but we all thought it deserved admiration: in other respects the gun was, after a full year broken, as good as new. I gave the carpenter a crate of beer, and we were both delighted.

Mail from home continued to be the main prop to our morale, with the postal service taking under a week, which considering the planes and the route, was very good. I had carried on a sporadic correspondence with Judy, the girl I had taken to my last May Ball, but now had to write quite firmly in reply to her "we were much amused by you sitting on that iron picket". Sitting indeed! I had to explain that, being no contortionist, I was not in the habit of sitting on the inside of my thighs.

Angus and I had been waiting for the First of October and the start of the pheasant season, but that proved to be a particularly busy day with plenty of minor Chinese activity and, most unfairly, the Imjin flooded again, just when we had assumed that the rains were over for the year. Despite this we managed to get out on my favourite marsh by the airstrip for an hour and shot two cock and two hen pheasants.

As if to give official blessing to my excursions, I was then asked to arrange some shooting for Lieutenant General Bridgeford, an Australian who was the Commonwealth Commander-in-Chief based in Japan. With him I was asked to take the Commander of the Canadian Brigade and the Colonel in charge of the Division's medical services, also a Canadian. It turned out that none of them knew much of pheasant shooting in the English sense and, much too late, I was told that the General couldn't walk far. I did my best, but to me he was "a poor old man" and there was not time to organise a driven shoot with lots of beaters. As it was, the few pheasants we could find near a road flew the wrong way, and no one got a shot. This near disaster was, however, saved by the good grace in which everyone accepted the situation. After my guests had left me I walked up a valley with my batman and got a young cock pheasant and missed a hen.

My new boss, Colonel Hill, turned out to be a keen shot, which made my life much easier. On our first outing he and Angus and I brought home nine pheasants and, unhappily, left seven runners or dead birds behind. Again the question of using the mine dogs as retrievers came up and, with the Colonel to back us, it looked as if we would now be allowed to try one out. I was finding that my rebuilt gun, despite its appearance, suited me very well and I was shooting well above my normal standard. The Korean pheasants, to which many of the strains released in Britain must have been related, flew splendidly but tended to give fairly easy shots over the low scrub. We usually found them in the valleys, so there were not many high birds off the hills.

With shooting whenever the day would allow, my paperwork was starting to overtake me and I had to work into the nights, which were getting colder. Again we had been issued with excellent sleeping bags, their main disadvantage being that one never wanted to get up in the mornings. The thought of taking my boots to bed with me again, as otherwise they would freeze solid, did not add to the attractions of my second Korean winter in a small tent but, with my Balaclava helmet and bed socks which I unashamedly wore, I certainly slept well.

The Chinese attacks on the American First Marine Division continued into October, to the extent that our Corps Commander decided to help them by sidestepping our Division, which had six battalions on the line, by one battalion to the left. The previous year we had managed to knock the Chinese off their winter line just at this time, and now they were trying to do exactly the same to us, all most unfair. The piece of ground which would again come under our control after the move included a dull, but apparently vital, hill known as "The Hook", which covered the junction of the Samichon and Imjin rivers, near which any breakthrough would be likely to pass.

Plans for the change were made in great secrecy. The week before, I was sent to the Marine Division to discover the engineer implications of the move and to gain approval for one of our officers to join the Marines immediately to start taking over the minefields. They readily agreed, but said that he had better be dressed as a US Marine, and so Ian Thompson, our officer, was. As we had expected, due to the many changes of units and much fighting in the area, the minefield plans were by our standards, chaotic. Ian, who was soon joined by John Hackford, spent many dangerous days locating what they could of the almost non-existent fences.

The Americans had started to tunnel the Hook, and the Black Watch, who took over that particularly undesirable piece of real estate, continued the task knowing that those above ground would have very little chance of surviving the attack that would surely come. In the meanwhile, it was upon the Royal Canadian Regiment at the other end of our line that the strongest attack on our Division for many months fell. They lost some ground temporarily, but soon regained it, at considerable cost.

The number of casualties caused by our own mines continued to rise and caused increasing concern, not just to me, to whom all accidents were reported, but to the senior members of the staff. Although the totals of casualties directly caused by mines were appreciable, the overall effect of the mines on our minor tactics were even greater. The minefields much restricted the movement of the Infantry and it became known, but not publicised, that some of our patrols were not going out through the minefields to their destinations. This was understandable, as it only took one shell splinter to cut a minefield fence and then it was only too easy for a patrol to stumble into a minefield. The M2 bouncing anti-personnel mines were proving their effectiveness all too conclusively. One, that was set off by a patrol of nine of our men, killed three and wounded five, and after such an incident the worse problem of rescue from a minefield in the dark remained.

The Chinese devised an effective answer to patrols which might not follow their prescribed route in No Man's Land. The patrol leader would be given one or more placards, which he had to plant at designated points, a sport rather akin to orienteering. The next morning the Chinese officer would look through his binoculars, and woe betide any patrol leader whose placards were not correctly displayed. For those who had been visited, the emergence of a placard on their perimeter wire out of the dawn mist caused much embarrassment, but even greater delight to friends in view who were not directly concerned.

The war for which I had volunteered was very different from the one in which we were now involved. Then there had been hordes of Chinamen supported by nothing bigger than a few mortars. Now, on average, there were more United Nations' forces on the front line than Chinese, an enemy who was massively supported by all types of artillery. In No Man's Land there was nothing second rate about the Chinese patrolling, and both sides had gained a healthy respect for each other. All that remained unchanged was the endless expanse of rolling brown hills and, praise be, a plentiful supply of pheasants!

Those well intended lectures that I and others gave to incoming units about our minefields were, hardly surprisingly, proving insufficient. Everyone was sure that practical training was required, but our rivals, the Royal Artillery, doubted the motives of the Royal Engineers when we chose the best venue for pheasant shooting to make into the Divisional minefield training area. It was then fenced off and marked up with red triangles, just like a live minefield, so we should never, of course, have entered it, except to search for mines. For some of us, who were sure that the area contained no live mines, the temptation soon proved too great.

The day at last came when I was permitted to select the most likely of the mine dogs as a companion for a shooting outing. It may have been that, in the company of his mine finding handler, the dog managed to keep his instincts under control, but, although he was a big, friendly Springer spaniel type, he made it quite clear that pheasants had not been part of his training. After hoping for so long for a gundog, this was a sad disappointment, but Angus and I still managed to shoot on two or three afternoons each week, and the produce was much appreciated in our Messes.

At the end of our previous shooting season, in February, the Divisional NAAFI store proudly announced that they were expecting a shipment of 12 bore shotgun cartridges. We were delighted, as none of us had as many as we would have wished, but it was sad that they were coming too late. When September came we tried to buy some, to be told, "Oh, what a shame, we did have some, but as there was no demand for six months, we have backloaded them." The story of the ice skates, when the Imjin froze two months later, was very similar. Never mind, the NAAFI kept us supplied with most of the necessities of life, including a plentiful variety of drink, so much could be forgiven.

October 1952 proved to be a disturbed month but, apart from the attack on the Canadians, nothing major befell us. However, the news of the War as reported in Britain was of sufficient concern for me to write:—

19 Oct '52

Don't worry about the fighting. We *still* stay unmolested, and I believe the reasons are:—

1. We have no outposts, just a solid main line, in depth.
2. We have tremendous minefields.

The Americans have outposts and very little depth and, poor fellows, take a lot of casualties.

"Kelly" used to be in our Div area, as were "Tessie", "Nicky" and "Norrie" (all outposts). I went onto all of them, except "Norrie", last year. So were "Seattle", "Frisco" and "Detroit", on the other end of our line: all Chinese held at present and bare as drums, not a single blade of grass left. Hill 395, White Horse Ridge, twenty miles NE of here has just changed hands twenty times in a week, so Thank Goodness we aren't there! Needless to say, both sides had very heavy casualties.

23 Oct '52

Don't worry about the news from here. All the fighting is for the very front line hills and, No, we certainly haven't had to move.

I've spent a very pleasant couple of days visiting the US Marines, next

door. Masses of pheasants in their area, but mostly in the minefields. Autumn
colours really wonderful, yellow poplar, red giant oak and green fir.
  We had a marvellous show by Ted Ray and his party, and then supper
with them afterwards in the Field Park Mess. He had a girl with him,
Julia Shelley, with a really lovely voice. The blokes nearly went mad.

At last, after continued effort in the office and on the ground, we had
sufficient confidence in the location of our minefields to have them
overprinted directly onto the 1:25000 scale maps which had now
become available. However, the boundaries covered the join of four
map sheets, thus introducing errors in the overprinting. A hundred
yards wrong, or even less in the location of a minefield could be a matter
of life or death.

I heard that there was an American map printing unit down in Seoul,
so booked an Auster to fly down, to save both time and the terribly
dusty drive. The Americans proved highly co-operative, but spent some
while explaining to me the inaccuracies that would probably be
introduced if they photographed four maps which had been joined
together, also that the tone of the new map, which could only be in one
colour, would be horrible, as the parent maps had all been coloured
differently. "Nothing ventured, nothing gained" I thought and as it
was costing Her Majesty nothing, asked for a thousand copies of the
new sheet to be overprinted with our minefields in black. Judging by
the number of observations we received on the result, the new map at
least aroused interest. The amended version was much better and, for
those who bothered to use it properly, a valuable document. In the
meanwhile, mercifully, we had not suffered any casualties attributable
to the map errors.

I went on The Hook a couple of times, once with Colonel Hill and
once with Ian Gilmore, the Australian who had taken over from me as
the Intelligence Officer in the Engineer Regiment, to see the
fortifications which the Black Watch, with liberal Sapper assistance,
had been building. I had never been taught even the rudiments of
tunnelling and, the more I saw, the more glad I was that I was not
involved in the work. It was certainly impressive how far into and
through the hill the tunnels went, or so I was assured: from the moment
I entered a tunnel I was almost totally blind, as my specs, from being
cold outside, fogged up immediately. The lighting was dim, and many
off duty soldiers sleeping on the floor proved to be frequent, and
sometimes grumpy, obstacles. Luckily I could not understand most of

what was addressed at us in broad Scots by those who had been kicked.

The fug was repulsive, but not as beastly as down those Chinese tunnels I had visited a year before. Nevertheless, it was an enormous relief to come out into the open air again on the side of The Hook, where my immediate actions were to gulp fresh air and try to clean my specs. It was as I came out of a tunnel that I heard a shell coming in very close, so demonstrated the agility that only came to me on these occasions, and was down on the ground well before it burst in the valley below. This delighted the Scotsmen, as it had been one of our own going out, not Chinese coming in. I had come out of the tunnel on the same side of the hill as I had entered.

These seemingly warlike excursions were welcome compared to the embarrassingly peaceful job which was now added to my duties in Divisional Headquarters. It was true that the squad tents which we junior staff officers used as our Mess were squalid, if one came to

Entrance to the Yong Dong Tunnel. Typical of 1952/53 fortifications.

consider them, but we seldom did. They met our basic needs, and with a tin pot of hot toddy on the stove, and more rum available at very little cost, there was no great problem in keeping warm in good company. However, as the war became ever more static, and duller, more and more parties of entertainers were arriving from England to enliven us. They had to stay and eat somewhere and, though I never heard any of them complain, the conditions we offered were perhaps excessively rustic.

Major Joe Black, the Royal Canadian Engineer under whom I worked and who, as a resourceful fellow, saw no need to make war an excuse for discomfort, managed to procure, by means unspecified, a splendid shed for use as a new "B" Mess. It was seventy-two feet long by twenty-four feet wide, huge by Korean standards, and the sort of thing that was probably intended for hospital use. Joe told me where to find the materials for the shed and added, "Please would you, Dan, get on and build it." Would I also please note, he added, that the project was unofficial and so could be given no priority, but the Mess was needed quickly.

Joe had worked hard to scrounge the shed, but scrounging the labour to build it was difficult too. At its peak my work force consisted of three

"B" Mess 1st Commonwealth Division. The author, Jerry Mott, Tony Rawlence, Bryan Smith, Bruce Robinson and Frank Lewis.

Canadian carpenters, of whom two were reputed to be of doubtful character, a New Zealand and a Korean carpenter, both good men, six infantrymen from the Divisional Headquarters Defence Platoon, two Korean labourers to build the front door steps and three Sappers from the Regiment, all defaulters, to dig a deep ditch under the building site in which to lay a long metal culvert. Not everyone builds a palace across a stream, but that was the only site on offer to me.

This was not the kind of task I had expected as a staff officer and, at first, my pride was hurt. I soon discovered, however, that the job had its compensations, as the number of free drinks stood to me by other prospective users of the Mess increased dramatically. Now I was into my last three months of my Korean tour, more glamorous tasks were losing some of their previous attraction.

Despite my constructional duties, my desk continued to be inundated with intelligence reports, but they seldom contained anything of great substance. At least once a week new aerial photographs were taken of the Chinese positions in front of us and our air photo interpreters probably worked consistently longer hours than anyone else to see if they could leach anything new from the pictures. The United Nations' command of the air had always been overwhelming and now was, relatively, stronger than ever. Unless our neighbouring divisions were heavily involved, close air support strikes became easier to obtain, rather like my Auster flights, and if the interpreters could identify a target, there was no doubt that it would soon be attacked. By night the main role of the US Air Force close to our front line was to fly flare ship missions, when a bomber aircraft would fly slowly up and down the Chinese front line dropping large parachute flares every few minutes. For good measure they would also throw out wodges of pamphlets, which were intended to impress any Chinaman who cared to pick one up. From a distance, as we were, those flares were very pretty, but close to, they showed up our own forces, including minelaying parties, as much as the enemy, so proved a mixed blessing.

I usually had great faith in the views of our air photo interpreters, but was roused when a track to Hill 317, now two miles beyond our front line, was reported to be four feet wide. Of course it was unfair and thoroughly ungentlemanly of me, but I could not resist asking them for confirmation before announcing that I, personally, had built that particular "road" a year ago and it was then, and probably still was, fully eight feet wide. They were grateful for, but rather dismayed by the observation.

When information on the enemy was scant, which was almost always, it was worth studying the daily intelligence summaries from Army Headquarters with a view to extracting more about the plans from our own forces than may have been intended. I had now been seeing these summaries almost every day for a year: they included a fold out map of the war zone in colour, red for the believed dispositions of the Chinese and North Korean formations, blue for the headquarters of the United Nations' divisions which, apart from the Commonwealth Division, were all American or South Korean. Almost all the dozen, or so, UN divisions on the front line used to be relieved by one of the six reserve divisions every few months. A pattern soon built up, and it was possible to predict which two divisions would swap over. If this did not occur, then the chances were that something of interest was about to happen. My predictions started to gain some credence, to the extent that when a new United States division appeared on the map in the reserve areas, I foresaw a very interesting task, including a seaborne landing up the west coast, for it. At that stage I was ordered to stop anticipating our own plans, or at least to keep my speculations private.

It was evident that the Chinese interest in The Hook was increasing, and the defensive preparation for the impending battle accelerated accordingly, with the Royal Engineers much involved with the technicalities of tunnelling and of bunker building. Meanwhile, on a lovely Saturday afternoon in mid-November, Colonel Hill and I, with his batman as a beater, bettered our Korean shooting record, bringing home ten pheasants and seeing many more.

The attack on the Black Watch on The Hook came on the night of 18th November, 1952. Our Gunners had only recently received supplies of proximity fuzes for their shells, and the tactics for the defence of the hill depended upon their use. These fuzes were shrouded in some secrecy, and known by the code letters "V T", which was said to stand for variable time. In fact each fuze contained a tiny radar set which sensed the approach of the shell to the ground and then set it off at its most lethal height.

The Chinese preceded their attack by a tremendous bombardment, so intense that the shell holes overlapped to the extent that a normal trench would have provided negligible protection. Their infantry, who must have had a very unpleasant time in their forming up areas from the attention of over 100 United Nations' guns and mortars, then swarmed onto The Hook, many of them carrying pole charges to blow down the mouths of tunnels. By this stage most of the Black Watch and those supporting them were under ground and the fire from our guns, using the special airburst fuzes, was directed over their own heads.

All this was thoroughly unpleasant for the defenders, but worse for the attackers. Such Chinese as were left alive withdrew before dawn, leaving the surface of The Hook a powdered shambles covered in their own dead. They also left some of the Black Watch buried in their tunnels: luckily most were dug out alive but, of over 100 casualties in the battalion that night, twenty were listed as missing.

Safe and sound seven miles away, I was in no way involved in the action on The Hook, but when we heard what a high proportion of casualties had been suffered by the Black Watch pipers, we in Divisional Headquarters, were particularly sad. Only recently had they put on a memorable display for us at General Cassels' farewell party, and never had we imagined them in their battle role as stretcher bearers. There can have been few nastier jobs that night on The Hook.

CHAPTER FIFTEEN

PHEASANTS AND FINAL FORAYS

I would have liked to visit The Hook soon after the Black Watch battle to see how the tunnels and Sapper defences had fared, but managed with no difficulty to convince myself that my presence there was not essential. A few days later, I was most impressed by a squashed jeep on the side of the approach road. During the night of the battle a lone tank of the Skins had been sent up the hill to give what assistance it could. The only sure way up at night had been by that track, but it turned out to be blocked by a jeep. The young officer commanding the Centurion tank reported this to his Squadron Leader over his wireless. "If it's a jeep, what are you?" asked the major. "A tank," was the obvious reply. "Then behave line one," was the order given to the 50 ton tank, which drove straight over the jeep, resulting in an unusual piece of metallic sculpture, of which Carl Milles could have been proud.

With Christmas under a month off and with our new Mess open, more and more parties were being thrown, and many of them became very good parties. Rather like a doctor always being on call, so we were all theoretically on call should a battle brew up: fortunately most people's heads remained remarkably clear, perhaps due to the fresh air and cold climate. The main difficulty with the parties was to avoid repetition. With no female company, and only a limited number of officers living locally, the need for originality was apparent. Some thought the pursuance of this went too far when "Bowling for a Pig" was announced as a forthcoming attraction before a poor piglet was flown in from Japan. On the same plane there happened to be travelling a visiting General, who, apart from disliking the behaviour of his companion animal, gained quite the wrong impression of the rigours of the Korean campaign.

Staying eighteen months in Korea, to count as a complete overseas tour, had its attractions, but I felt a wrench when units that had arrived after me left again after a year or less. My friends the Skins were due to go on 8th December and Peter Duckworth came to see me in "B" Mess to say goodbye. I was genuinely embarrassed when he saw our plywood palace, as I had had to tell him on various occasions that plywood simply was not available. Being a polite fellow, all he did was to compliment us on the excellent fireplace which had been built onto the end wall.

With a view to keeping in touch with any changes, I aimed to visit the Divsions on either side of us once a week. With the First Marine Division on our left, this was a pleasant and often social outing, but with the First Republic of Korea Division on our right, matters were rather more formal, though I usually tried to deal with them through one of the American liaison officers. In fact, there were remarkably few Americans in the Divisional Headquarters and I was immensely impressed at the strides the South Koreans had made in such a short time since their Army was all but destroyed. However, I found that successive visits to 1 ROK Div were progressively less productive, so as the weeks went by I tended to visit them less and the Marines more. It was on my way across to the First Marine Division on one occasion that I found myself passing under a constant stream of helicopters flying over the Imjin and up to the front line. I was told that I was seeing a heli-borne battalion attack, one of the first that had been mounted.

When President-elect Eisenhower visited our Division on 4th December, 1952, it was not by helicopter, but with a fleet of fixed wing planes, thirteen of them, the same number as had accompanied Field Marshal Alexander when he visited us earlier in the year, but these planes were larger. Ike arrived at 8.15 a.m., with the temperature just above zero Fahrenheit. We could only watch through binoculars, but it was generally agreed that he looked fatter and older than we had expected, and very like Winston Churchill from behind.

Although the serious likelihood of us shooting pheasants on the same ground two seasons running in war had seemed remote, here we were putting into effect the plans that Angus and I had made during the summer. There was no doubt that the second season proved to be better, as regards numbers of birds shot, but, with more and more people wanting to join in, some of the spontaneity of the sport was lost.

As Sappers, our trump card remained our assumed knowledge of the minefields and, although all areas were freely available to everyone, others tended to keep further away from the minefields than was absolutely necessary.

As if the increased interest in shooting pheasants within the Division were not bad enough, American helicopters now entered the scene. A pilot had discovered that, if, by flying low, he could put up a pheasant and then follow its flight precisely, the bird presented the equivalent of a sitting shot to a crewman pointing a shotgun through the window. Quite apart from this practice being, to our minds, most unsporting, we could see no reason why our personal preserves needed to be poached. We managed to trace the helicopter concerned and let it be known that one of the places it had landed to pick up a dead pheasant had been inside a minefield. We also mentioned that we were very busy, and would be unlikly to have any effort available to help if they got into difficulties. If we appeared inhospitable, that was just what was intended, and those guests never visited us again, and our pheasants were safe.

The Chinese is front of our Division were taking the approach of the festive season even more seriously than had their predecessors the year before. Great numbers of boxes of Christmas gifts, including well indoctrinated 1953 diaries and English extracts from Mao's little red book, all liberally interleaved with safe conduct passes for prospective deserters, were left in No Man's Land on the wire in front of our positions. A gentleman with a loud hailer shouted the position of any that had not been found, adding that no dirty tricks (his wording was more polite) would be attempted and, so far as I know, they weren't. If his aim was to tickle the Commonwealth sense of humour, he achieved it, but I never heard of anyone accepting the invitation to desert to the North.

We doubted if our allies, the South Koreans next door, could be receiving the same treatment, as in a battle for the "Norrie" outpost the United Nations had just fired 70,000 shells against an estimated 30,000 Chinese in return. On a pretext that cannot have been very strong, I was flown on 17th December close to "Norrie" in an Auster, as usual at 7,000 feet, and the air in the closed plane was soon smelling strongly of explosive.

Our preparations for Christmas were, like our pheasant shooting, better organised than the year before, but I never expected the Engineer

Intelligence Officer of the First Marine Division to bring me across a parcel, which turned out to be a really good cake. He stayed to lunch in our new Mess, which suitably impressed, if not amazed, him, and I gave him a bottle of cointreau to take away.

I knew of a good bunch of mistletoe well up on an eating chestnut tree, and was asked to pick it. Just who there might be to kiss under it remained in grave doubt, but I set off to climb the tree. As could have been expected, that was too much for me, so I went back and collected my shotgun and shot the branch off with cartridges loaded with No. 3 shot. These could have been used for duck shooting, but ever since the Turkish Brigade had mined the best part of the Imjin, the sport had lost its attractions.

The occurrence that really made our Christmas Day was the personal foray of a Canadian platoon commander across No Man's Land in broad daylight. To cap his seasonal celebrations he announced that he was going to capture a Chinaman. His sergeant sensibly managed to make him hand over his pistol, but, undeterred, the officer then set off armed with a couple of empty bottles. Watched by many pairs of binoculars he reached the first Chinese position after staggering several hundred yards completely in the open, and even found a couple of Chinamen at whom to shout. This was a considerable achievement, as the Chinese had, for a long while, made a point of not emerging from their holes in daylight. The officer threw his bottles, whereupon the Chinamen said, "Shoo," or something equivalent. At that stage the officer took their good advice, and made his way back to his own lines. His commanding officer was not overjoyed to see him back.

I spent my Christmas Day much as the one before, except that no one asked me to mix the brandy butter. Our sergeant clerk and I served gunfire tea to the soldiers in bed, then there was the eight o'clock service and a hearty breakfast before I visited the Gunners to get their bar open. The officers and sergeants then served lunch to the soldiers, after which I went for a hitch hike north of the river, visiting various friends, getting lifts from three Australians, a Canadian Colonel and a Royal Fusilier, and walking five miles. We had an excellent Christmas dinner, but No, we did not find anyone to kiss under the mistletoe!

I ended 1952 by spending a couple of days in Seoul, where I had been sent to meet Colonel Donald Portway. He was Master of St. Catherine's College, Cambridge and a Royal Engineers Territorial Officer of great repute. His visit to Korea was in connection with a United Nations' education commission, but his train from Pusan was cancelled, so my task became more challenging.

I spent the night at the British officers' transit Mess, which had been much improved and where I met friends. I spent the next morning meeting planes at Seoul airport, as I thought the Professor might have hitched a lift, but the informality of air travel in Korea must have been too difficult for a newcomer to grasp immediately. Just to see the traffic, though, was interesting, with all sizes of aircraft from British Austers to American Globemasters, certainly the biggest planes I had seen.

I went back into Seoul to our military headquarters where I heard that "the UN Reconstruction Advisers" might know something of Colonel Portway, so I then managed to find a very rugged, but pleasant, Australian retired Major General called Lloyd, who had been Adjutant General of the Australian Army at the end of the war. He gave me lunch and offered me a bed, as he had heard that Colonel Portway was coming on the evening train. The hot and cold running water, steam heating and a real spring bed much impressed me, and made me wish that I, too could one day be a reconstruction adviser.

I got Donald Portway off the train, and remembered him well from Cambridge. He was pleasantly surprised to hear that I had been to his own College's May Ball in 1950, but much more interested in any of our more warlike doings. He was a real old warrior, longing to see a battle, so I brought him back to our Division via the Marines, as I thought there might be more activity there. They didn't oblige, but he appreciated the gesture.

Although, but the start of 1953, the River Imjin was fully frozen, it was generally agreed that the previous winter had been colder. Cold or not, I found getting in and out of my canvas camp bath just as bad as the year before and convinced myself that once a fortnight was quite frequent enough for the activity. I had heard of eskimos seldom bathing, lest they lost their natural oils, and felt they had a point. Although we may not have been quite as clean as others would hope, daily shaving remained mandatory and setting that standard kept hygiene within sensible bounds. Ice hockey on the river became highly popular, where jeep skidding also offered excitement, until the General himself, complete with his ADC, went through. Neither they nor the jeep came to any great harm.

Our new Divisional Commander, who had taken over from General

Cassels, was Major General Mike Alston-Roberts-West. He was an even taller man than his predecessor and shared his gift of finding a smile, or an interested word, for everyone. He changed very little of what General Cassels had started, but an obvious small innovation was his requirement for everyone within normal range of Chinese guns to wear steel helmets. With the much increased level of enemy shelling, this was a thoroughly sensible precaution.

I attended the daily session at nine in the morning when the General was briefed. We heard of the work of the Air Forces, of our own actions during the previous night, which all too often included mention of accidents in our minefields, and of the affairs of our neighbours. The briefing only took ten or fifteen minutes and, as the tent was much warmer than the one I worked in, proved an interesting and usually social start to the day.

I had asked the Intelligence Officers of all three of our Brigades to let me know if a Chinaman were ever captured who might be prepared to give me his views on our minefields. So that the questions could be asked to best advantage, all had agreed to keep off this subject until I arrived to pose them myself.

Early on a particularly cold morning I was rung from 28th Commonwealth Brigade. "Dan, we got a Chinaman last night who seems so co-operative that we think he must have been on the point of deserting. We've got to send him back past you, so you ought to see him. I'm sure he'll tell you everything you want." I was thrilled, and left my regrets for my Colonel that I would not be at the General's briefing.

The Chinese prisoner was not the greatest specimen of humanity, but he was unusually alive and talkative, just what we wanted. "Please ask him," I said to the interpreter, "what he thinks of our mines." A lengthy conversation in a Chinese tongue followed, to the extent that I wondered if either the prisoner or the interpreter, or both, understood the term "mine". The prisoner looked puzzled, as if he very much hoped he was giving the right answer, but wasn't sure. "He says," and it was the interpreter who now looked ill at ease, "that when they are short of explosive, they go and lift what mines they need."

It was then my turn to stumble over my words, as none of my carefully prepared questions fell into that sequence. "Ask him if he and his comrades are frightened by our new very strong fields, with the mines laid close together," was the best I could do. The answer "No" came back quite quickly, then, thinking he ought to be more helpful, the prisoner added, "we can collect more mines quicker when the mines are close together." I waived the opportunity to ask further questions, and went across to the Mess for a second breakfast.

Despite the increased interest in pheasant shooting around the Division, Angus and I still had some pet spots which others did not frequent, and we managed to add another dozen birds to our bag on some beautiful January days. Very appropriately, my shooting in Korea reached a climax at the end of the month:—

25 Jan '53

We had a memorable day's shooting yesterday. The British Gunner Regiment organised a vast shoot, as they thought they knew where there were lots of birds. We met at midday about three miles behind our forward position, nineteen guns and forty-five beaters, and if the Chinese could have seen us they would have run for their lives! Angus, Lieutenant Colonel Arthur Field (the new CO of the Engineer Regiment who had taken over from Lieutenant Colonel Peter Moore two months before), and I and others, were put to stand along the banks of the Samichon River, a tributary of the Imjin. The beaters came in an enormous line over some small hills, through a first line of guns, which included Colonel Hill, the CRE, then on across several hundred yards more of frozen, reed covered, marsh.

There was a good strong wind, but there were very few birds. Each of the guns in our line on the river bank got about three shots, but Angus got the one and only cock picked up. The pheasants were miles up and much faster than bullets, and I just didn't know what to do with them. All this took about an hour, and the party on Colonel Hill's side of the river only got a brace, or at least initially they did. Eventually one of the Gunner beaters, seeing how meagre the bag was, surrendered another bird out of his pocket. That made four pheasants, and a very dead deer which one of the soldiers had found and was determined to bring home, much to the envy of others who wanted their photos taken with it.

Having so poor a bag, the organisers rather lost heart and control, but after a little beer and confusion, we decided to walk a piece towards the Imjin with roads on two sides and a small river on the third. It was about a mile, into and across the wind, and Angus and I had the sense to get right at the down-wind end of the vast line. We had some lovely birds, curling right back over us after having been missed by six or seven pairs of barrels. We missed most of them too, but did get some, including what looked like an impossibly high hen that we both fired at at once. We also had a smack at a duck. The barrage was terrific and we picked up fourteen birds, of which Angus and I had six, more than our share.

After that everyone seemed to be going home but, as there was just time, Lieutenant Colonel Field, Angus, self, a Gunner and his batman decided to walk the four miles home along the north bank of the Imjin. We only saw thirteen birds and brought home ten of them, seven cocks and three hens, and were back by 5.30 having had quite enough. I fired a total of thirty cartridges in the day for seven birds, and Angus had the same for fewer cartridges, so we had fourteen between us, half the day's bag for nineteen guns! That makes thirty-seven I've had this year, and I reckon that the Div area north of the Imjin, about 32,000 acres, must have produced over a thousand birds in the season.

Something tells me that I'll be leaving Korea at just the right time, as if one side or the other doesn't do something in the Spring, I'll be amazed. If it's us, I can't see what possible good it can do, and if it's them, it would have to be to knock us right out of Korea, which I suppose would mean us bombing China and a world war. Wait and see!

Must stop. Masses of unexpected Americans have just arrived.

From those daily studies of the United States Army intelligence maps I had prided myself on being able to anticipate the moves of our divisions along the line. Now it turned out that I had completely missed the most important move of all. The impossible was now to happen, with the First Commonwealth Division going into reserve at the end of January 1953. When the awful truth dawned, I was at least glad to have the chance of thanking General West for not moving us until the end of the pheasant shooting season. In fact, like General Cassels before him he had probably resisted the move because the administrative problems, with all the Commonwealth units needing special supplies and special ammunition, looked so overwhelming. The answer in the end was to bring only the front line infantry into reserve, to positions behind the artillery and the service units who stayed where they were.

We had always foreseen chaos if we had to move in winter. Luckily we had three days' warning in Div HQ, but there was still plenty to occupy us. One of the worst problems proved to be the long steel pickets which had been driven well into the ground to support wind breaks around tents and vehicles. Now, the pickets were set in the deeply frosted ground like concrete and the only way to move the vehicles was to cut the pickets off at ground level with oxy-acetylene torches, of which not many were available. So much for the mobility which had always been plugged at us in England! There was no doubt that in Korea, mainly due to the complete lack of enemy aircraft, we broke many well founded rules, but presumably, those who knew the form had weighed the risks. Meanwhile, it was just as well that the gentlemen of the Press, particularly cartoonists, were not present. As we moved out, so the American 2nd Infantry Division moved in.

I had always imagined that being in reserve would prove boring, so was pleased when Colonel Hill told me that he wanted me to stay behind for a few days with the incoming American Army Engineers, to help them in any way I could. Pohibi, my Maori driver, took me across to the 2 Div Engineers the next morning, but, as he did not consider himself to be part of the liaison deal, took himself and his jeep back to the new location of the Commonwealth Division Headquarters, a few miles to the south-west on the Seoul side of Gloucester Valley.

After experiencing the US Army Transit Camp at Sasebo, I had already surmised that the conditions under which the Americans lived in the field might not be as plush as some fondly imagined, but had not expected comfort to be so entirely lacking. Hardly surprisingly, no red carpet awaited me, in fact the only officer who might be expecting me, "The Three", was out. I knew, from my reading of many US Army reports, that the figure 3 meant operations, so "The Three" would be the operations officer of the battalion, what we then called the Adjutant. I also knew that, as an intelligence staff officer, I would be known as a "Two", and promptly was. Instead of "The Three", I was taken to the commanding officer, who was putting up his tent and introduced me to his second-in-command who was also putting up another small tent nearby. Neither of them had anyone to help him, and both were showing that they were not in practice at the job. It struck me that the British system of soldier batmen undertaking such tasks, whilst their officers planned, or gave orders, was, even if less democratic, not a bad one.

Luckily I had not taken much kit with me and was soon asked to take it to the BOQ, which I learnt stood for Bachelor Officer Quarters. This consisted of a single squad tent, with room for seven or eight camp beds on either side. I had just put my bed together and unrolled my bedding roll when the order came to move. As I had nothing to do, I offered a hand to the commanding officer and his senior major to pack up the tents they had only just erected. They were most grateful, and turned out to be the nicest of chaps.

We moved just a couple of miles, we were never told why, so were fortunately able to put up the tents up again before dark. There was every excuse for our feeding routine to be disrupted, but it would have taken me a long while to settle to the normal "chow" hours of 0645, 1200 and 1700 hours, and nothing else. "The Three" arrived back that evening and told me that he'd let me know what they wanted me to do in the morning, so off I went to my bedspace in the BOQ and found that I was not alone in having a bottle or two in my kit. Even if the circumstances were uncomfortable, my companions were congenial and genuinely interested to hear of the engineering tasks in progress in our old area.

It was a cold night, so the cooks did well to have breakfast ready on time, which consisted of flap-jacks and treacle and scrambled egg, all served on the same plate. The milk was frozen, but the coffee was hot and, with all this being consumed standing in the open at dawn at zero Fahrenheit, a memorable meal resulted. We really were camping and, for a short while, it was fun.

After breakfast "The Three" came across and said, "Now, you, me and the Colonel will go up The Hook." There was I, the survivor of seventeen months of rugged warfare (or so I had inferred), and now they were asking me to show them round The Hook, where no sane man had gone in daylight for weeks. I must have looked horrified, and was in no way reassured when they told me that we would wear their new bulletproof waistcoats. I suggested that we should go at dusk, or before dawn the next day, but couldn't be too forceful, lest I let the Commonwealth down by showing my true cowardice. We did go to The Hook, and not for months can that nasty hill have been more peaceful. We wended our way through the tunnels, with my specs fogged up as usual and with the waistcoat, into which many hard and uncomfortable steel plates had been sewn, proving much heavier than I had been promised. It was a wonderful thought, though, that I should never need to go onto The Hook, or through its tunnels, again.

I spent the remainder of that day with the American "Two" explaining our minefield maps and records, which he kindly said were much better than any others he had met. So they should have been, with us having lived in the same place for so long, but all very gratifying it was to hear. The next day we went to check the location of a couple of fields, so as to validate the map, but the event of most note was the arrival of a French officer in the evening with a gift of a couple of bottles of champagne. The Engineers of the US 2nd Division had made him a nice gap through a minefield, and this was his small gesture of thanks. I made it clear that I, personally, would be very happy to make him a gap any day for a single bottle of champagne, but the Frenchman regretted that his unit was moving further up the United Nations' line to the east. The French Battalion had made an excellent name for itself in Korea, but, with their own war in Indo-China becoming ever hotter, we wondered how long they would be left in Korea.

Pohibi collected me the next day and I returned to my own Division, but continued to attend the American commanding officer's briefing each evening until the end of the week. Once I had settled into the routine, I had started to enjoy my life with the American Army, but my main thoughts now were on going home on the March boat. Meanwhile, many more of my old friends were arriving in the country, including George Cooper (later General Sir George, Adjutant General), to whom I gave my shotgun. He offered to pay for it, but with its improvised stock and barrels of doubtful strength, its value to me was more sentimental than monetary.

As if matters social in the Commonwealth Division had previously been lacking, the crescendo of party giving, with the Division out of the line, now reached unprecedented heights. The parties provided a perfect setting for my handover as the Sapper Intelligence Officer to Don Cameron, who had just commanded a Troop with distinction. In particular I remember a lunch party with the Black Watch, with their commanding officer, Colonel Rose, dispensing "Bull's Blood", red wine and champagne mixed in equal quantities, as liberally as I ever could have wished.

I took Don over to meet the US Marines one afternoon, and we stayed until nearly midnight. Our jeep had been behaving badly, but was still going as we passed between minefield fences close up to the road on either side. Suddenly a deer, which must have been frightened by our lights, ran out of the minefield on our right, across the road, and through the minefield on our left. Nothing happened, but I was so near to going home that I felt more than usually frightened. Shortly afterwards the jeep's radiator packed up, so we had to make our own way home. We got a couple of lifts, but still had to walk eight miles, which included the full length of Gloucester Valley, where the Chinese had been finally stopped on their way south nearly two years before. Everything was very still, very cold and very ghostly.

No junior officer could have asked for a better send off than I had from Korea. Colonel Hill took me to dinner in "A" Mess, where General West proved to be a most gracious and highly amusing host, then I was dined out in my own "B" Mess. I had dinner with the Engineer Regiment on my last night, just one mile from where I had spent my first in the country, then flew from Seoul to Kure in Japan. The date was 26th February, 1953, so my eighteen month tour in Korea had exceeded the prescribed maximum by three days.

POSTSCRIPT

Perhaps it was due to the silence, but now that I had time to reflect on my excursion to Korea, gunfire came quickly to mind. I had heard the guns in our Division alone fire some one and a half million rounds, a figure which the New Zealand Gunners confirmed by celebrating the despatch of their own first half million 25 pounder shells. Much of my work and thinking had been on mines and minefields, and I had learnt more than I would have wished about them. In particular I now knew how I, and others, felt to live amongst the beastly things.

Since my arrival in Korea 550 days before, the First Commonwealth Division had recrossed the Imjin, a memorable river on its own account, advanced over only six miles of derelict country, lost a little of it again, and then dug in to stay. In so doing the Division had suffered nearly 4,000 casualties, mainly amongst the Infantry for whom I had gained an ever increasing respect. I had also formed an uneasy respect for the Chinese and felt that, another time, I would rather have them on our side.

The remarkable achievements of the Americans, to whom we seldom gave credit, were not fully appreciated by 27-year-old Dan, but it was obvious that it was they who had held the United Nations together and that it was they who were putting South Korea on a promising footing. I had enjoyed meeting them, and representatives of so many other nations, and had made more friends than many may in a lifetime. The Royal Engineers seemed to meet more people than most, and I was indeed proud to have served with them in our unique Division.

One statistic stood out above the rest in my memories. I had shot fifty-one pheasants, a far greater number than would have come my way in England, and had achieved the intended purpose of my Korean War much more successfully than I could ever have dreamt possible. Yes, I was glad I had volunteered!

The peace talks at Pan Mun Jon lingered on into the summer of

1953, the main point of disagreement being the repatriation of prisoners. The Chinese and North Koreans wanted them all sent back, which would have suited almost all the United States and Commonwealth prisoners, but not a large number of the Koreans and Chinese. At last voluntary repatriation was accepted, and an armistice was signed on 27th July, 1953.

The fighting ended almost precisely where it had started, with the North Koreans and Chinese having gained nothing, which represented a major, if somewhat negative, achievement by the United Nations. And so it turned out that the Korean War had lasted just over three years, and that I had been there for nearly half of it.